ULTIMATE COMICS SPIDER-MAN

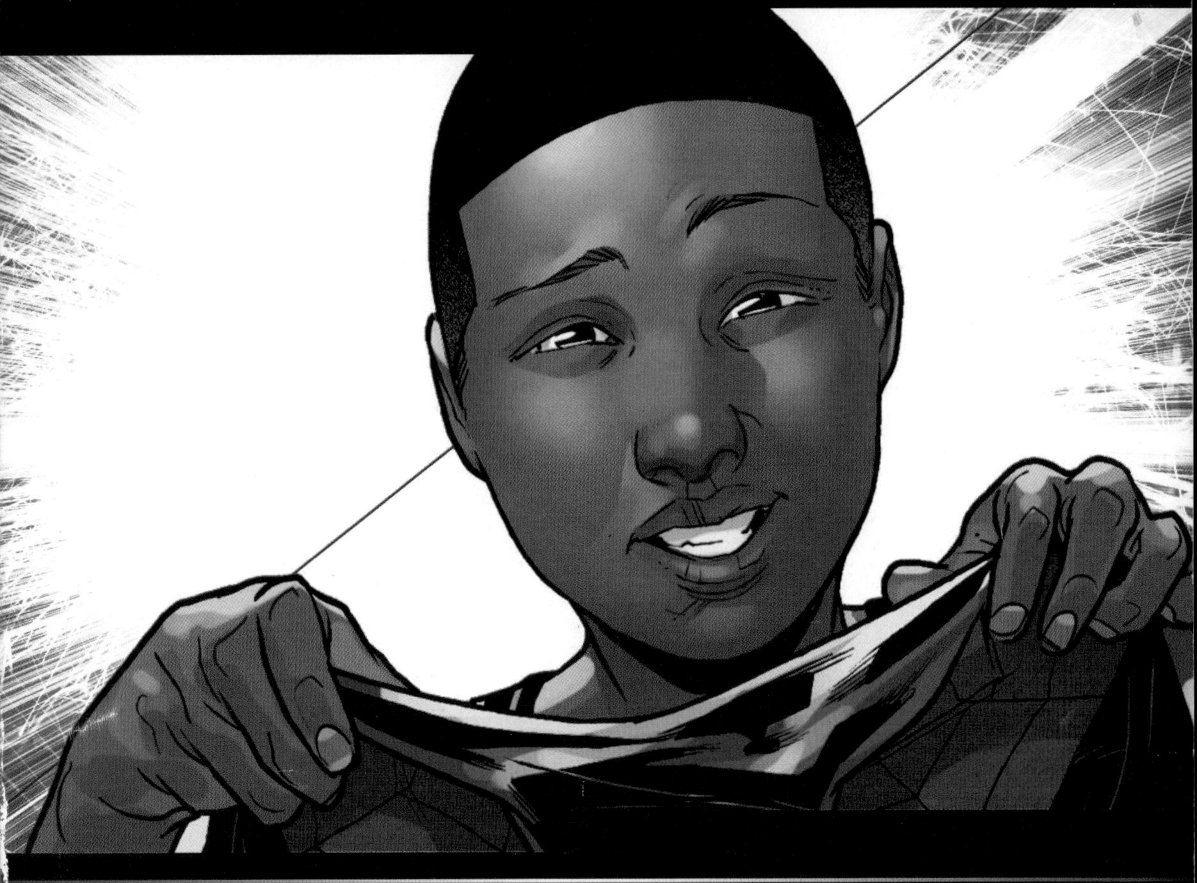

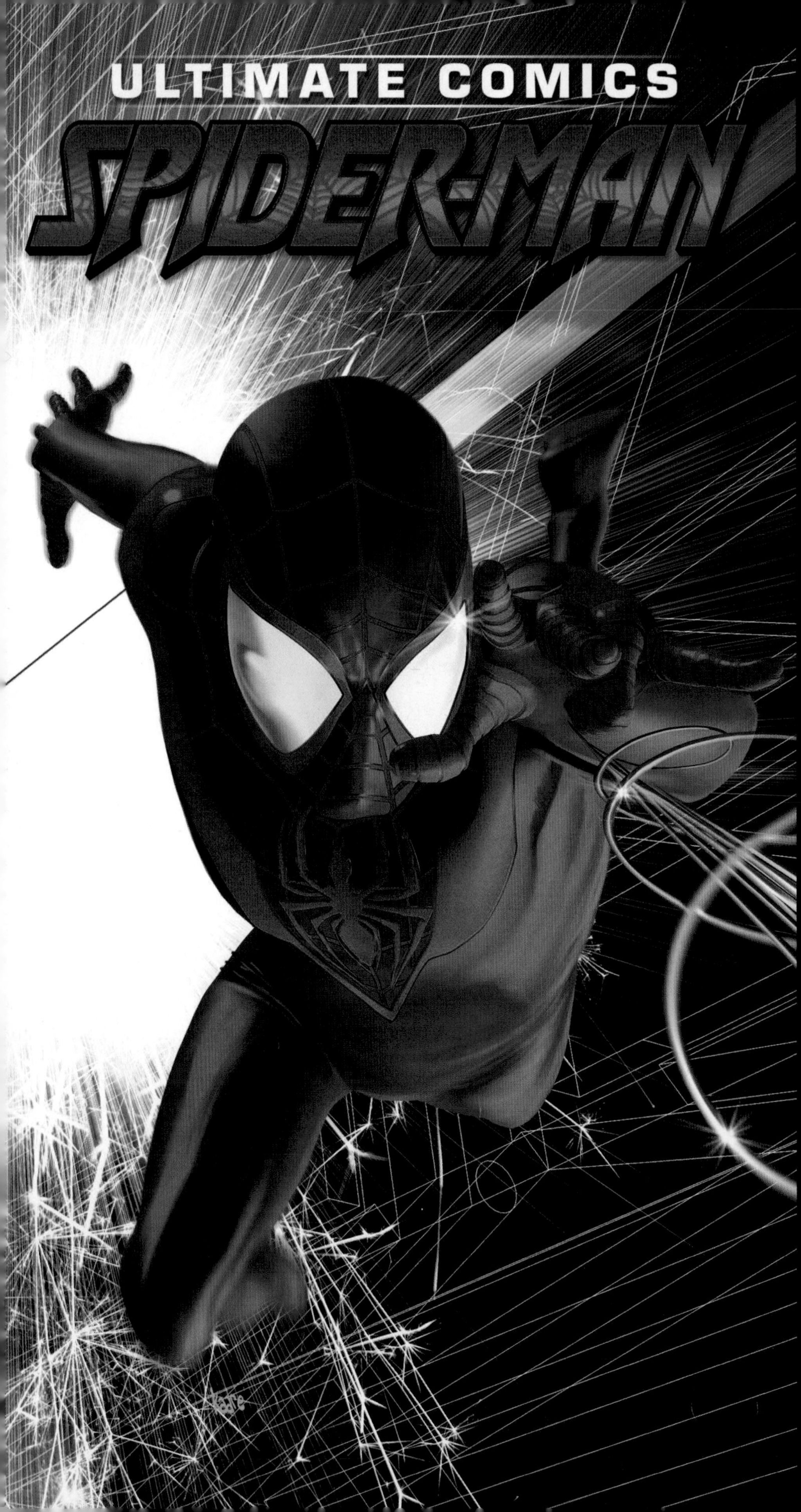
ULTIMATE COMICS
SPIDER-MAN

WRITER: **BRIAN MICHAEL BENDIS**
ARTIST: **SARA PICHELLI**
FINISHES, ISSUE #5: **DAVID MESSINA**
COLORIST: **JUSTIN PONSOR**
LETTERER: **VC'S CORY PETIT**
COVER ART: **KAARE ANDREWS**

ULTIMATE COMICS FALLOUT #4
REED RICHARDS
    WRITER: **JONATHAN HICKMAN**
    ARTIST: **SALVADOR LARROCA**
    COLORIST: **FRANK D'ARMATA**
VALERIE COOPER
    WRITER: **NICK SPENCER**
    ARTIST: **CLAYTON CRAIN**
LETTERERS: **VC'S CORY PETIT & CLAYTON COWLES**
COVER ART: **MARK BAGLEY, ANDY LANNING & JUSTIN PONSOR**

ASSISTANT EDITOR: **JON MOISAN**
ASSOCIATE EDITOR: **SANA AMANAT**
SENIOR EDITOR: **MARK PANICCIA**

COLLECTION EDITOR: **JENNIFER GRÜNWALD**
ASSISTANT EDITORS: **ALEX STARBUCK** & **NELSON RIBEIRO**
EDITOR, SPECIAL PROJECTS: **MARK D. BEAZLEY**
SENIOR EDITOR, SPECIAL PROJECTS: **JEFF YOUNGQUIST**
SENIOR VICE PRESIDENT OF SALES: **DAVID GABRIEL**
SVP OF BRAND PLANNING & COMMUNICATIONS: **MICHAEL PASCIULLO**

EDITOR IN CHIEF: **AXEL ALONSO**
CHIEF CREATIVE OFFICER: **JOE QUESADA**
PUBLISHER: **DAN BUCKLEY**
EXECUTIVE PRODUCER: **ALAN FINE**

...MAN BY BRIAN MICHAEL BENDIS VOL. 1. Contains material originally published in magazine form as ULTIMATE COMICS SPIDER-MAN #1-5 and ULTIMATE COMICS FALLOUT #4. First ...N# 978-0-7851-5712-0. Softcover ISBN# 978-0-7851-5713-7. Published by MARVEL WORLDWIDE, INC., a subsidiary of MARVEL ENTERTAINMENT, LLC. OFFICE OF PUBLICATION: 135 ...Y 10020. Copyright © 2011 and 2012 Marvel Characters, Inc. All rights reserved. Hardcover: $24.99 per copy in the U.S. and $27.99 in Canada (GST #R127032852). Softcover: $19.99 ...99 in Canada (GST #R127032852). Canadian Agreement #40668537. All characters featured in this issue and the distinctive names and likenesses thereof, and all related indicia are ...ters, Inc. No similarity between any of the names, characters, persons, and/or institutions in this magazine with those of any living or dead person or institution is intended, and any ...cist is purely coincidental. **Printed in the U.S.A.** ALAN FINE, EVP - Office of the President, Marvel Worldwide, Inc. and EVP & CMO Marvel Characters B.V.; DAN BUCKLEY, Publisher & ...Digital Divisions; JOE QUESADA, Chief Creative Officer; DAVID BOGART, SVP of Business Affairs & Talent Management; TOM BREVOORT, SVP of Publishing; C.B. CEBULSKI, SVP of Creator ...D GABRIEL, SVP of Publishing Sales & Circulation; MICHAEL PASCIULLO, SVP of Brand Planning & Communications; JIM O'KEEFE, VP of Operations & Logistics; DAN CARR, Executive ...logy; SUSAN CRESPI, Editorial Operations Manager; ALEX MORALES, Publishing Operations Manager; STAN LEE, Chairman Emeritus. For information regarding advertising in Marvel ...ase contact John Dokes, SVP Integrated Sales and Marketing, at jdokes@marvel.com. For Marvel subscription inquiries, please call 800-217-9158. **Manufactured between 1/2/2012** ...and 1/2/2012 and 7/30/2012 (softcover), by R.R. DONNELLEY, INC., SALEM, VA, USA.

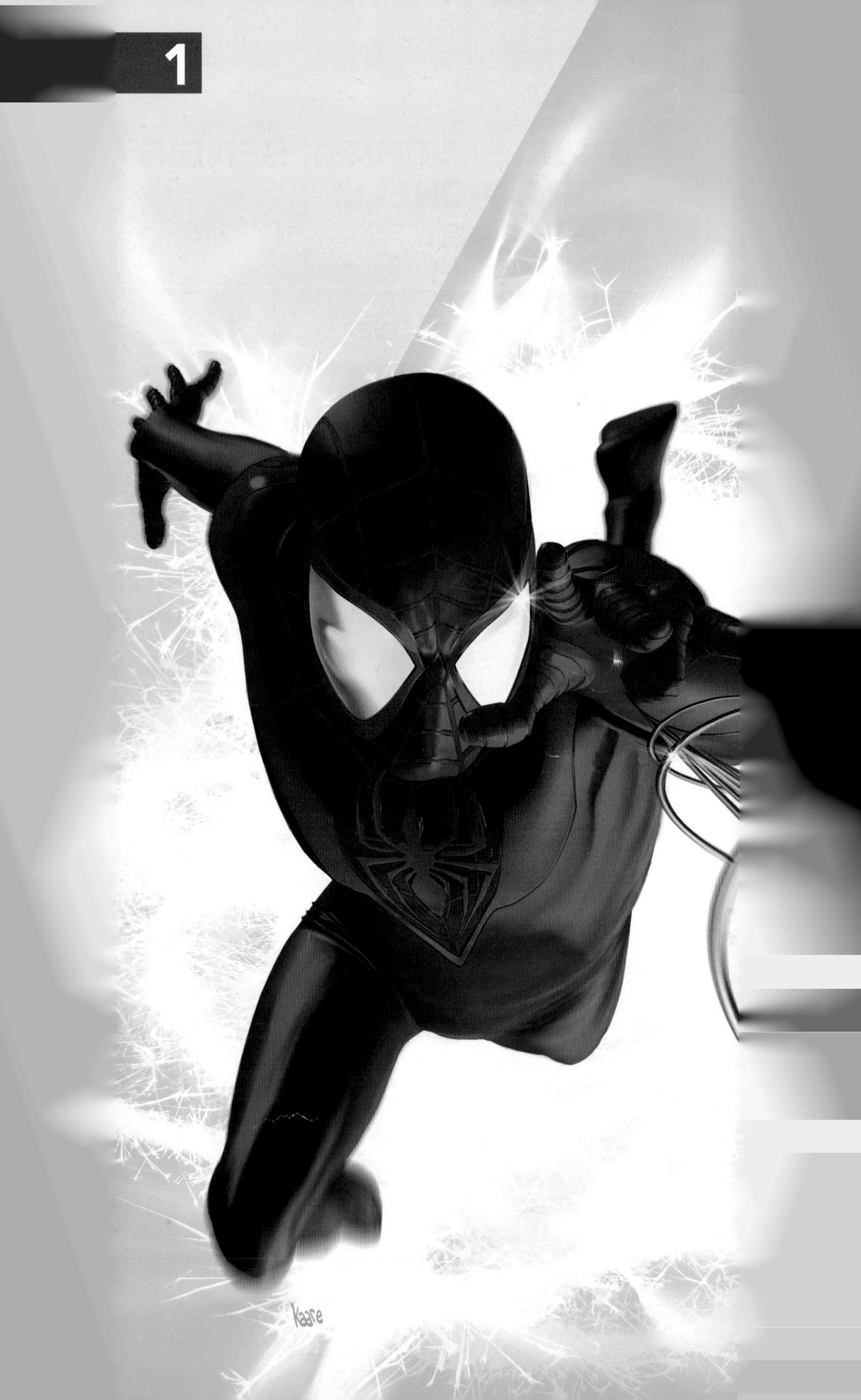
1
Kaare

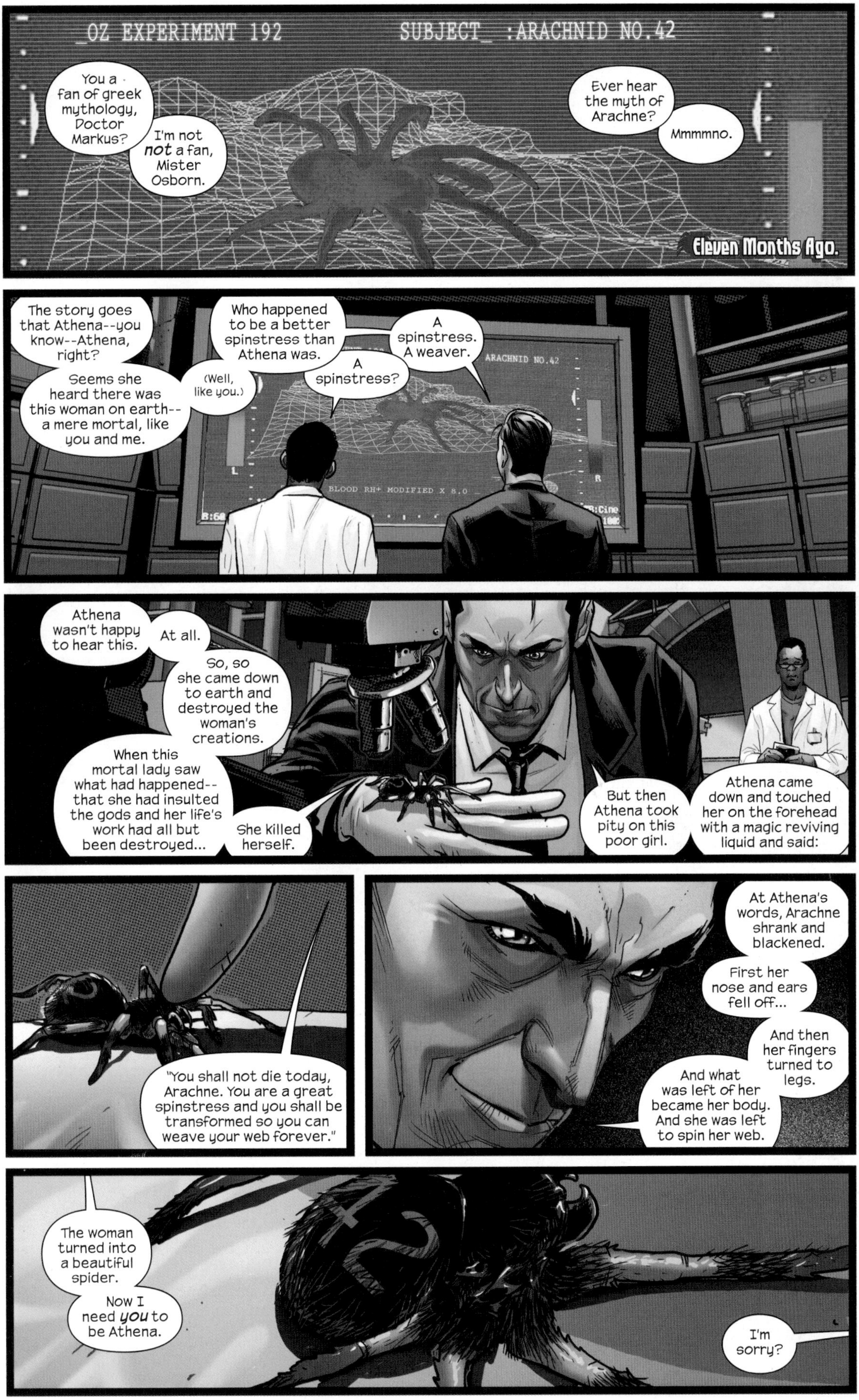

_OZ EXPERIMENT 192
SUBJECT_ :ARACHNID NO.42
Eleven Months Ago.
You a fan of greek mythology, Doctor Markus?
I'm not *not* a fan, Mister Osborn.
Ever hear the myth of Arachne?
Mmmmno.
The story goes that Athena--you know--Athena, right?
Who happened to be a better spinstress than Athena was.
A spinstress. A weaver.
ARACHNID NO.42
Seems she heard there was this woman on earth--a mere mortal, like you and me.
(Well, like you.)
A spinstress?
BLOOD RH+ MODIFIED X 8.0
Athena wasn't happy to hear this.
At all.
So, so she came down to earth and destroyed the woman's creations.
When this mortal lady saw what had happened--that she had insulted the gods and her life's work had all but been destroyed...
She killed herself.
But then Athena took pity on this poor girl.
Athena came down and touched her on the forehead with a magic reviving liquid and said:
"You shall not die today, Arachne. You are a great spinstress and you shall be transformed so you can weave your web forever."
At Athena's words, Arachne shrank and blackened.
First her nose and ears fell off...
And then her fingers turned to legs.
And what was left of her became her body. And she was left to spin her web.
The woman turned into a beautiful spider.
Now I need *you* to be Athena.
I'm sorry?

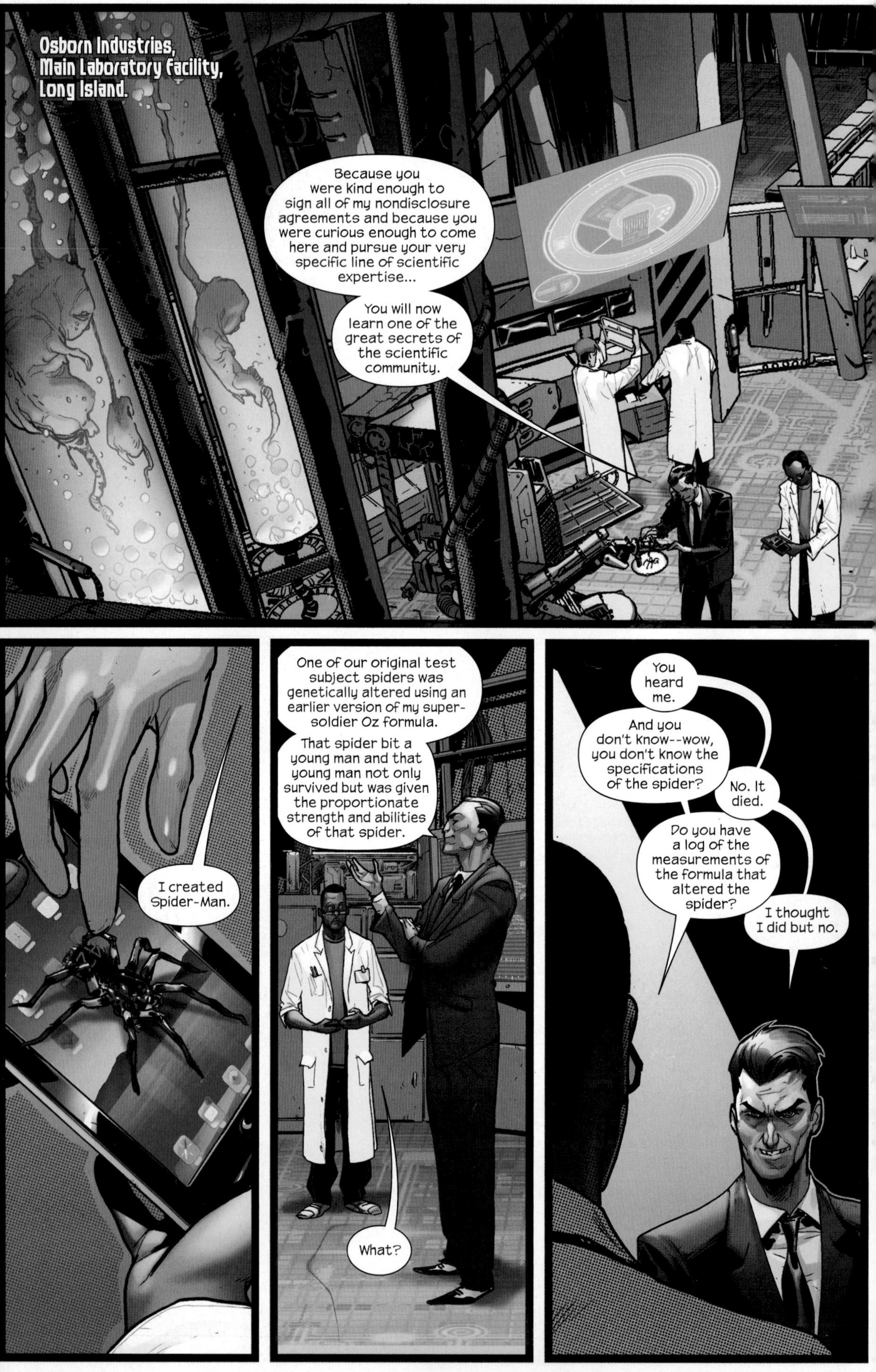
Osborn Industries, Main Laboratory Facility, Long Island.
Because you were kind enough to sign all of my nondisclosure agreements and because you were curious enough to come here and pursue your very specific line of scientific expertise...
You will now learn one of the great secrets of the scientific community.
I created Spider-Man.
One of our original test subject spiders was genetically altered using an earlier version of my super-soldier Oz formula.
That spider bit a young man and that young man not only survived but was given the proportionate strength and abilities of that spider.
What?
You heard me.
And you don't know--wow, you don't know the specifications of the spider?
No. It died.
Do you have a log of the measurements of the formula that altered the spider?
I thought I did but no.

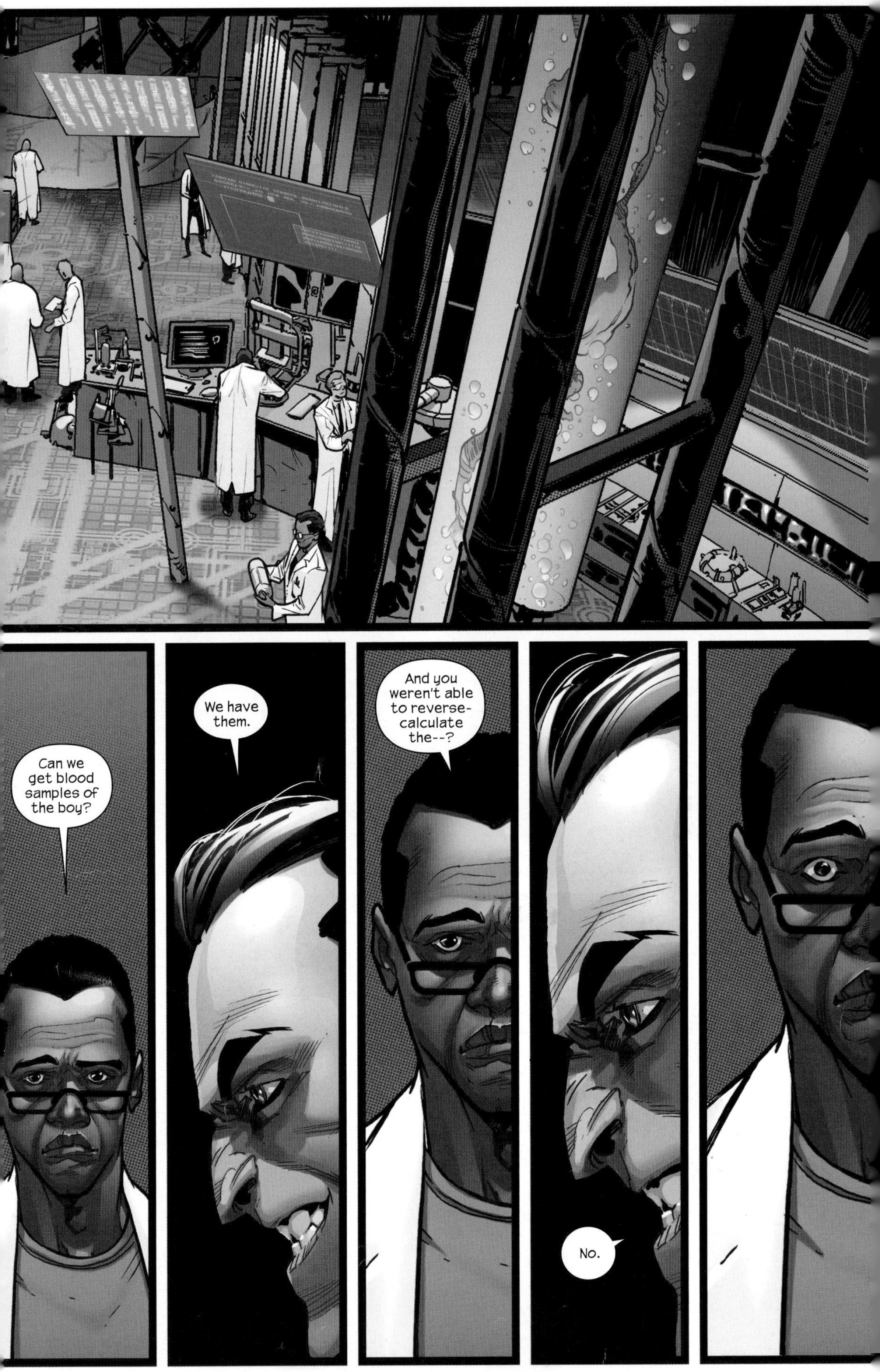
Can we get blood samples of the boy?
We have them.
And you weren't able to reverse-calculate the--?
No.

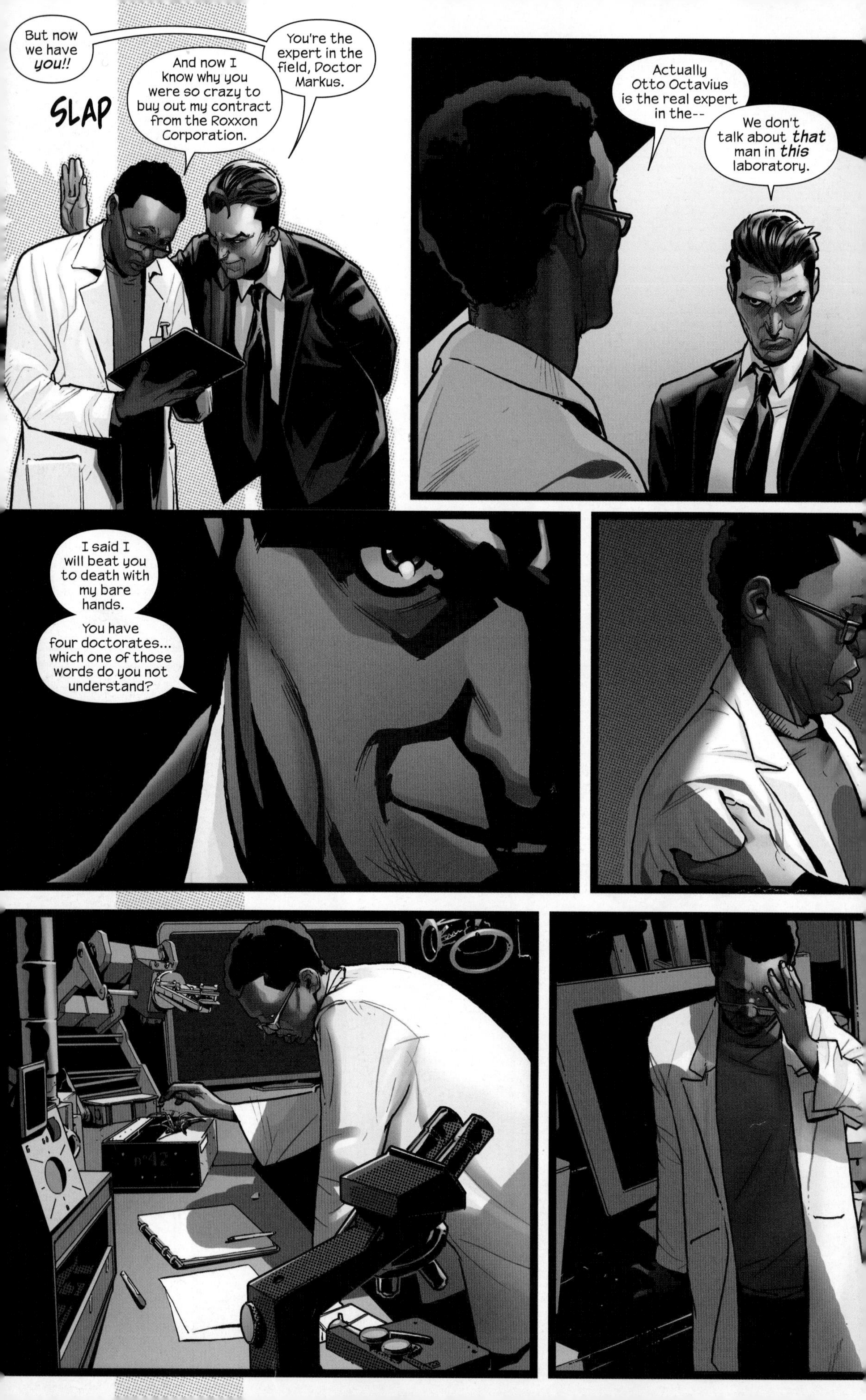
But now we have *you!!*
You're the expert in the field, Doctor Markus.
And now I know why you were so crazy to buy out my contract from the Roxxon Corporation.
SLAP
Actually Otto Octavius is the real expert in the--
We don't talk about *that* man in *this* laboratory.
I said I will beat you to death with my bare hands.
You have four doctorates... which one of those words do you not understand?

You created Spider-Man.

And I hope you understand that if this information leaves this building I will *kill* you.

Excuse me?

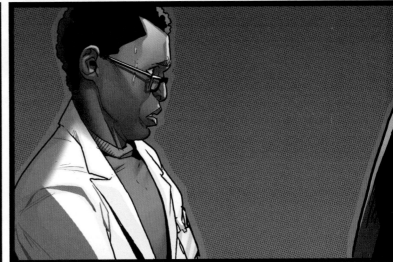

But if you solve this problem for me I will reward you to the point where I reinvent your life on every conceivable level.

LOCAL | INTERNATIONAL | ARTS & ENTERTAINMENT | OPINION | SPORTS

NORMAN OSBORN IS THE GREEN GOBLIN!

CONTROVERSIAL INDUSTRIALIST IS REVEALED TO BE GENETICALLY ALTERED MONSTER NOW IN THE CUSTODY OF S.H.I.E.L.D.

Reporting by Frederick Fosswell

Agents of the world peacekeeping task force S.H.I.E.L.D. have confirmed to the Daily Bugle that controversial industrialist Norman Osborn had infected his own body with one of his experiments altering himself into what one of our S.H.I.E.L.D. sources are referring to as the Green Goblin.

Sources also confirm that this Green Goblin is the same one that attacked Midtown High School a few months ago, shutting the school down for weeks. It is also referred to as the public debut of the mystery man called Spider-Man. Whether or not there is a connection between Spider-Man and Norman Osborn's double life has yet to be revealed.

Speculation continues as to why Norman Osborn would break one of the cardinal rules of science by experimenting on himself. Sources close to Norman say that certain pressures to create a workable version of his experimental "super-soldier" formula led him to use the formula on himself.

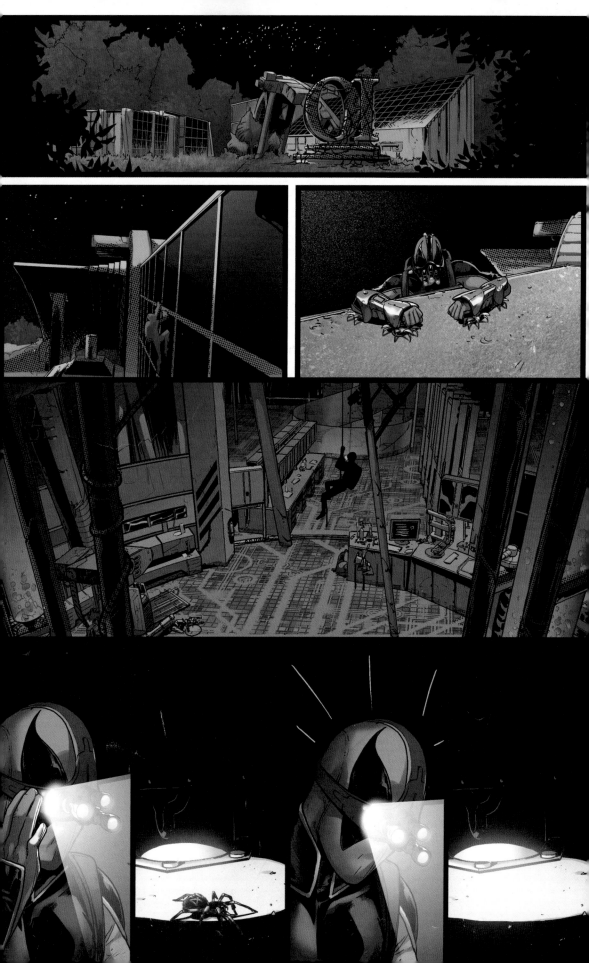

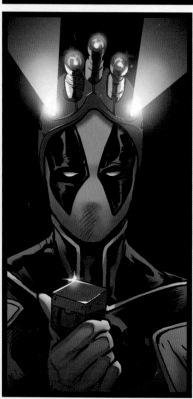

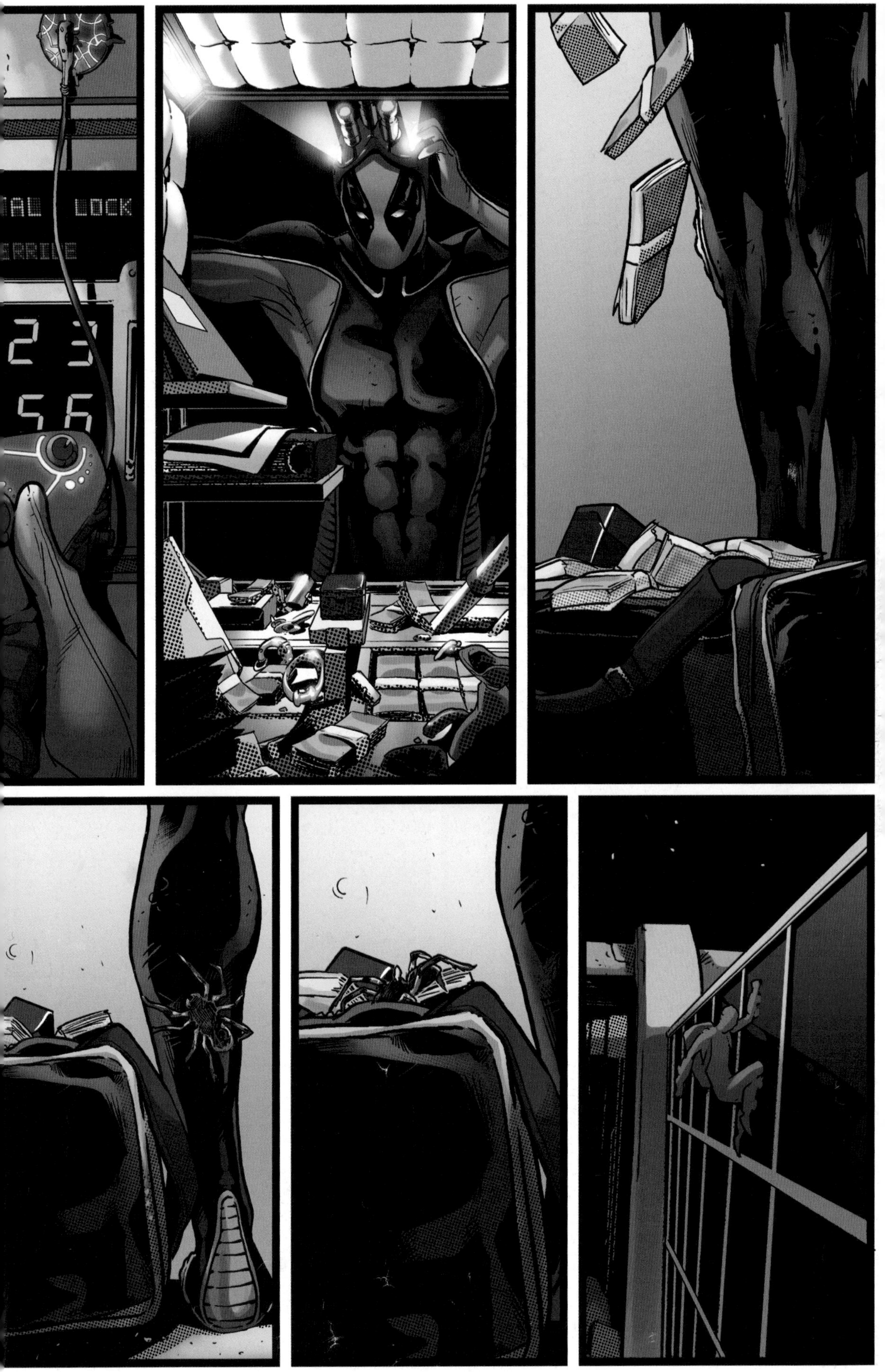
AL LOCK
RRIDE
23
56

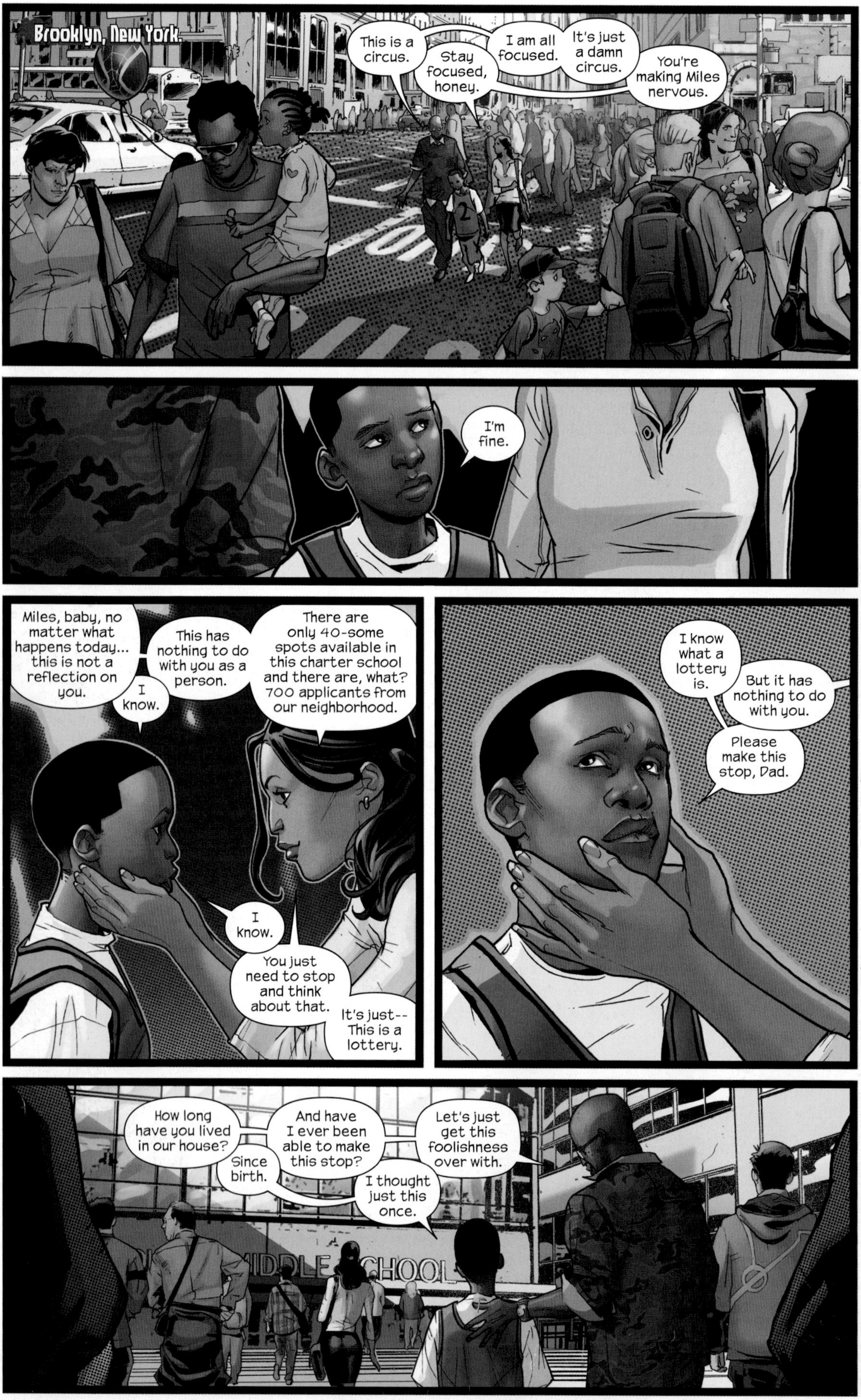
Brooklyn, New York.
This is a circus.
Stay focused, honey.
I am all focused.
It's just a damn circus.
You're making Miles nervous.
I'm fine.
Miles, baby, no matter what happens today... this is not a reflection on you.
I know.
This has nothing to do with you as a person.
There are only 40-some spots available in this charter school and there are, what? 700 applicants from our neighborhood.
I know.
You just need to stop and think about that.
It's just-- This is a lottery.
I know what a lottery is.
But it has nothing to do with you.
Please make this stop, Dad.
How long have you lived in our house?
Since birth.
And have I ever been able to make this stop?
I thought just this once.
Let's just get this foolishness over with.
MIDDLE SCHOOL

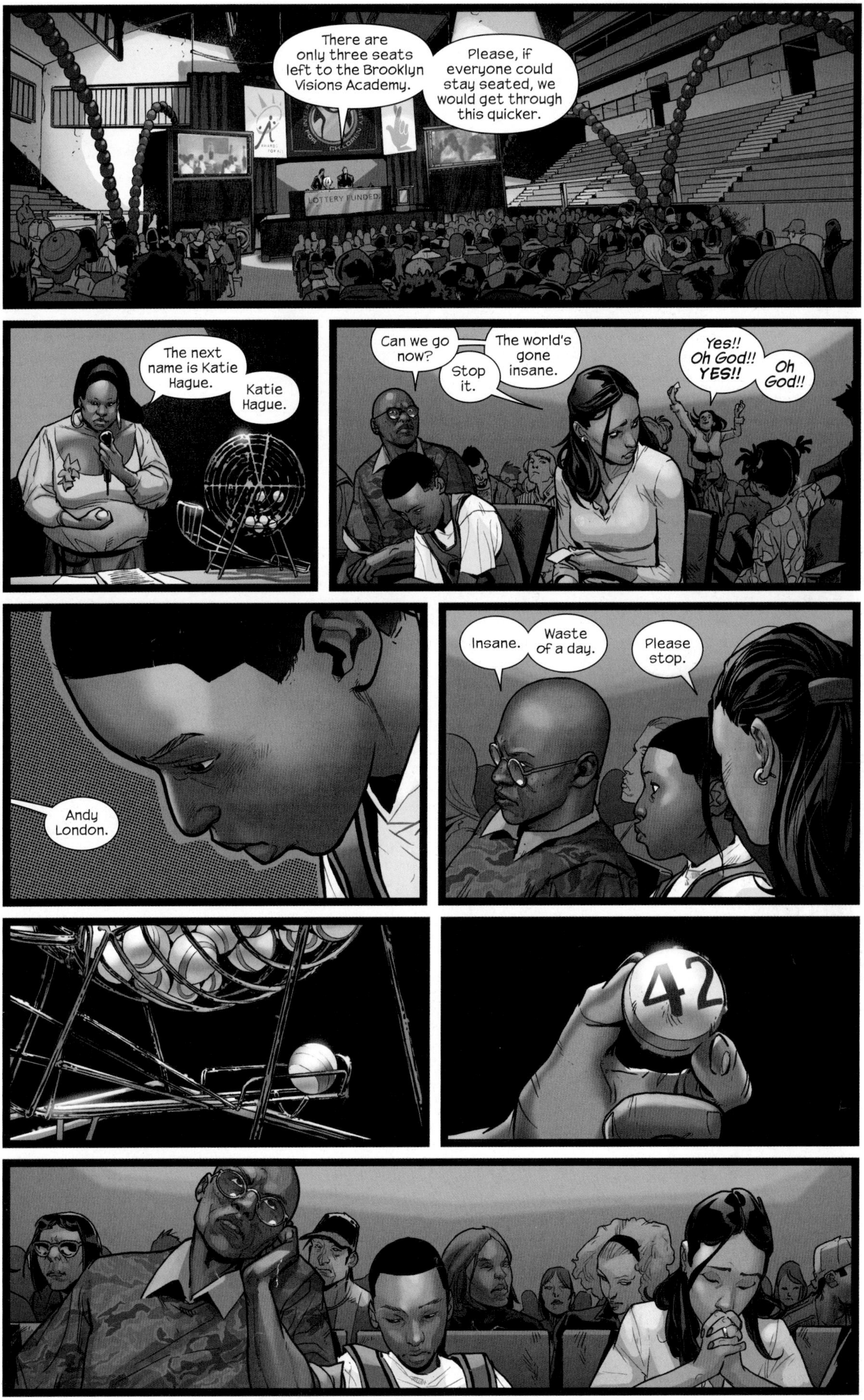
There are only three seats left to the Brooklyn Visions Academy.
Please, if everyone could stay seated, we would get through this quicker.
LOTTERY FUNDED.
The next name is Katie Hague.
Katie Hague.
Can we go now?
The world's gone insane.
Stop it.
Yes!! Oh God!! YES!!
Oh God!!
Andy London.
Insane.
Waste of a day.
Please stop.
42

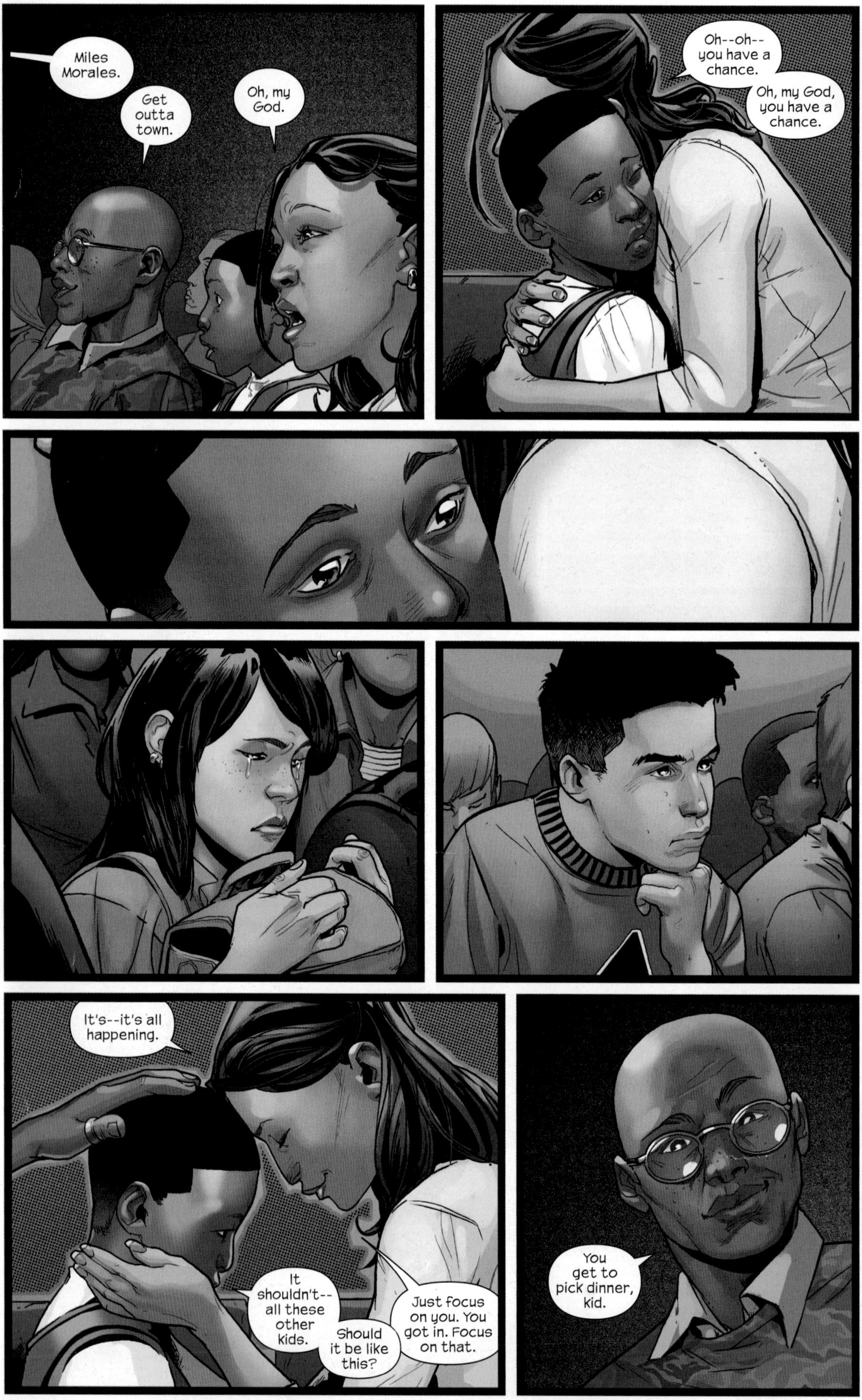
Miles Morales.
Get outta town.
Oh, my God.
Oh--oh-- you have a chance.
Oh, my God, you have a chance.
It's--it's all happening.
It shouldn't-- all these other kids.
Should it be like this?
Just focus on you. You got in. Focus on that.
You get to pick dinner, kid.

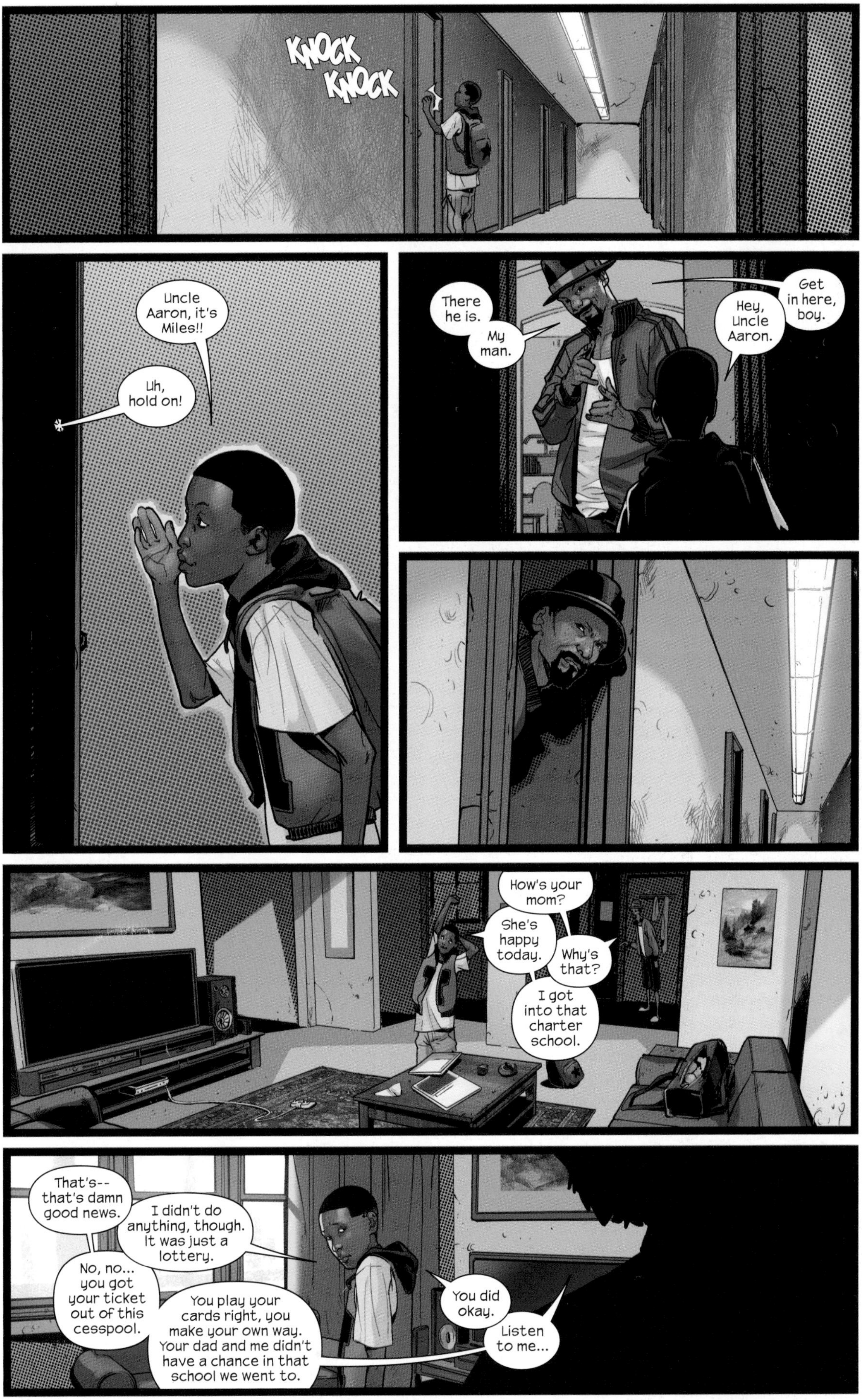
KNOCK KNOCK
Uncle Aaron, it's Miles!!
Uh, hold on!
There he is.
My man.
Get in here, boy.
Hey, Uncle Aaron.
How's your mom?
She's happy today.
Why's that?
I got into that charter school.
That's-- that's damn good news.
I didn't do anything, though. It was just a lottery.
No, no... you got your ticket out of this cesspool.
You play your cards right, you make your own way. Your dad and me didn't have a chance in that school we went to.
You did okay.
Listen to me...

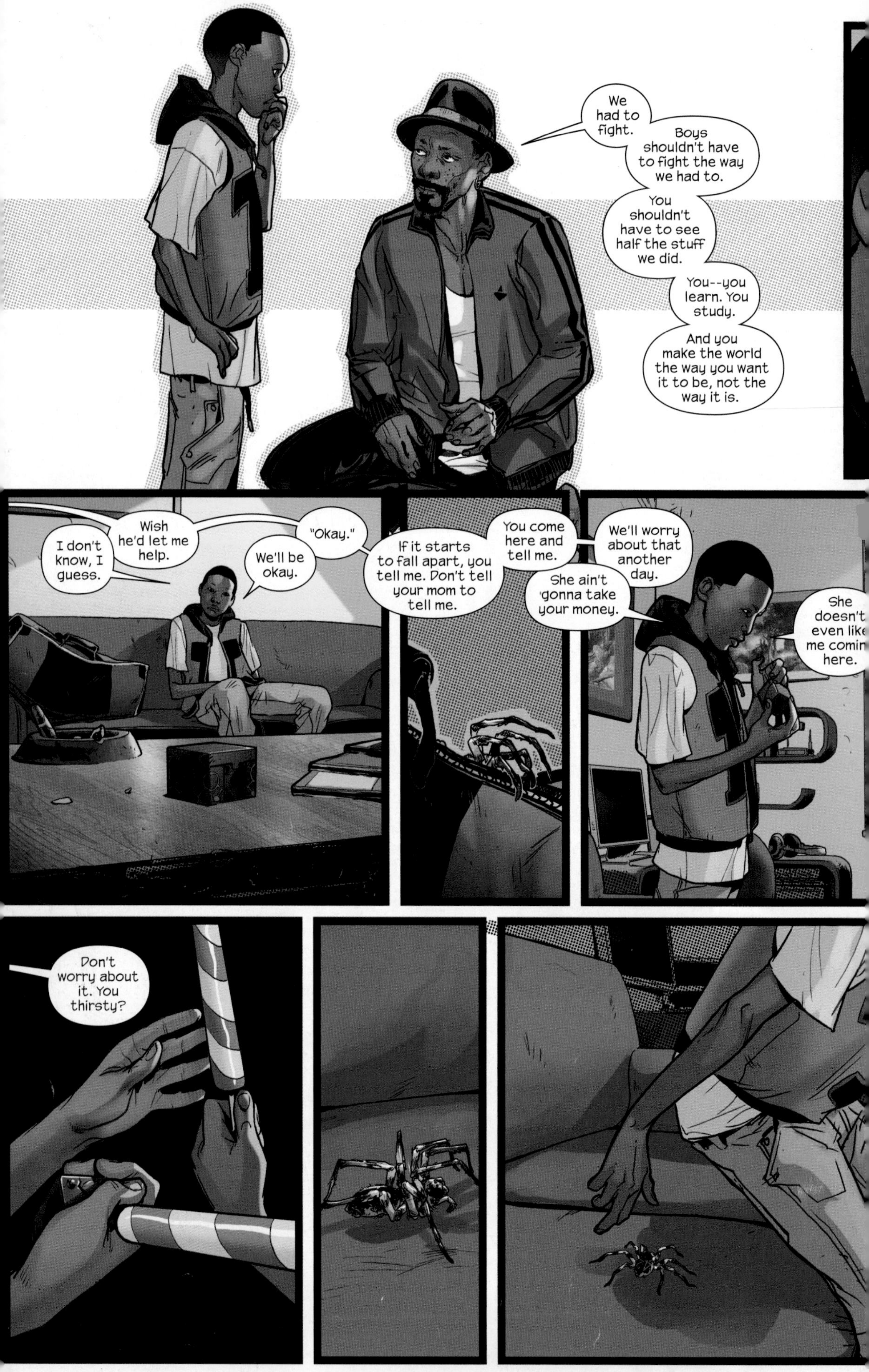
We had to fight.
Boys shouldn't have to fight the way we had to.
You shouldn't have to see half the stuff we did.
You--you learn. You study.
And you make the world the way you want it to be, not the way it is.
"Okay."
Wish he'd let me help.
I don't know, I guess.
We'll be okay.
If it starts to fall apart, you tell me. Don't tell your mom to tell me.
You come here and tell me.
We'll worry about that another day.
She ain't 'gonna take your money.
She doesn't even like me comin here.
Don't worry about it. You thirsty?

You make it.

Don't let people make it for you.

This is a good thing. This-- this calls for popsicles.

Right?

Yeah.

Your daddy gonna be able to pay for it?

What's this?

Oh hey no. That is something else--that is something for work.

What is it?

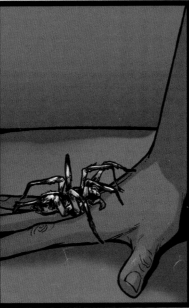

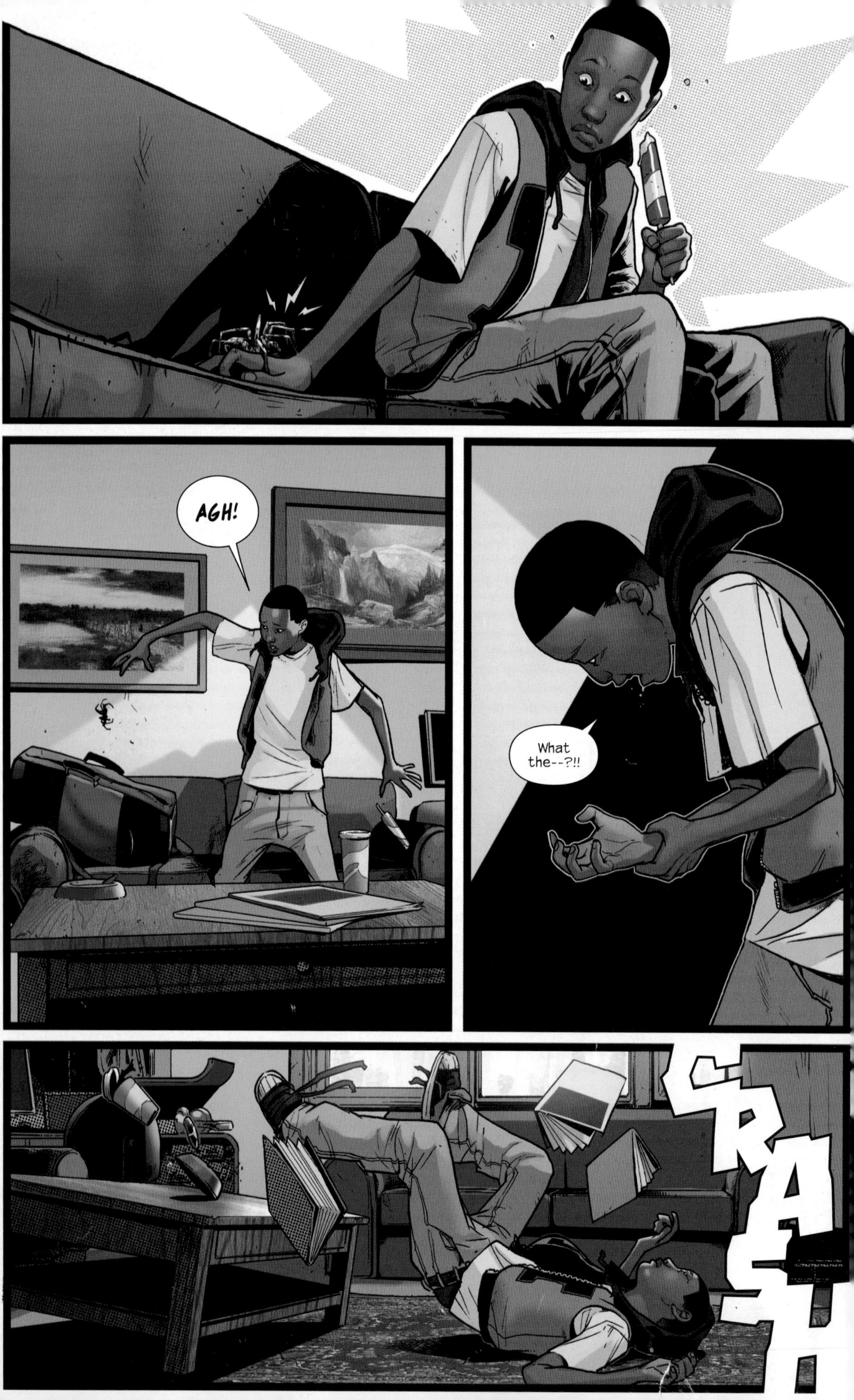
AGH!
What the--?!!
CRASH!

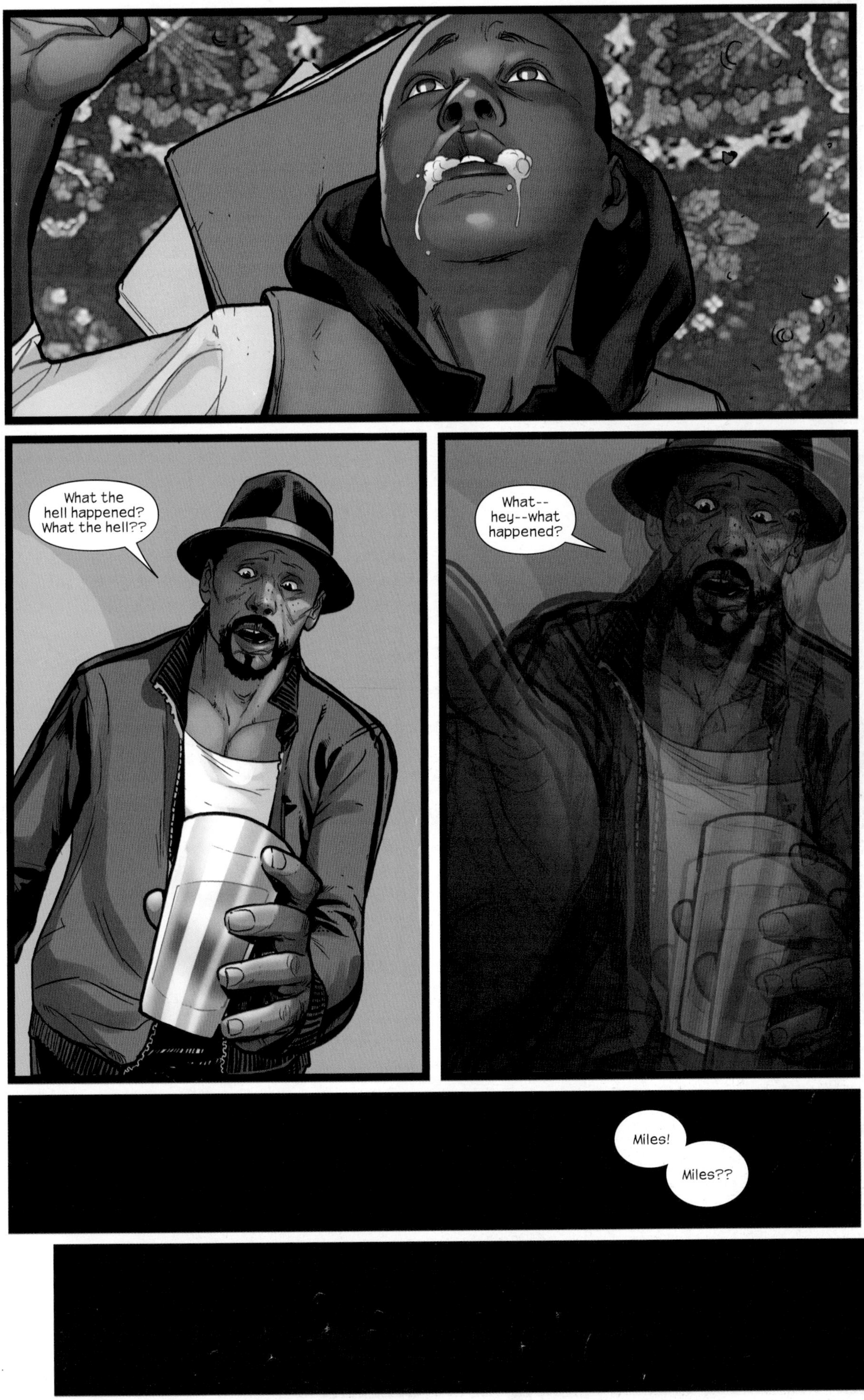
What the hell happened? What the hell??
What-- hey--what happened?
Miles!
Miles??

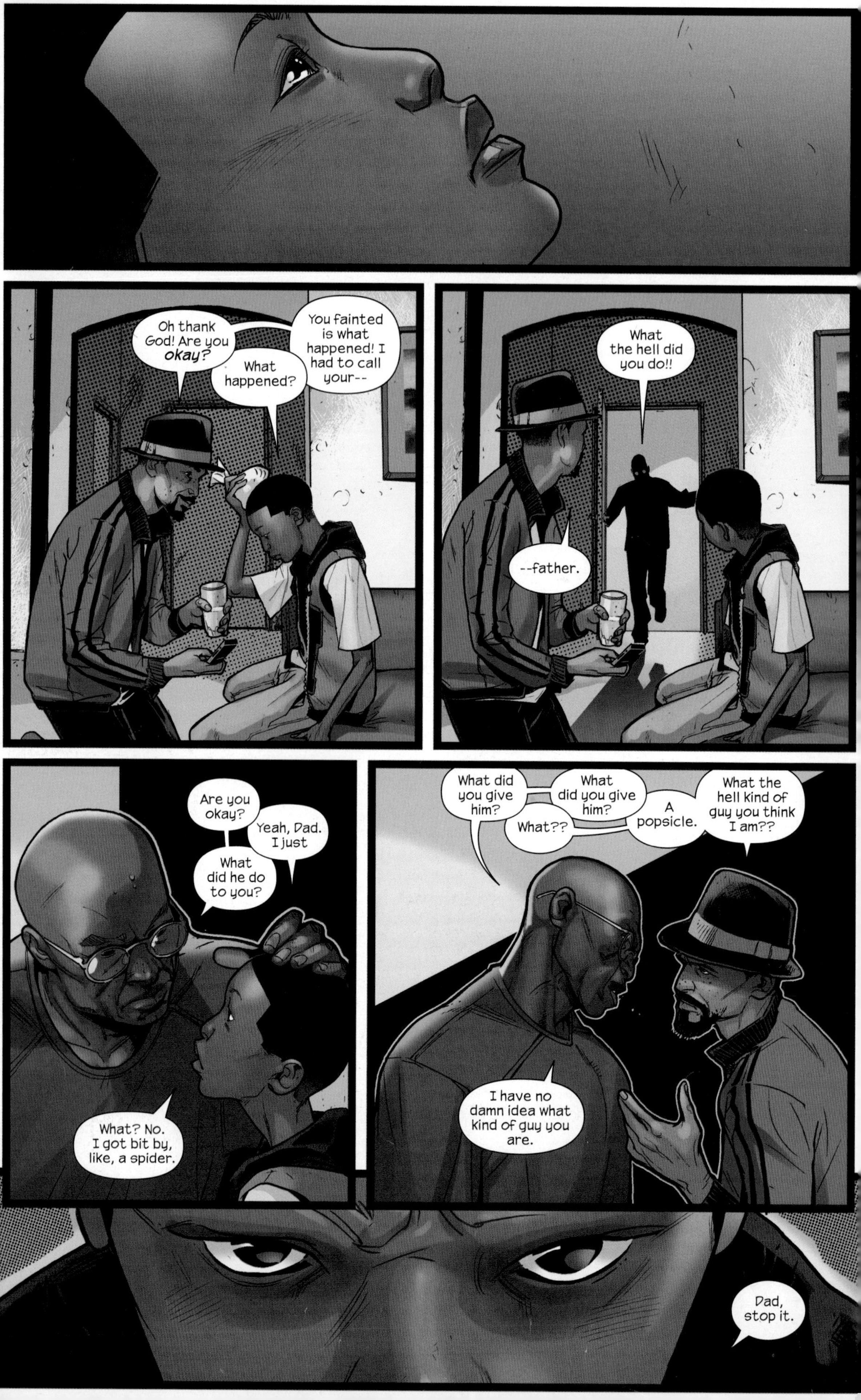
Oh thank God! Are you okay?
What happened?
You fainted is what happened! I had to call your--
--father.
What the hell did you do!!
Are you okay?
What did he do to you?
Yeah, Dad. I just
What? No. I got bit by, like, a spider.
What did you give him?
What??
What did you give him?
A popsicle.
What the hell kind of guy you think I am??
I have no damn idea what kind of guy you are.
Dad, stop it.

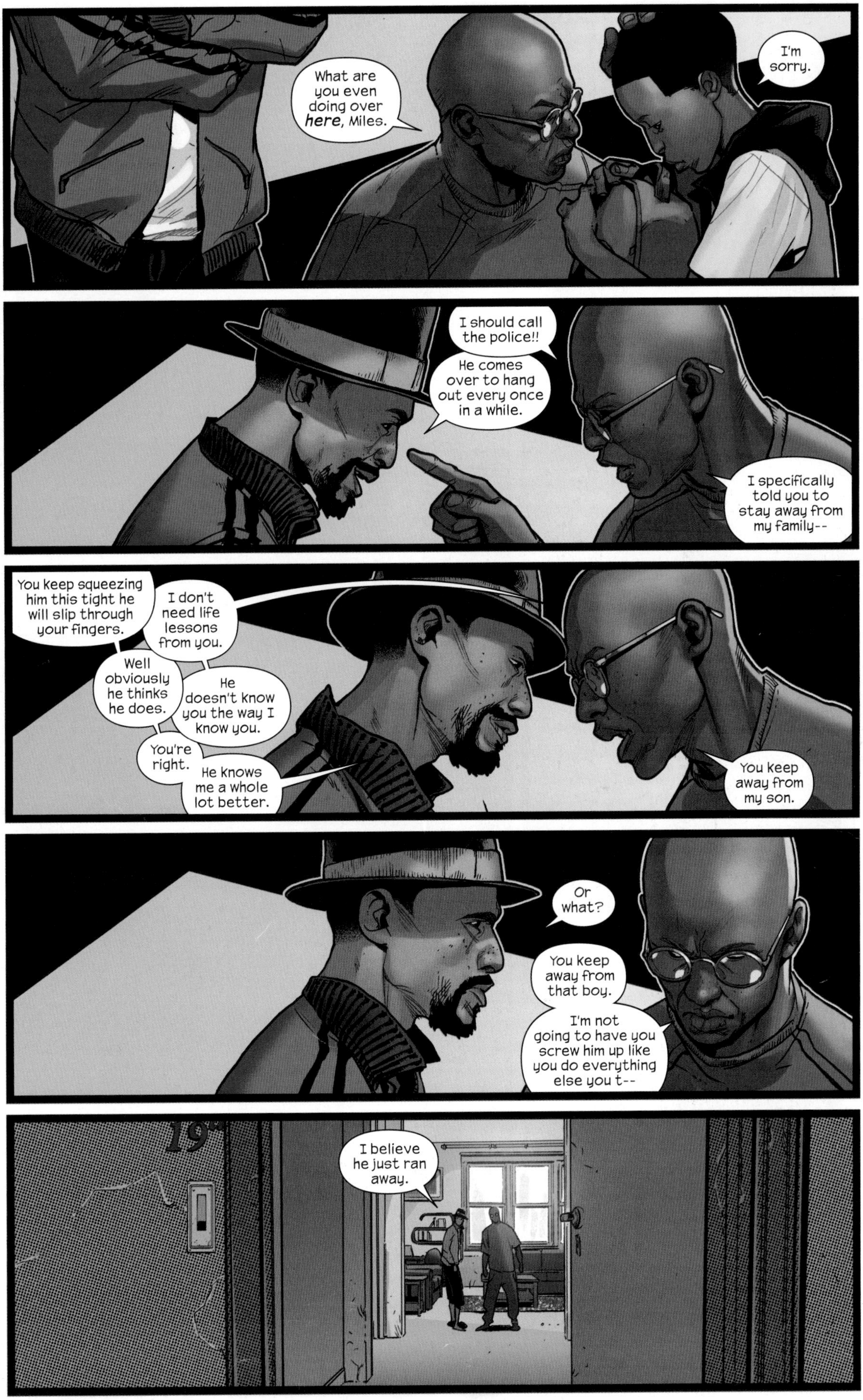

What are you even doing over *here*, Miles.
I'm sorry.
I should call the police!!
He comes over to hang out every once in a while.
I specifically told you to stay away from my family--
You keep squeezing him this tight he will slip through your fingers.
I don't need life lessons from you.
Well obviously he thinks he does.
He doesn't know you the way I know you.
You're right.
He knows me a whole lot better.
You keep away from my son.
Or what?
You keep away from that boy.
I'm not going to have you screw him up like you do everything else you t--
I believe he just ran away.

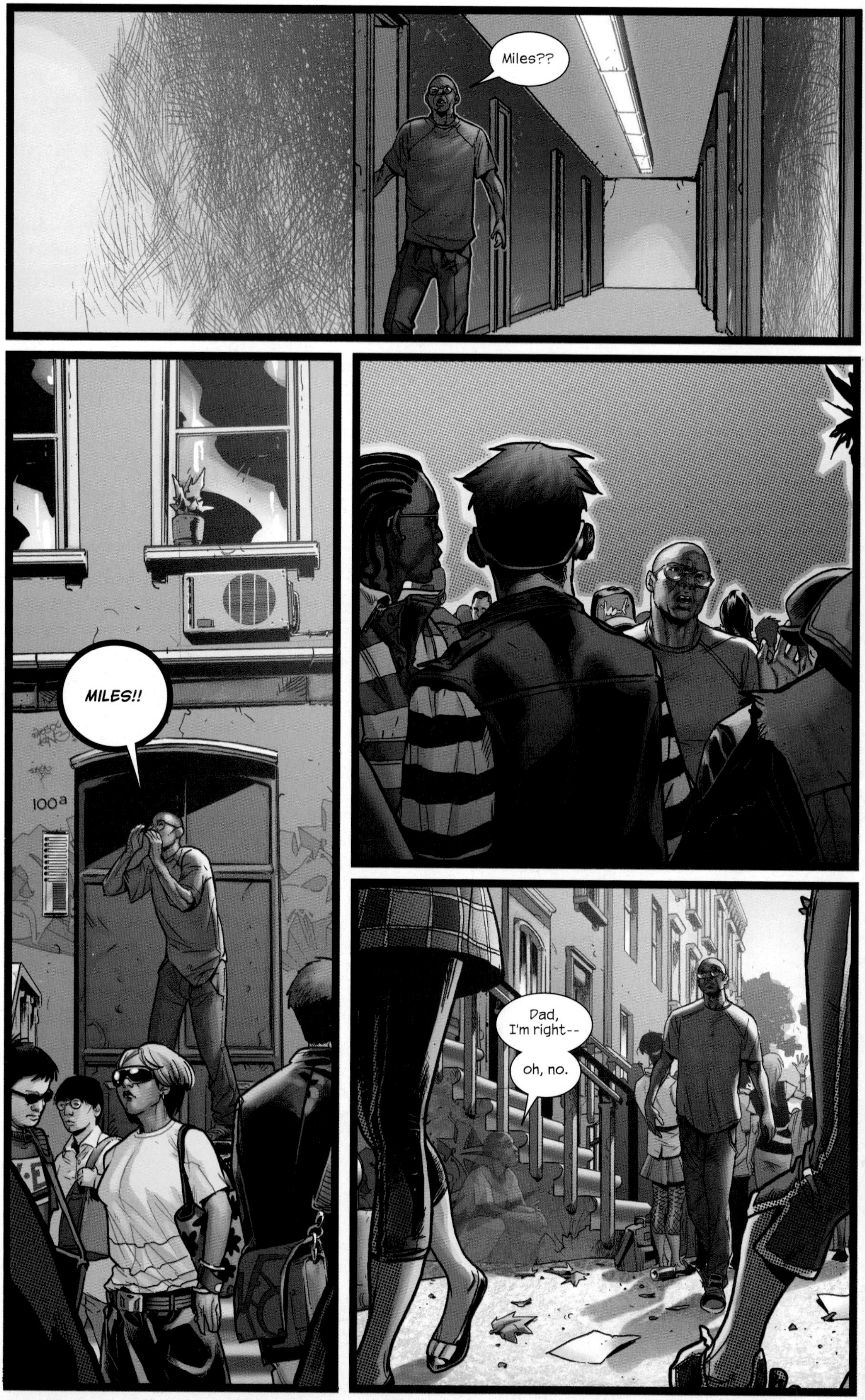
Miles??
MILES!!
Dad, I'm right--
oh, no.

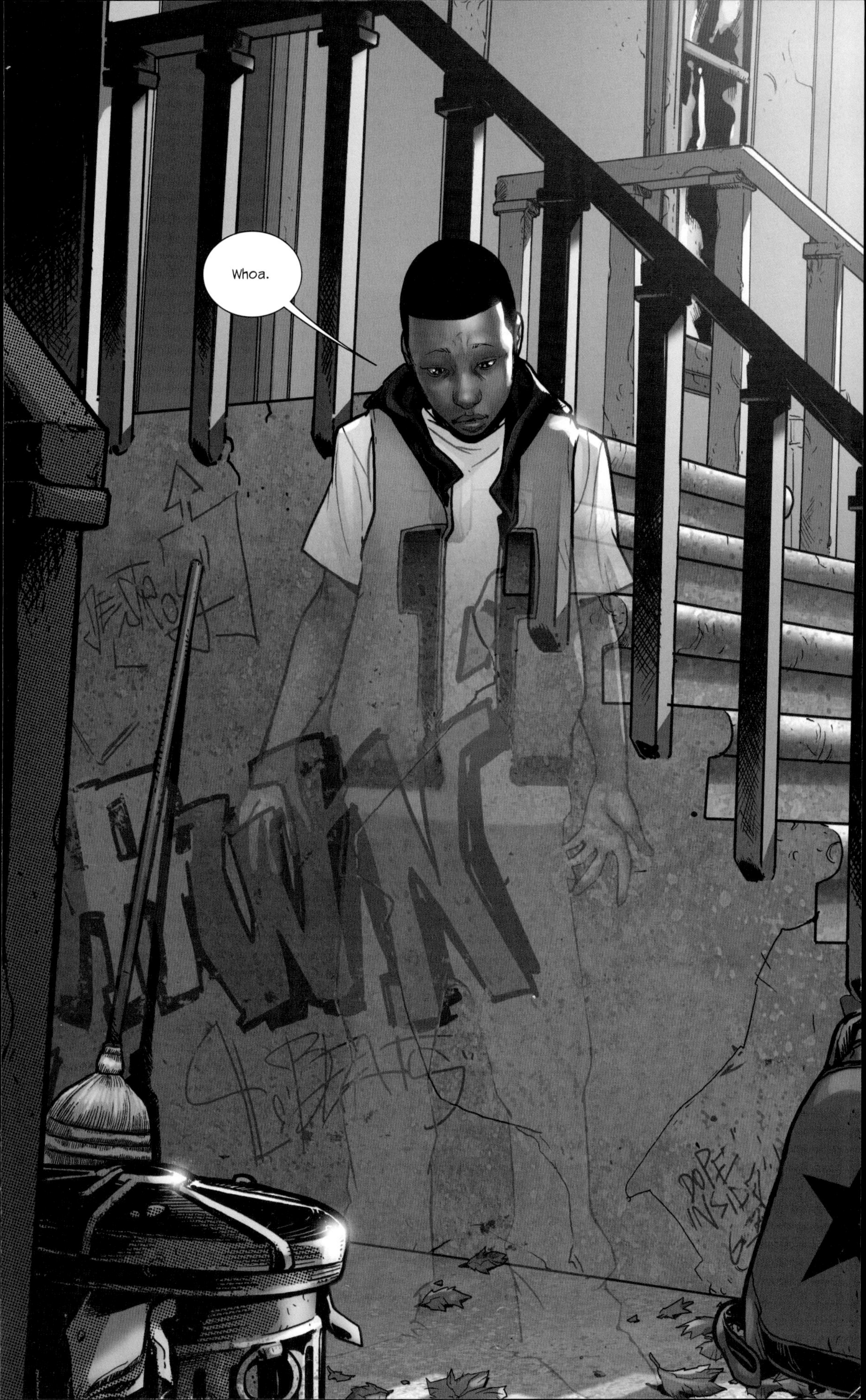
Whoa.

2

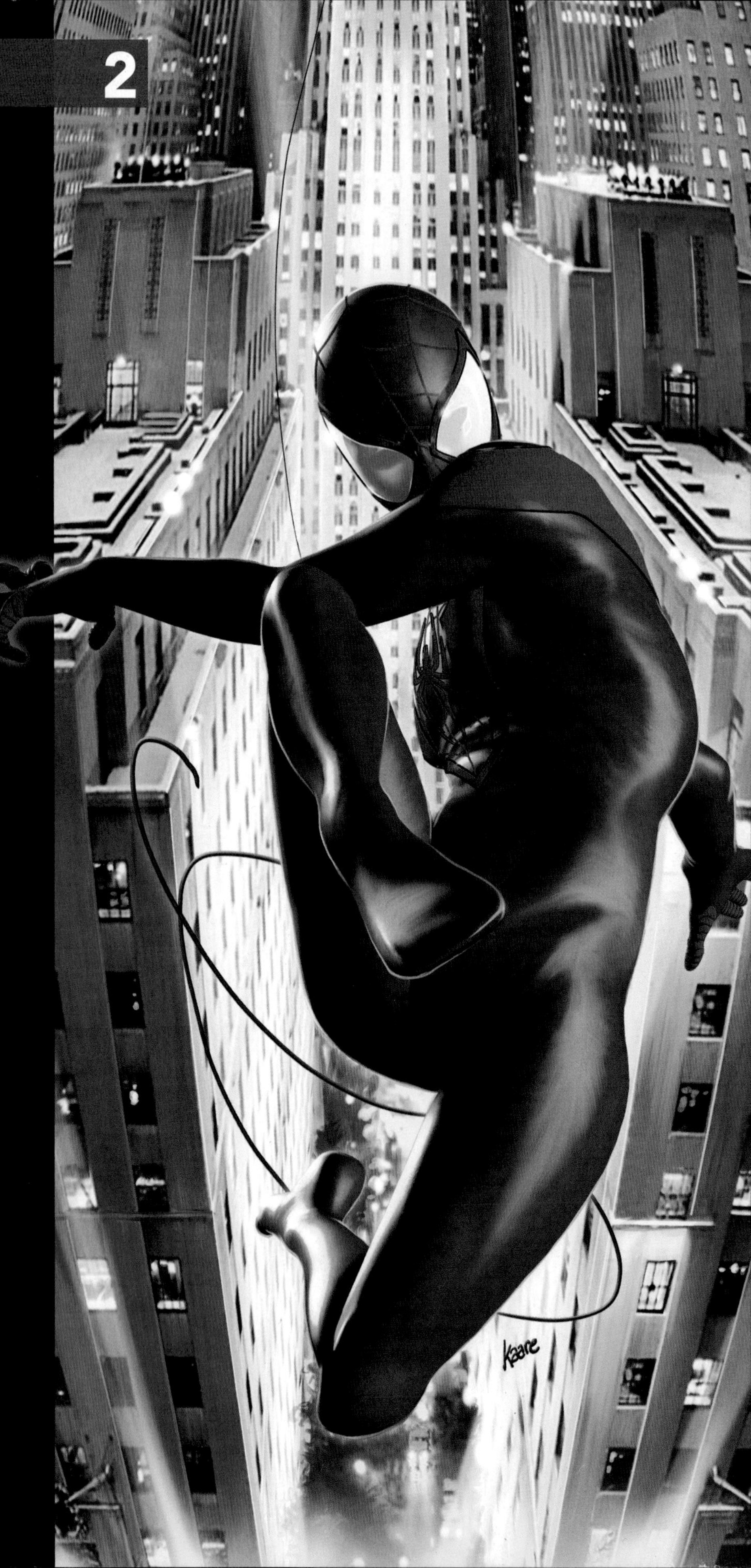
Kaare

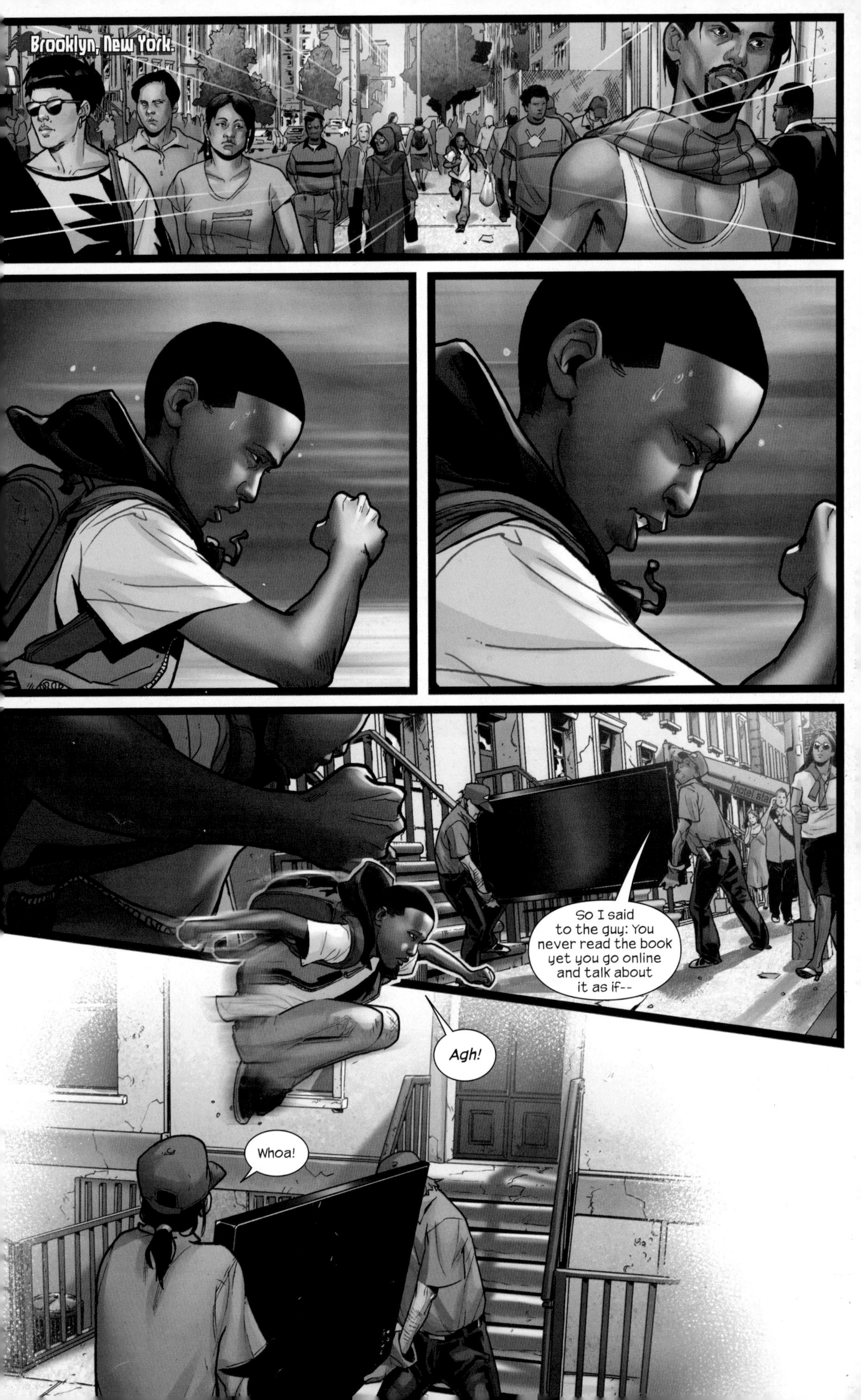
Brooklyn, New York.
So I said to the guy: You never read the book yet you go online and talk about it as if--
Agh!
Whoa!

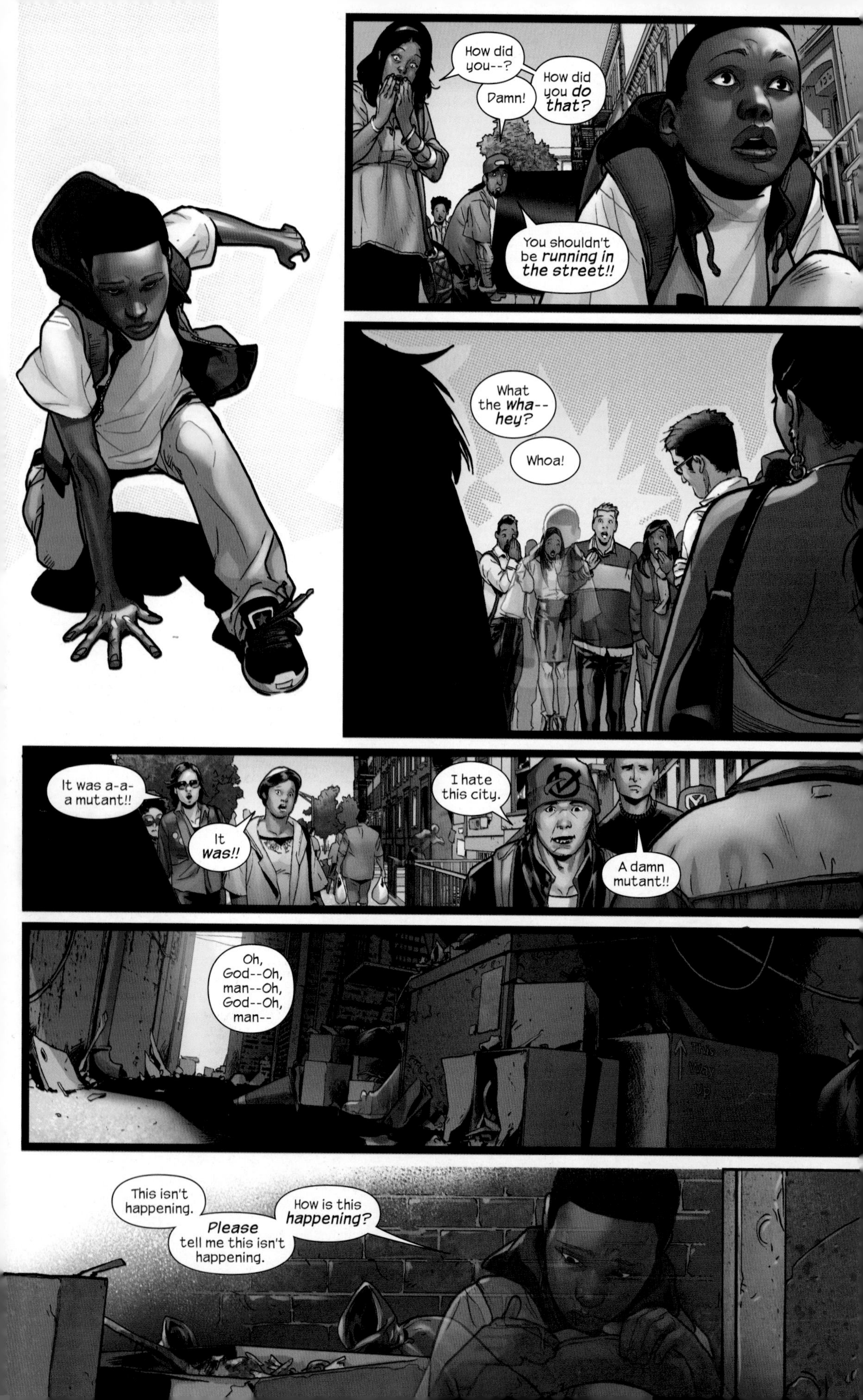

How did you--?
How did you *do that?*
Damn!
You shouldn't be *running in the street!!*
What the *wha-- hey?*
Whoa!
It was a-a-a mutant!!
It *was!!*
I hate this city.
A damn mutant!!
Oh, God--Oh, man--Oh, God--Oh, man--
This Way Up
This isn't happening.
Please tell me this isn't happening.
How is this *happening?*

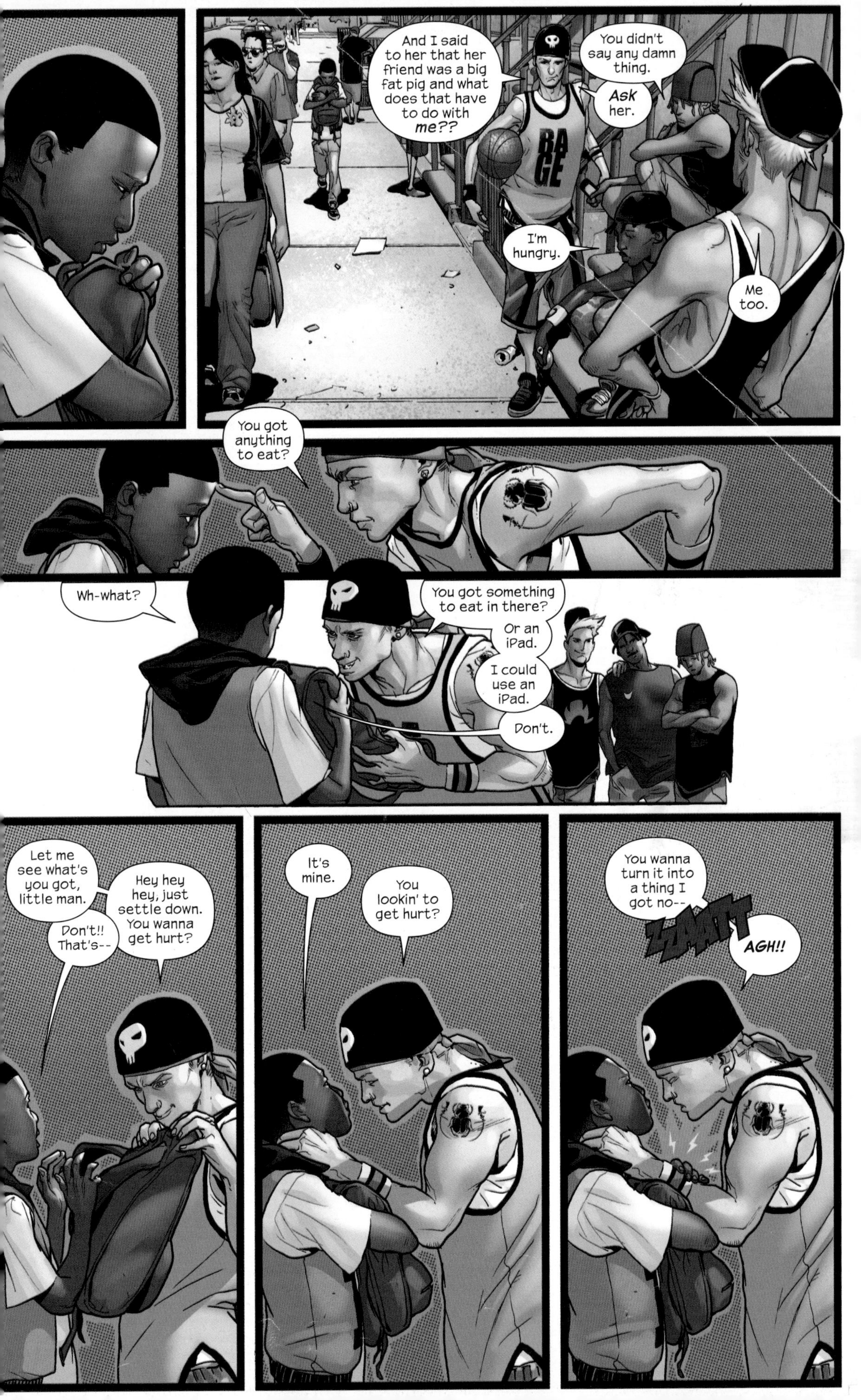
And I said to her that her friend was a big fat pig and what does that have to do with *me??*
You didn't say any damn thing.
Ask her.
I'm hungry.
Me too.
You got anything to eat?
Wh-what?
You got something to eat in there?
Or an iPad.
I could use an iPad.
Don't.
Let me see what's you got, little man.
Hey hey hey, just settle down. You wanna get hurt?
Don't!! That's--
It's mine.
You lookin' to get hurt?
You wanna turn it into a thing I got no--
ZZAATT
AGH!!

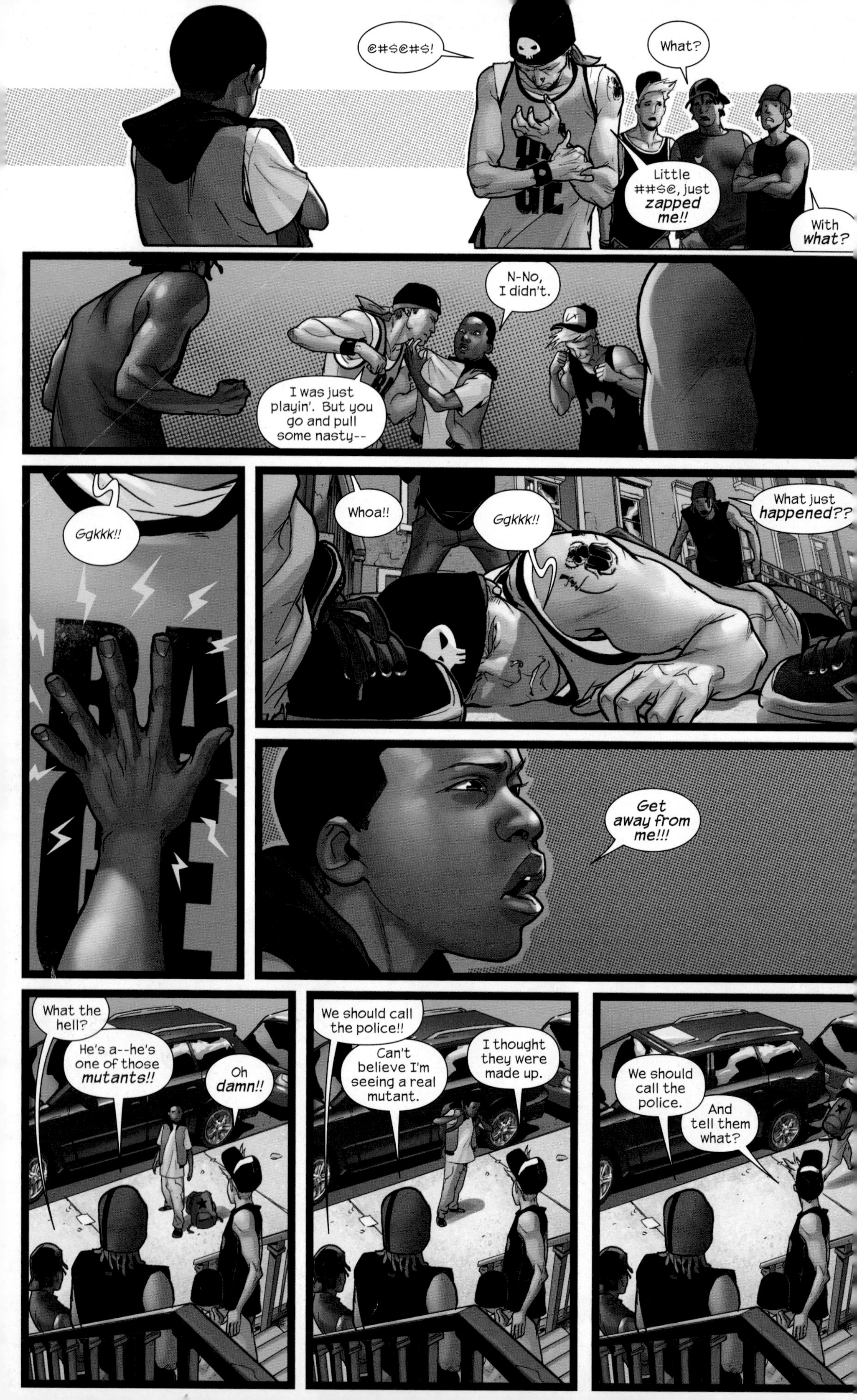
@#$@#$!
What?
Little
##$@, just
zapped
me!!
With
what?
N-No,
I didn't.
I was just
playin'. But you
go and pull
some nasty--
Ggkkk!!
Whoa!!
Ggkkk!!
What just
happened??
Get
away from
me!!!
What the
hell?
He's a--he's
one of those
mutants!!
Oh
damn!!
We should call
the police!!
Can't
believe I'm
seeing a real
mutant.
I thought
they were
made up.
We should
call the
police.
And
tell them
what?

Thank God you're home.

Miles!! Dude!

I need you, Ganke. I need your brain.

Just let me finish the masthead.

I need you to come back to real life and I need you to *help* me.

What's going on?

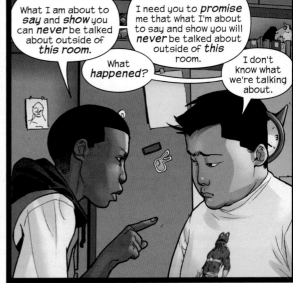

What I am about to *say* and *show* you can *never* be talked about outside of *this room.*

I need you to *promise* me that what I'm about to say and show you will *never* be talked about outside of *this* room.

What *happened?*

I don't know what we're talking about.

Promise me.

Tell me what we're talking about.

Promise me.

Dude.

Have I ever, ever screwed you over?

You're the only person I *talk* to.

Who am I going to tell whatever you're about to say?

Okay, I want you to *watch* this.

Okay.

Prepare to be freaked out like you've never been freaked out *before.*

Please don't take off your pants.

Just watch.

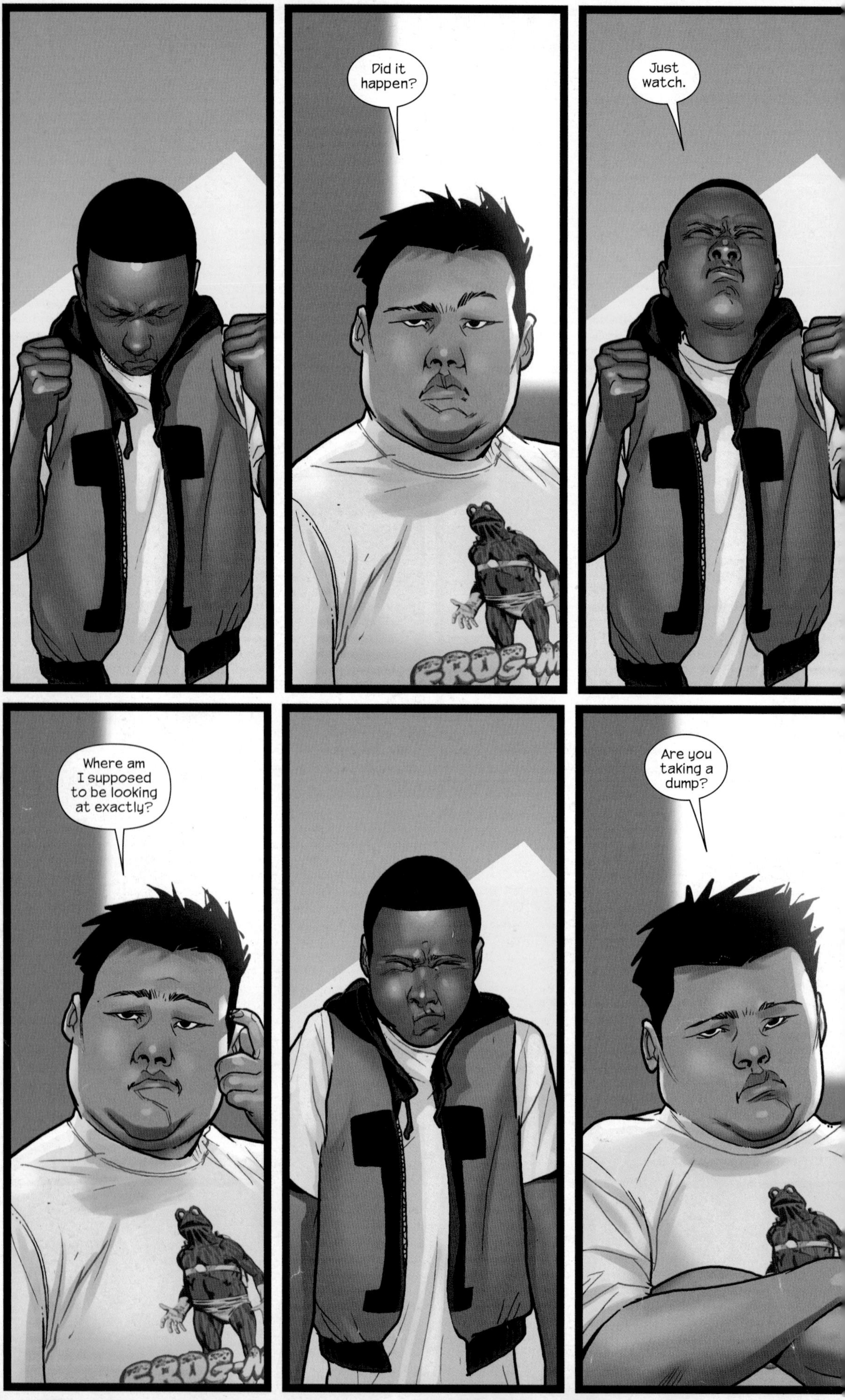
Did it happen?
Just watch.
Where am I supposed to be looking at exactly?
Are you taking a dump?

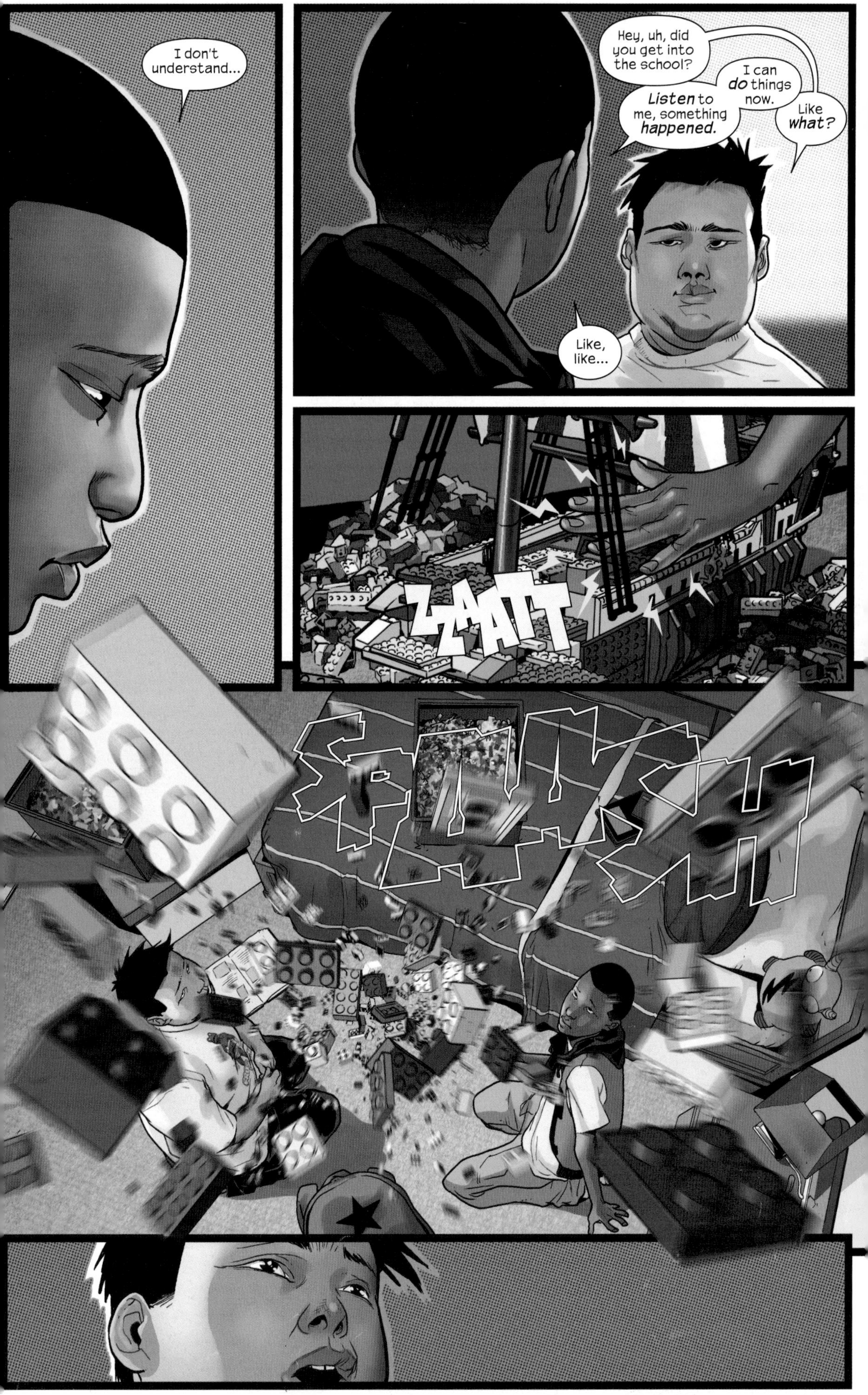
I don't understand...
Hey, uh, did you get into the school?
Listen to me, something happened.
I can do things now.
Like what?
Like, like...
ZZAATT

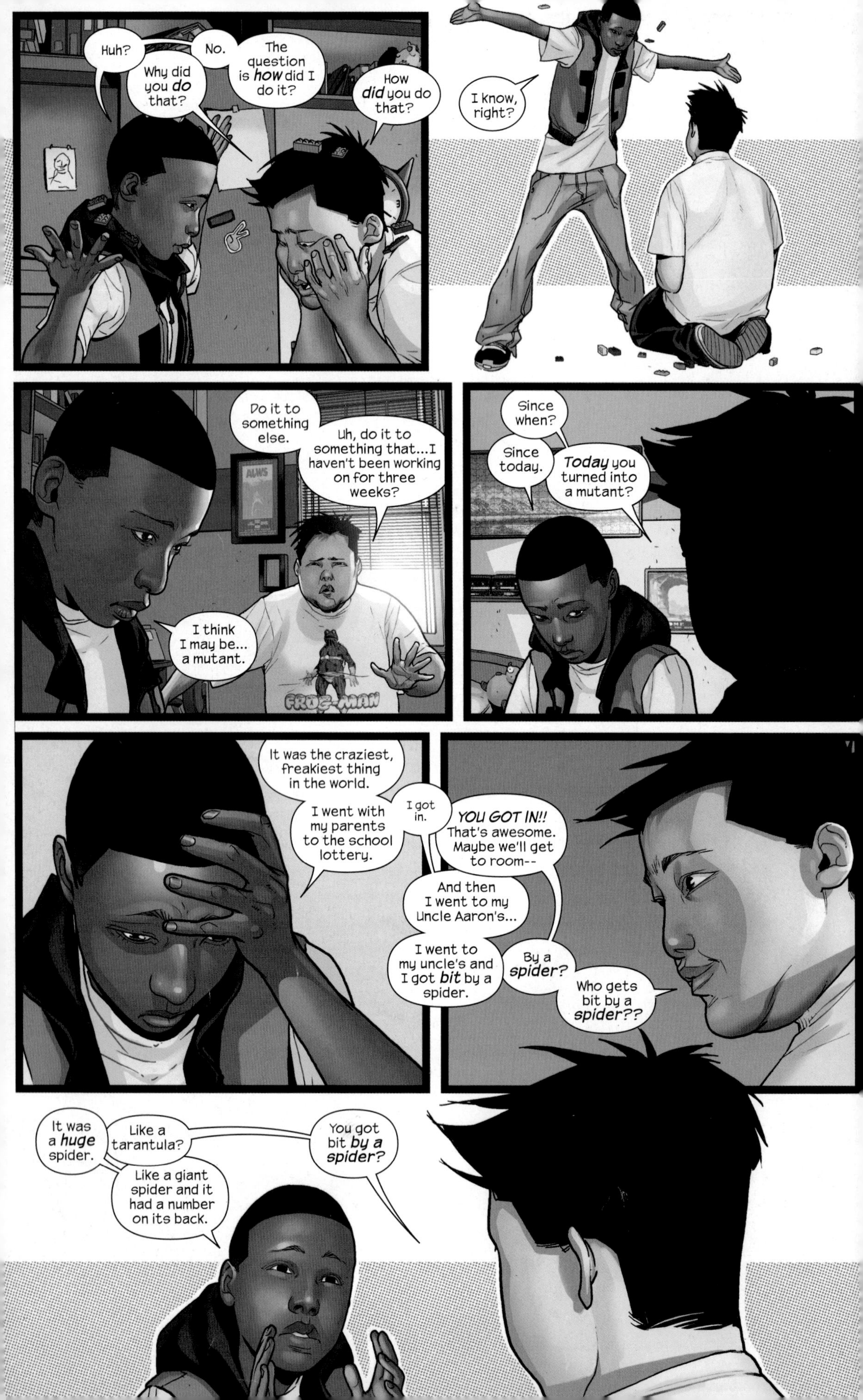

Huh?
Why did you do that?
No.
The question is how did I do it?
How did you do that?
I know, right?
Do it to something else.
Uh, do it to something that...I haven't been working on for three weeks?
I think I may be... a mutant.
FROG-MAN
Since when?
Since today.
Today you turned into a mutant?
It was the craziest, freakiest thing in the world.
I went with my parents to the school lottery.
I got in.
YOU GOT IN!! That's awesome. Maybe we'll get to room--
And then I went to my Uncle Aaron's...
I went to my uncle's and I got bit by a spider.
By a spider?
Who gets bit by a spider??
It was a huge spider.
Like a tarantula?
Like a giant spider and it had a number on its back.
You got bit by a spider?

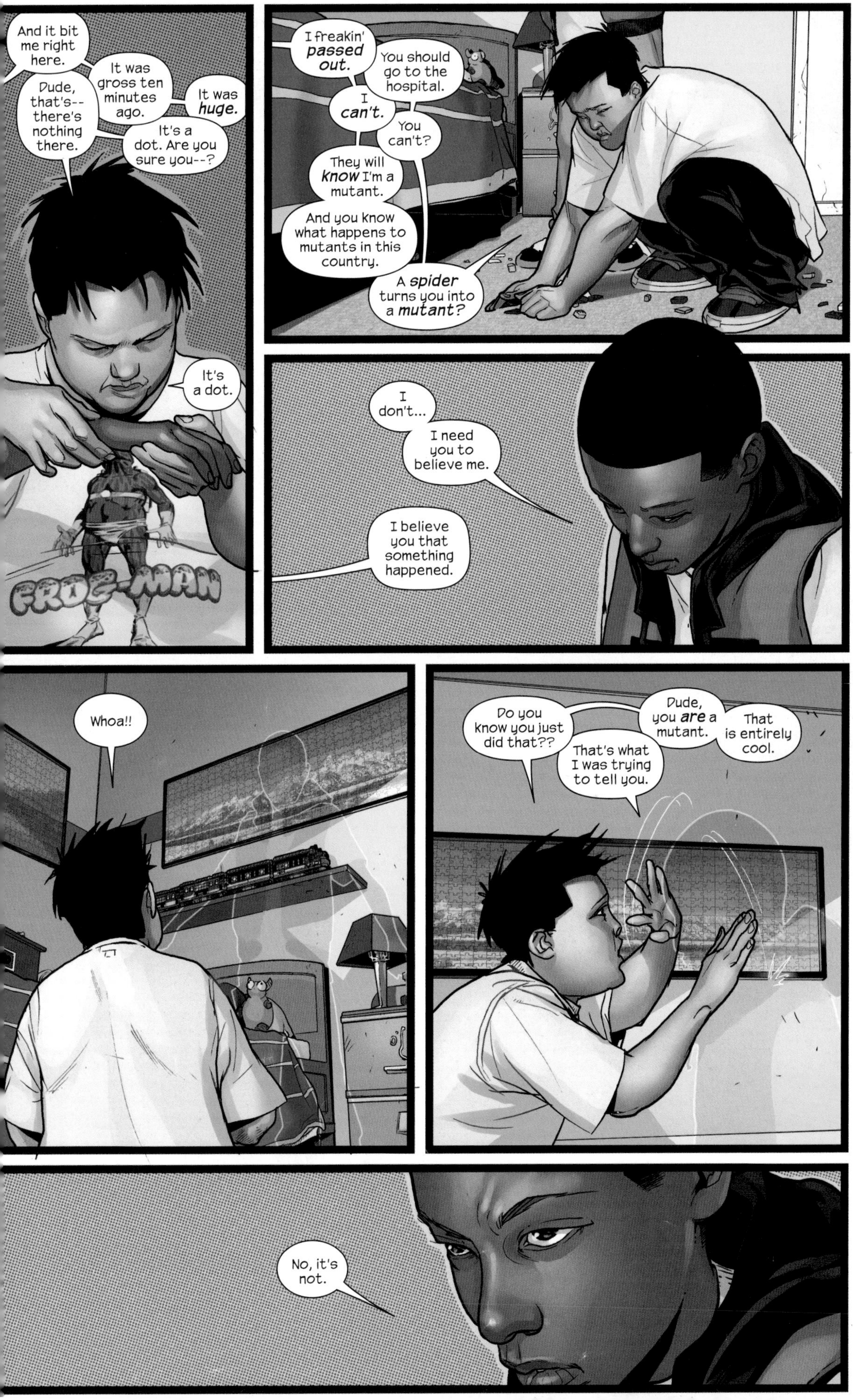

And it bit me right here.
It was gross ten minutes ago.
It was huge.
Dude, that's-- there's nothing there.
It's a dot. Are you sure you--?
It's a dot.
FROG-MAN
I freakin' passed out.
You should go to the hospital.
I can't.
You can't?
They will know I'm a mutant.
And you know what happens to mutants in this country.
A spider turns you into a mutant?
I don't...
I need you to believe me.
I believe you that something happened.
Whoa!!
Do you know you just did that??
Dude, you are a mutant.
That's what I was trying to tell you.
That is entirely cool.
No, it's not.

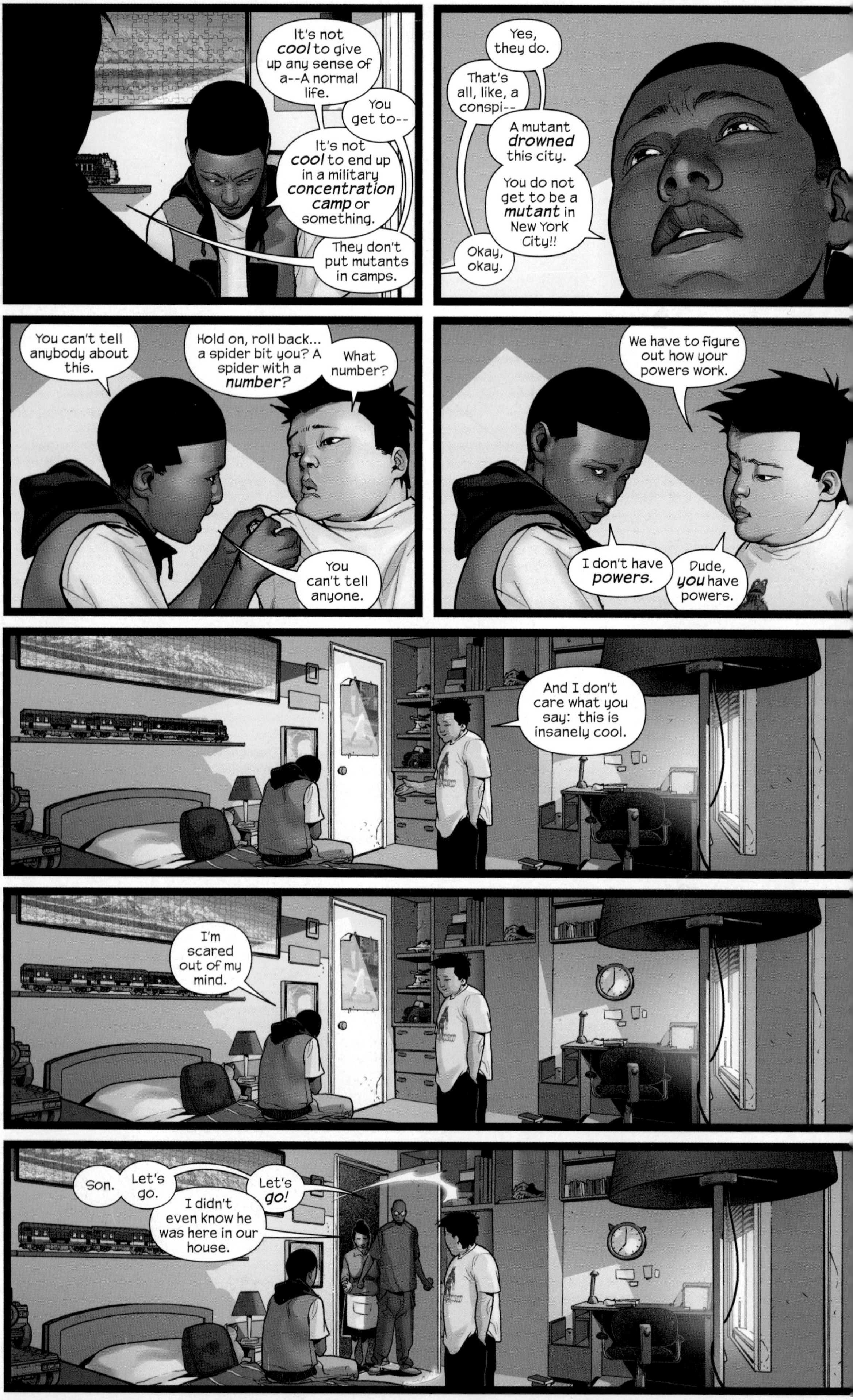
It's not cool to give up any sense of a--A normal life.
You get to--
It's not cool to end up in a military concentration camp or something.
They don't put mutants in camps.
Yes, they do.
That's all, like, a conspi--
A mutant drowned this city.
You do not get to be a mutant in New York City!!
Okay, okay.
You can't tell anybody about this.
Hold on, roll back... a spider bit you? A spider with a number?
What number?
You can't tell anyone.
We have to figure out how your powers work.
I don't have powers.
Dude, you have powers.
And I don't care what you say: this is insanely cool.
I'm scared out of my mind.
Son.
Let's go.
Let's go!
I didn't even know he was here in our house.

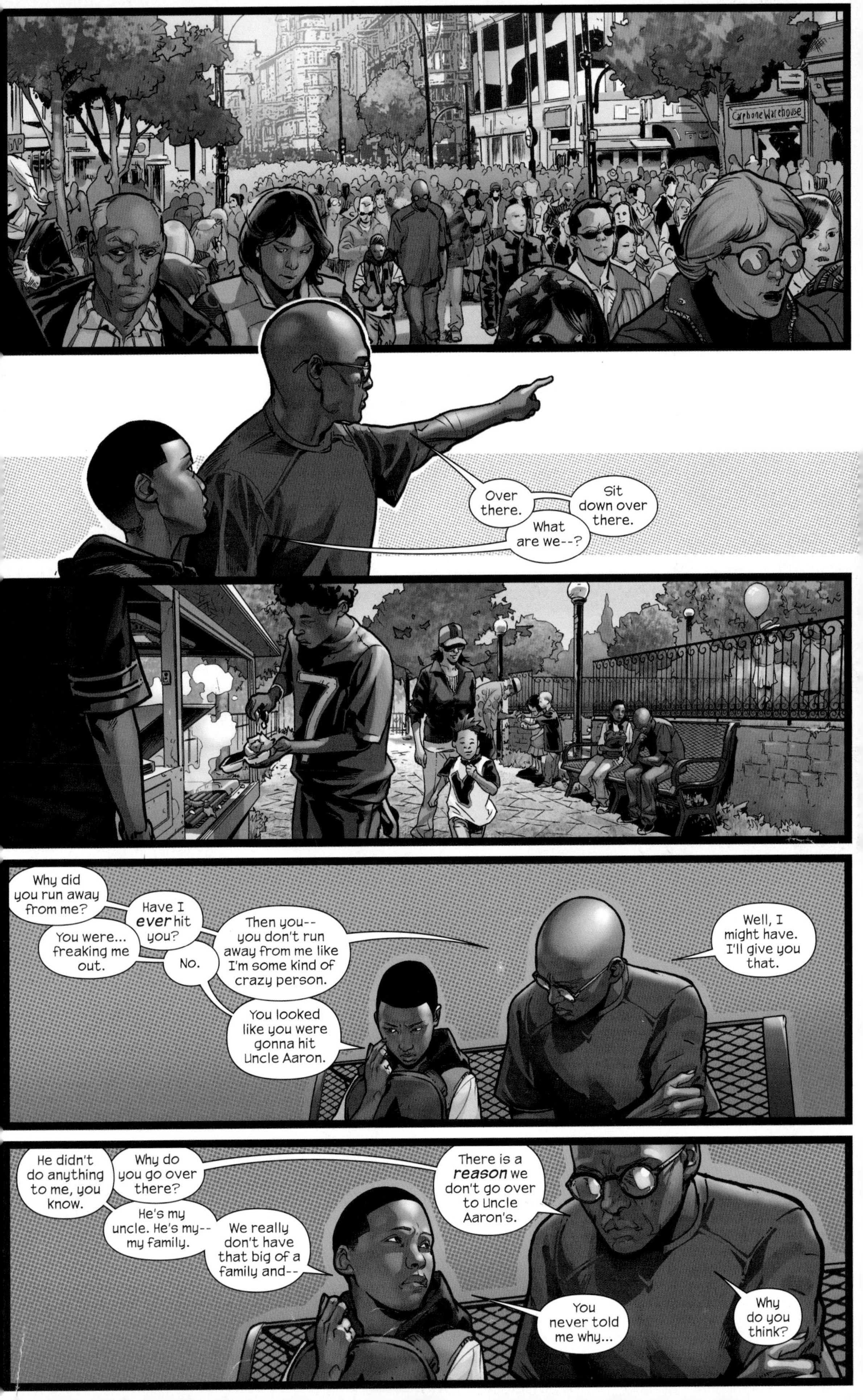
Carphone Warehouse
Over there.
What are we--?
Sit down over there.
Why did you run away from me?
You were... freaking me out.
Have I *ever* hit you?
No.
Then you-- you don't run away from me like I'm some kind of crazy person.
You looked like you were gonna hit Uncle Aaron.
Well, I might have. I'll give you that.
He didn't do anything to me, you know.
Why do you go over there?
He's my uncle. He's my-- my family.
We really don't have that big of a family and--
There is a *reason* we don't go over to Uncle Aaron's.
You never told me why...
Why do you think?

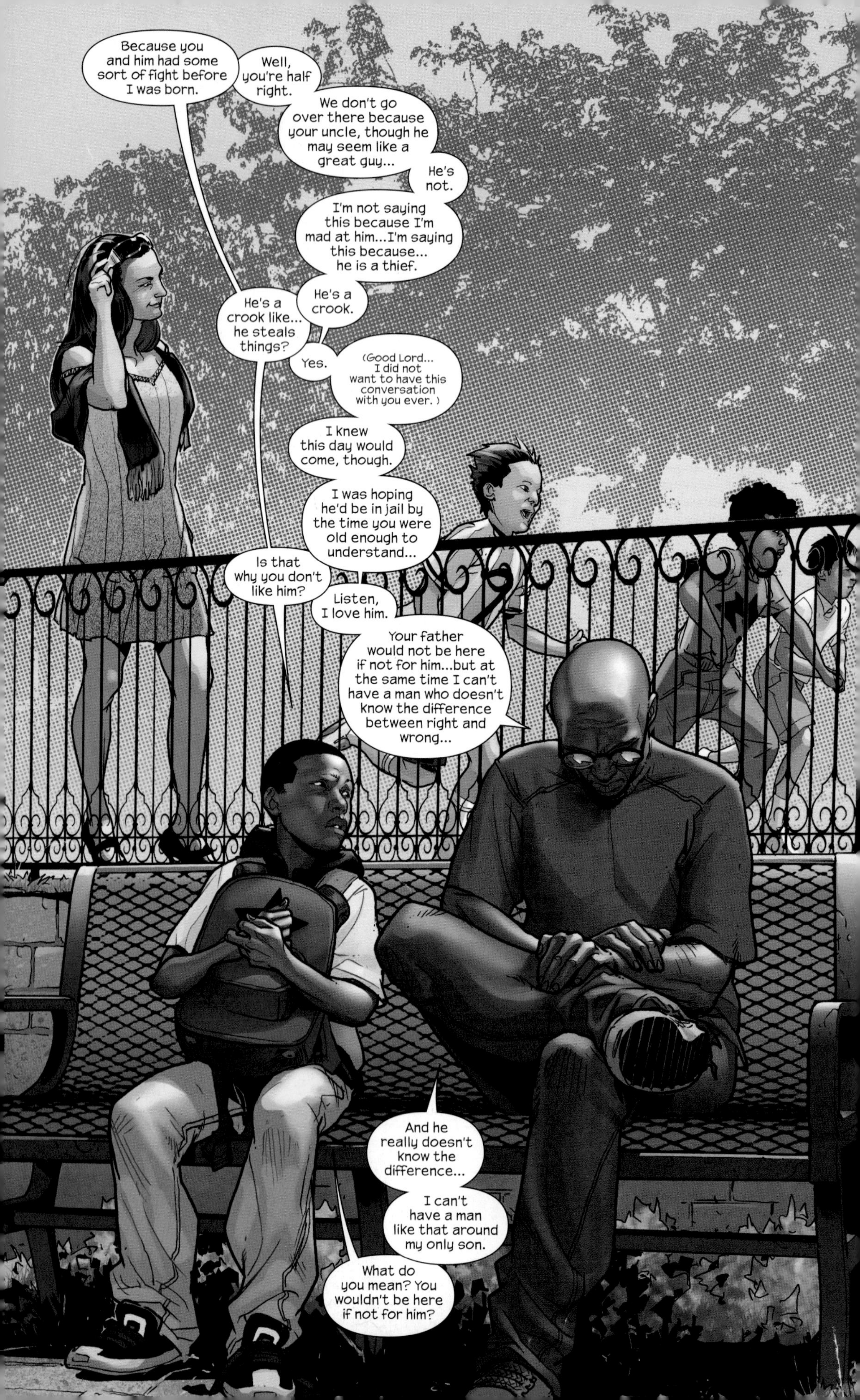
Because you and him had some sort of fight before I was born.
Well, you're half right.
We don't go over there because your uncle, though he may seem like a great guy...
He's not.
I'm not saying this because I'm mad at him...I'm saying this because... he is a thief.
He's a crook.
He's a crook like... he steals things?
Yes.
(Good Lord... I did not want to have this conversation with you ever.)
I knew this day would come, though.
I was hoping he'd be in jail by the time you were old enough to understand...
Is that why you don't like him?
Listen, I love him.
Your father would not be here if not for him...but at the same time I can't have a man who doesn't know the difference between right and wrong...
And he really doesn't know the difference...
I can't have a man like that around my only son.
What do you mean? You wouldn't be here if not for him?

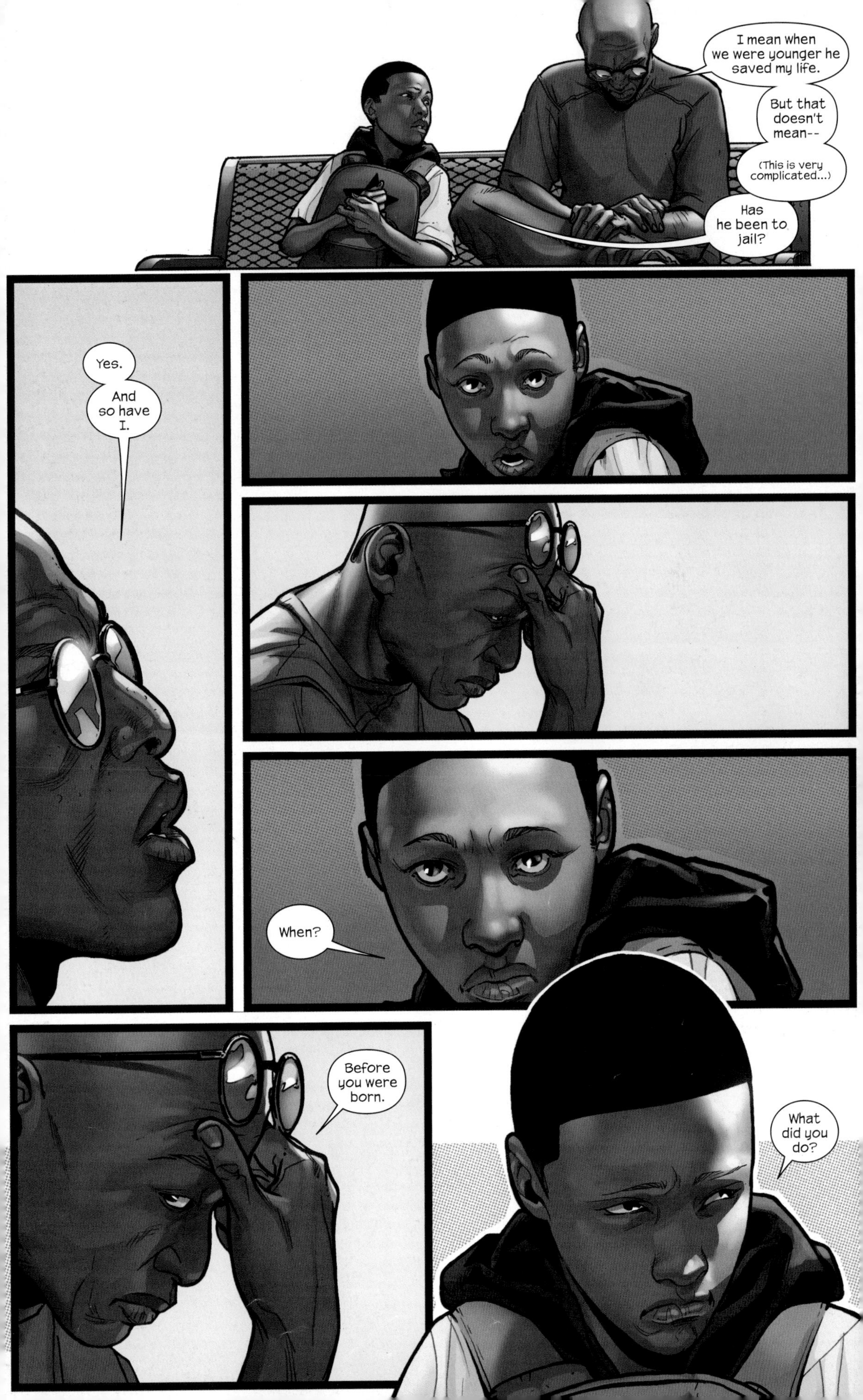
I mean when we were younger he saved my life.
But that doesn't mean--
(This is very complicated...)
Has he been to jail?
Yes.
And so have I.
When?
Before you were born.
What did you do?

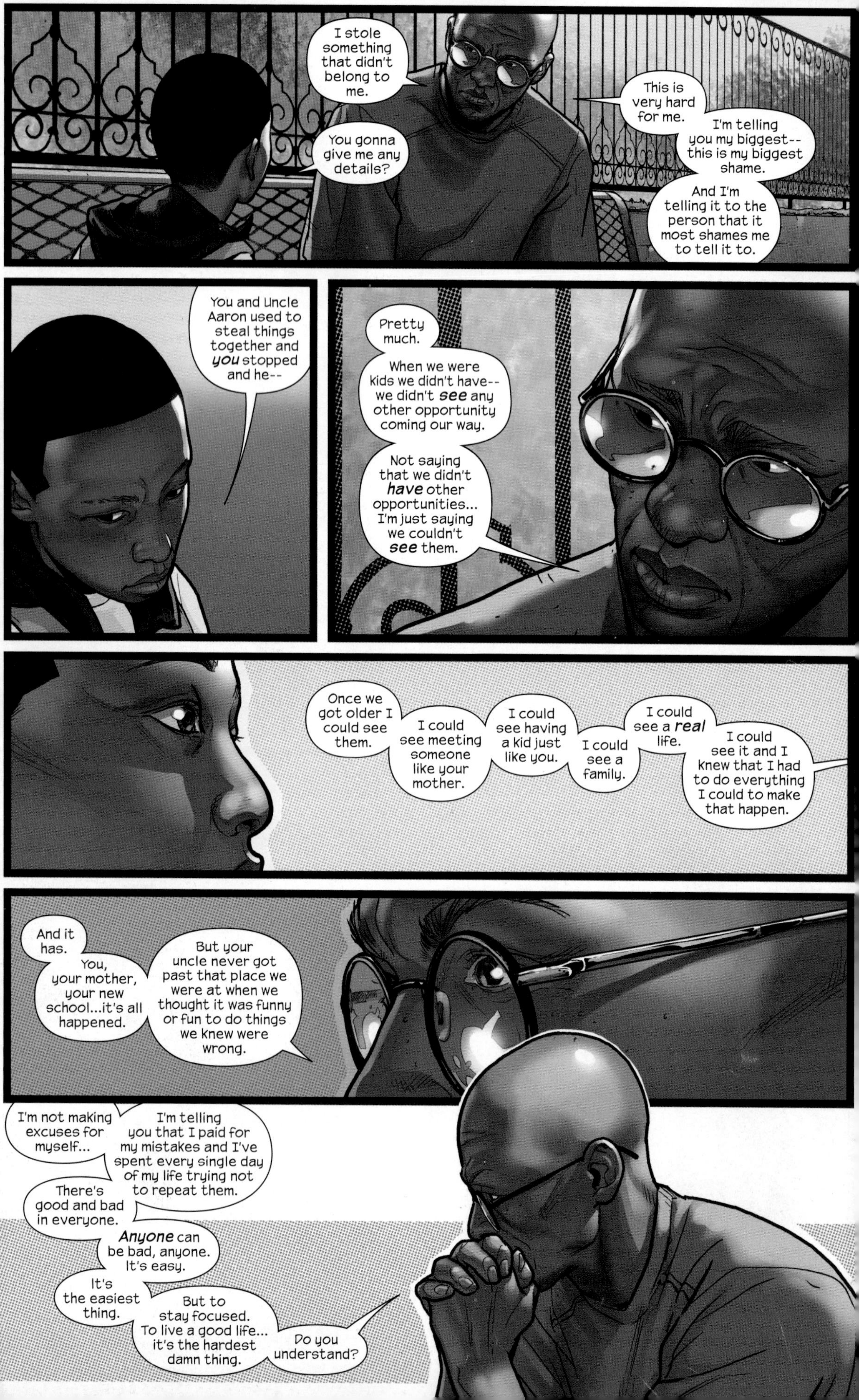
I stole something that didn't belong to me.
You gonna give me any details?
This is very hard for me.
I'm telling you my biggest-- this is my biggest shame.
And I'm telling it to the person that it most shames me to tell it to.
You and Uncle Aaron used to steal things together and *you* stopped and he--
Pretty much.
When we were kids we didn't have-- we didn't *see* any other opportunity coming our way.
Not saying that we didn't *have* other opportunities... I'm just saying we couldn't *see* them.
Once we got older I could see them.
I could see meeting someone like your mother.
I could see having a kid just like you.
I could see a family.
I could see a *real* life.
I could see it and I knew that I had to do everything I could to make that happen.
And it has.
You, your mother, your new school...it's all happened.
But your uncle never got past that place we were at when we thought it was funny or fun to do things we knew were wrong.
I'm not making excuses for myself...
I'm telling you that I paid for my mistakes and I've spent every single day of my life trying not to repeat them.
There's good and bad in everyone.
Anyone can be bad, anyone. It's easy.
It's the easiest thing.
But to stay focused. To live a good life... it's the hardest damn thing.
Do you understand?

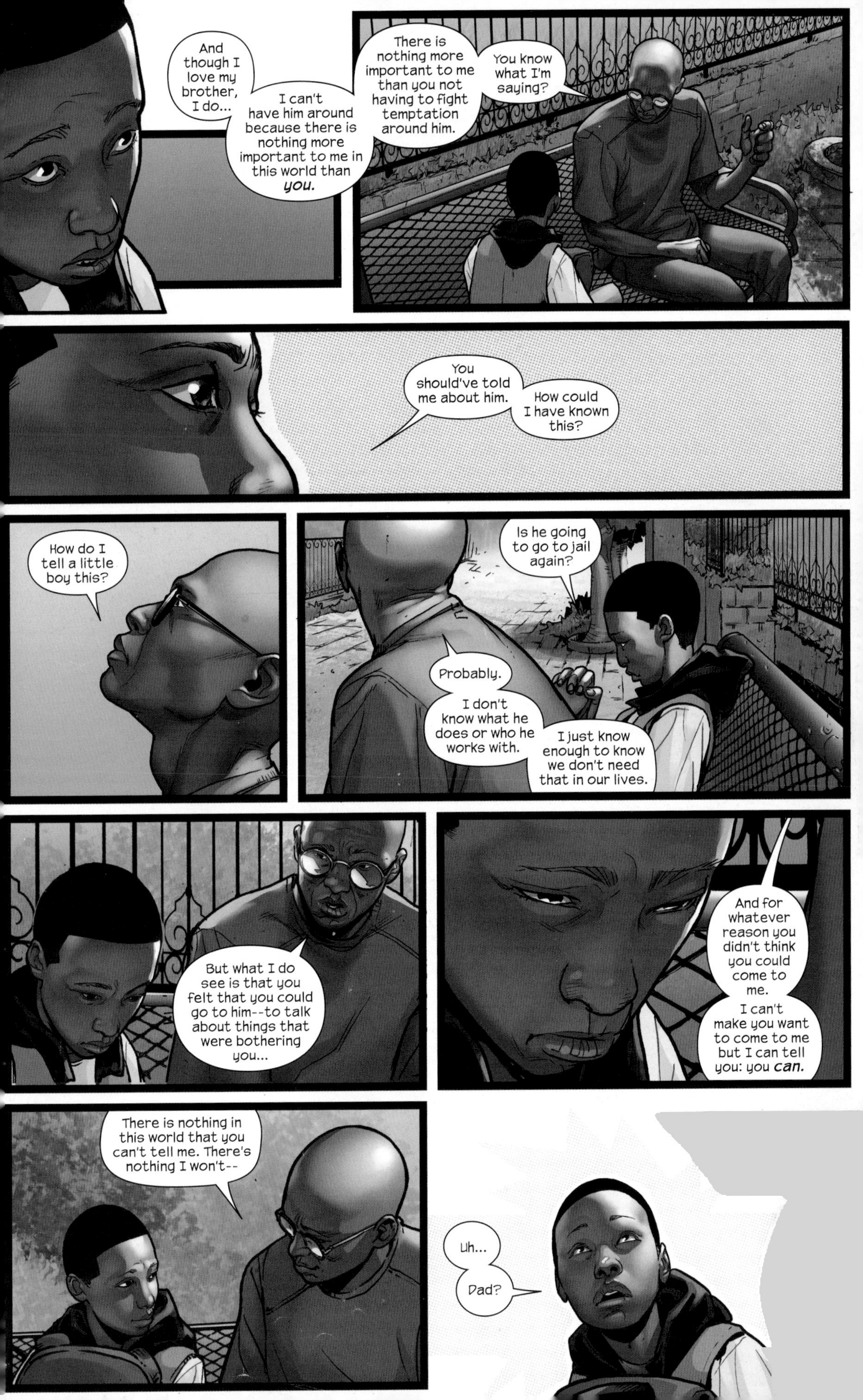
And though I love my brother, I do...
I can't have him around because there is nothing more important to me in this world than *you.*
There is nothing more important to me than you not having to fight temptation around him.
You know what I'm saying?
You should've told me about him.
How could I have known this?
How do I tell a little boy this?
Is he going to go to jail again?
Probably.
I don't know what he does or who he works with.
I just know enough to know we don't need that in our lives.
But what I do see is that you felt that you could go to him--to talk about things that were bothering you...
And for whatever reason you didn't think you could come to me.
I can't make you want to come to me but I can tell you: you *can.*
There is nothing in this world that you can't tell me. There's nothing I won't--
Uh...
Dad?

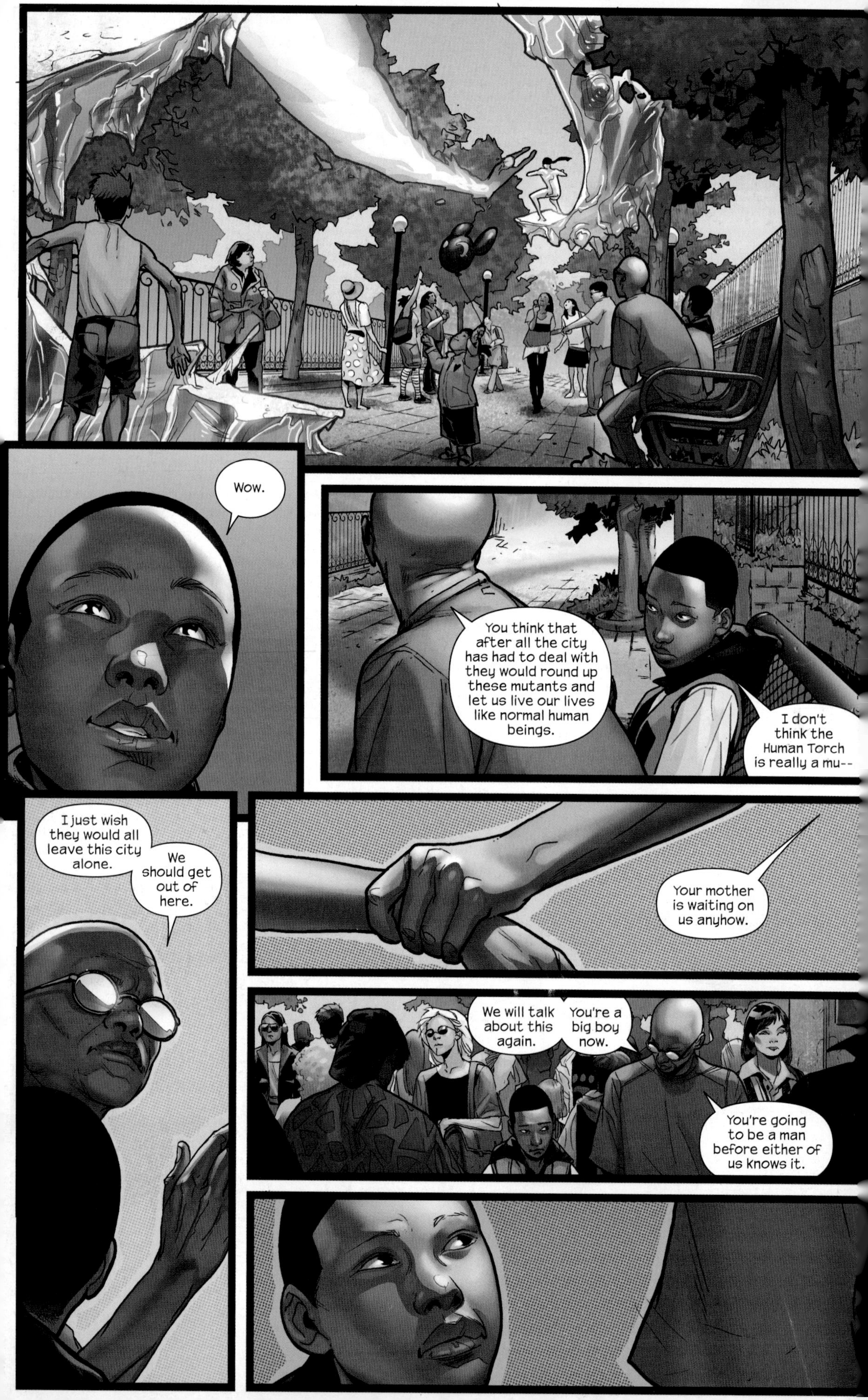
Wow.
You think that after all the city has had to deal with they would round up these mutants and let us live our lives like normal human beings.
I don't think the Human Torch is really a mu--
I just wish they would all leave this city alone.
We should get out of here.
Your mother is waiting on us anyhow.
We will talk about this again.
You're a big boy now.
You're going to be a man before either of us knows it.

STARPICS
Z100

Ganke THE AWESOME:
today, 1:07 am
you're not a mutant.

Ganke THE AWESOME:
today, 1:07 am
you're not a mutant.

Ganke THE AWESOME:
today, 1:08 am
u have chameleon like powers like some spiders do- & u have a venom strike, like some spiders have.

u have chameleon like powers like some spiders do- & u have a venom strike, like some spiders have.

Sir MILES:
today, 1:09 am
what r u talking about?

today, 1:09 am
what r u talking about?

Ganke THE AWESOME:
today, 1:10 am
Spider-Man was bit by a spider too.

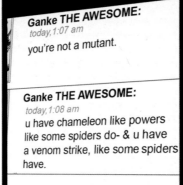

STARPICS

Z100

Spider-man was bit by a spider too.

Ganke THE AWESOME:
today,1:12 am
Spider-Man myth busted By Ben Urich

Ganke THE AWESOME:
today,1:12 am
Sp___ __n myth busted By

HOW SPIDER-MAN BECAME SPIDER-MAN

By BEN URICH

Last Updated: 3:37 PM, July 13, 2011
Posted: 5:54 AM, July 13, 2011

picture by Peter Parker

👍 Like   Send   7,042 people like this. Be the first of your friends.

+1   35   586

though said with levity, Spider-Man told police officers that he was bit by a spider that gave him spider-powers.

STARPICS

Z100

Ganke THE AWESOME:
today,1:10 am
sorry u'r not a mutant but...
R U Spider-Man?!!

Ganke THE AWESO
today,1:10 am
sorry u'r not a muta
R U Spider-Man?!!

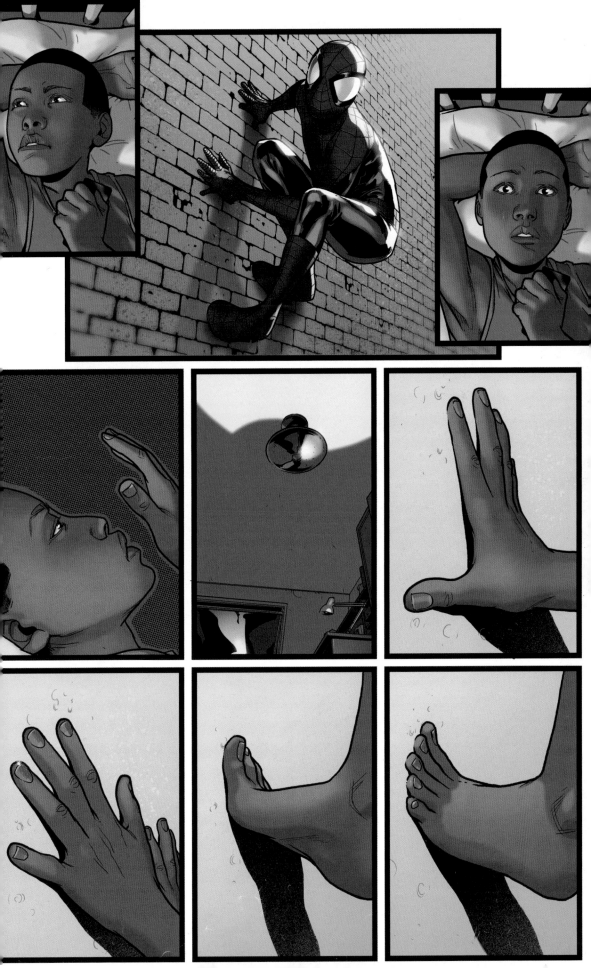

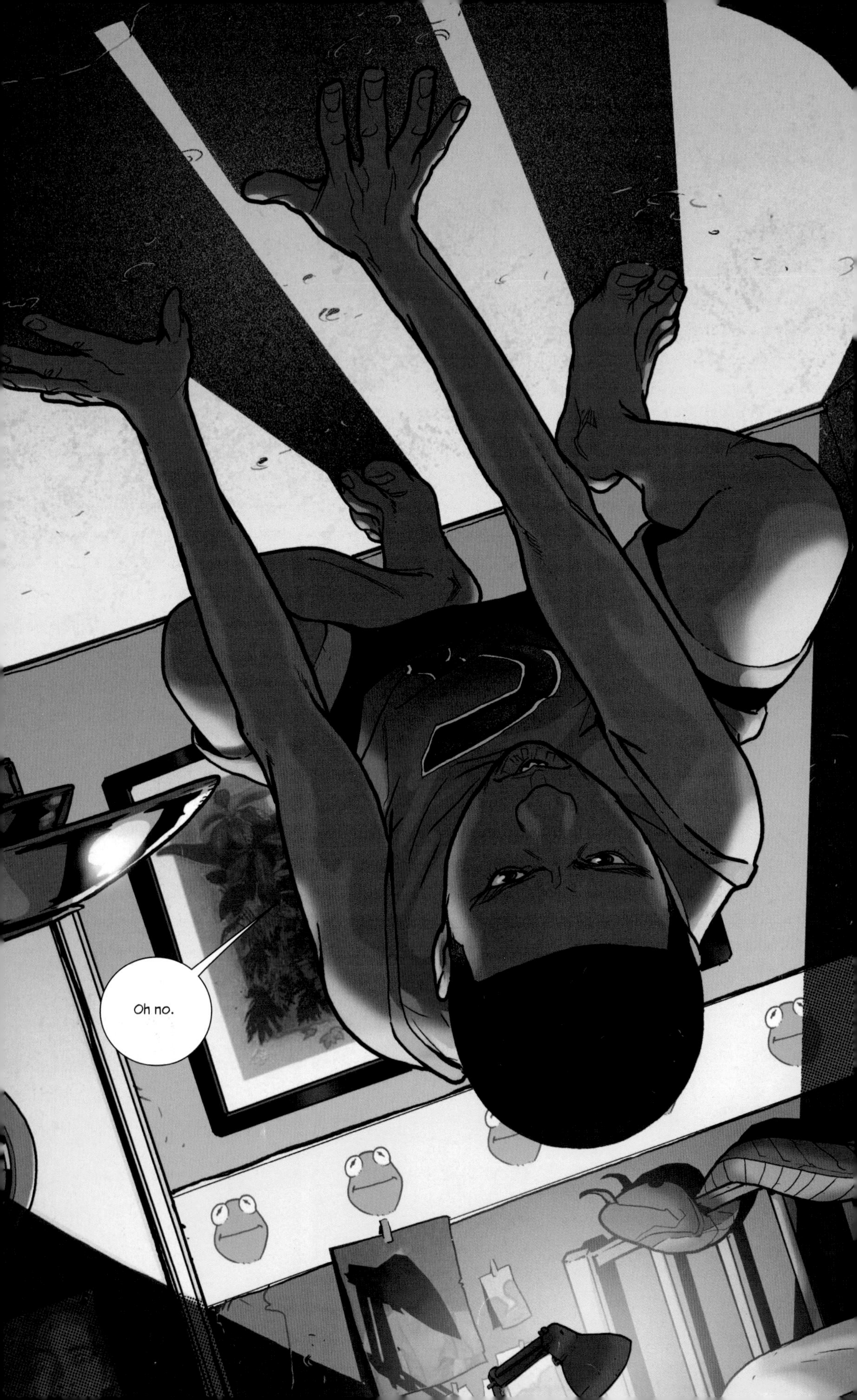
Oh no.

3

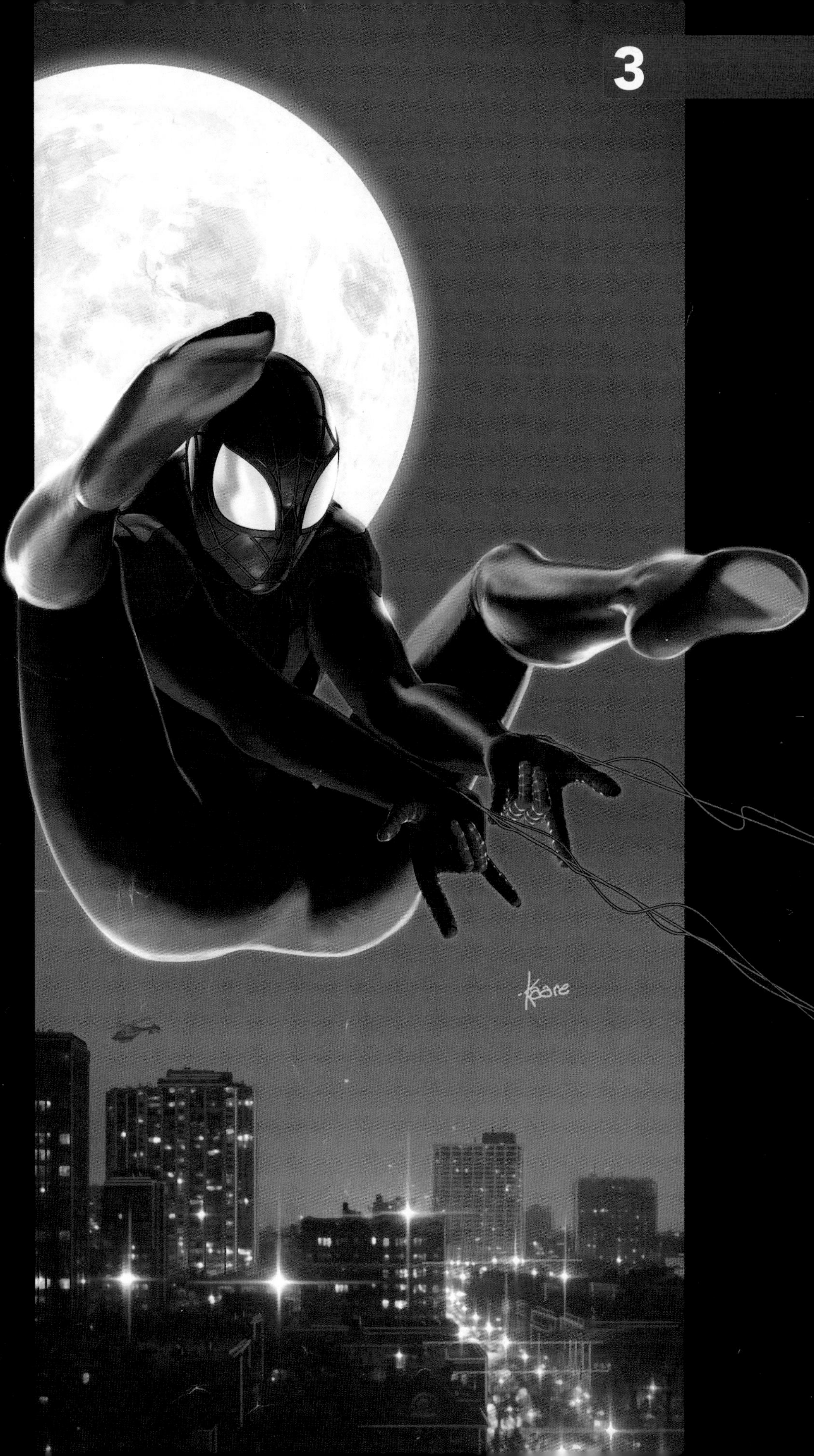

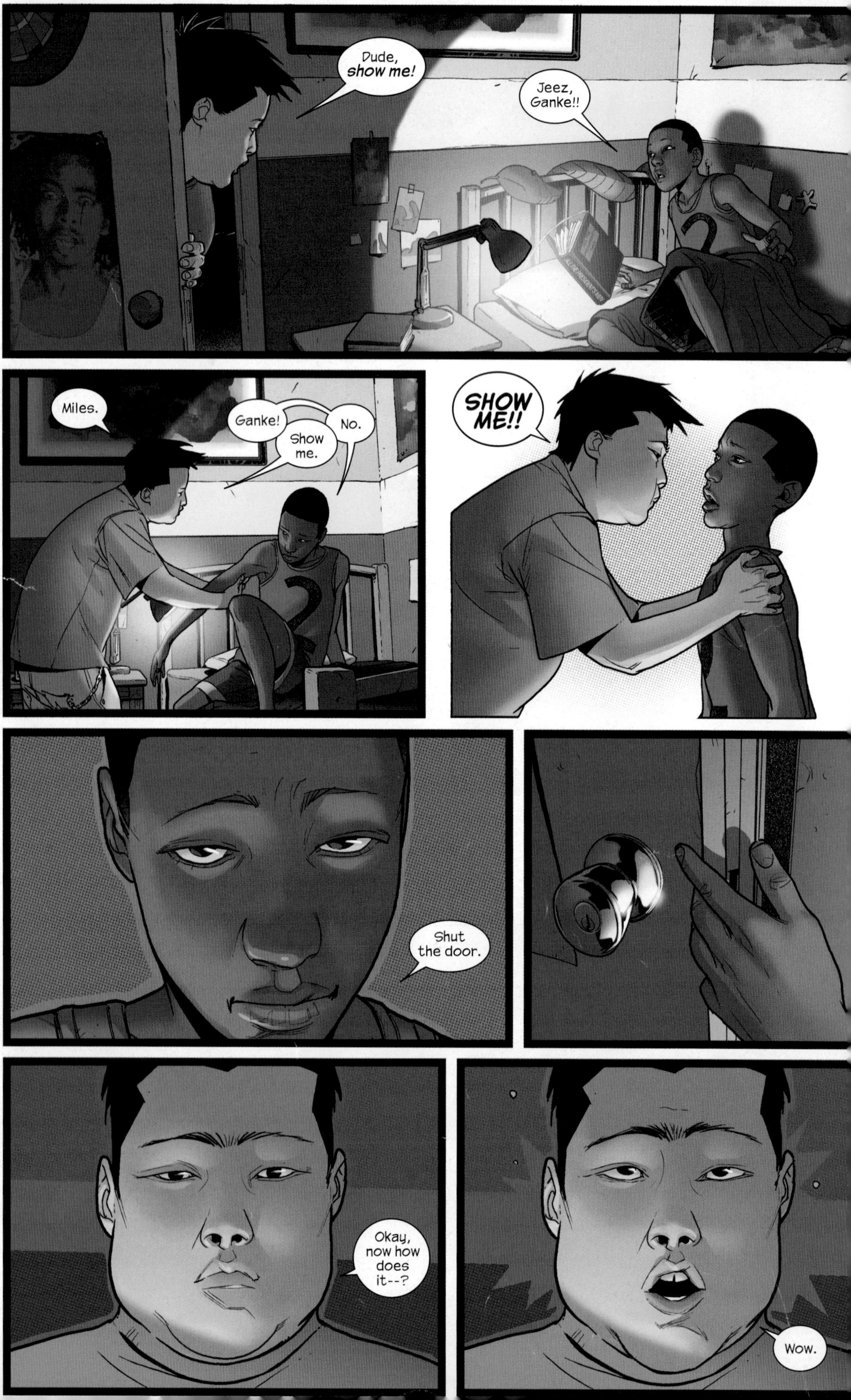

Dude, *show me!*
Jeez, Ganke!!
Miles.
Ganke!
Show me.
No.
SHOW ME!!
Shut the door.
Okay, now how does it--?
Wow.

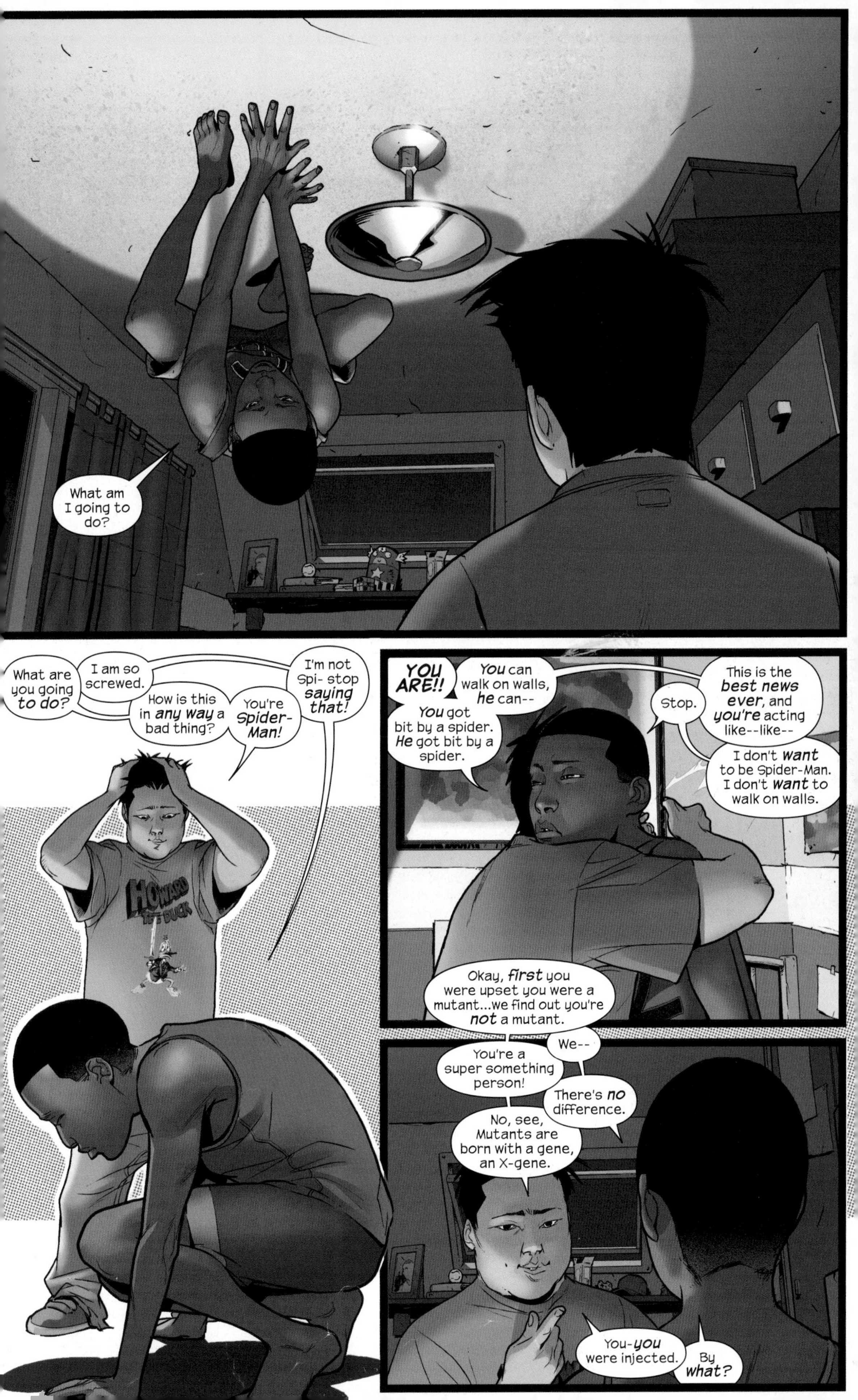

What am I going to do?
What are you going to do?
I am so screwed.
How is this in any way a bad thing?
You're Spider-Man!
I'm not Spi- stop saying that!
YOU ARE!!
You can walk on walls, he can--
You got bit by a spider. He got bit by a spider.
This is the best news ever, and you're acting like--like--
Stop.
I don't want to be Spider-Man. I don't want to walk on walls.
Okay, first you were upset you were a mutant...we find out you're not a mutant.
You're a super something person!
We--
There's no difference.
No, see, Mutants are born with a gene, an X-gene.
You-you were injected.
By what?

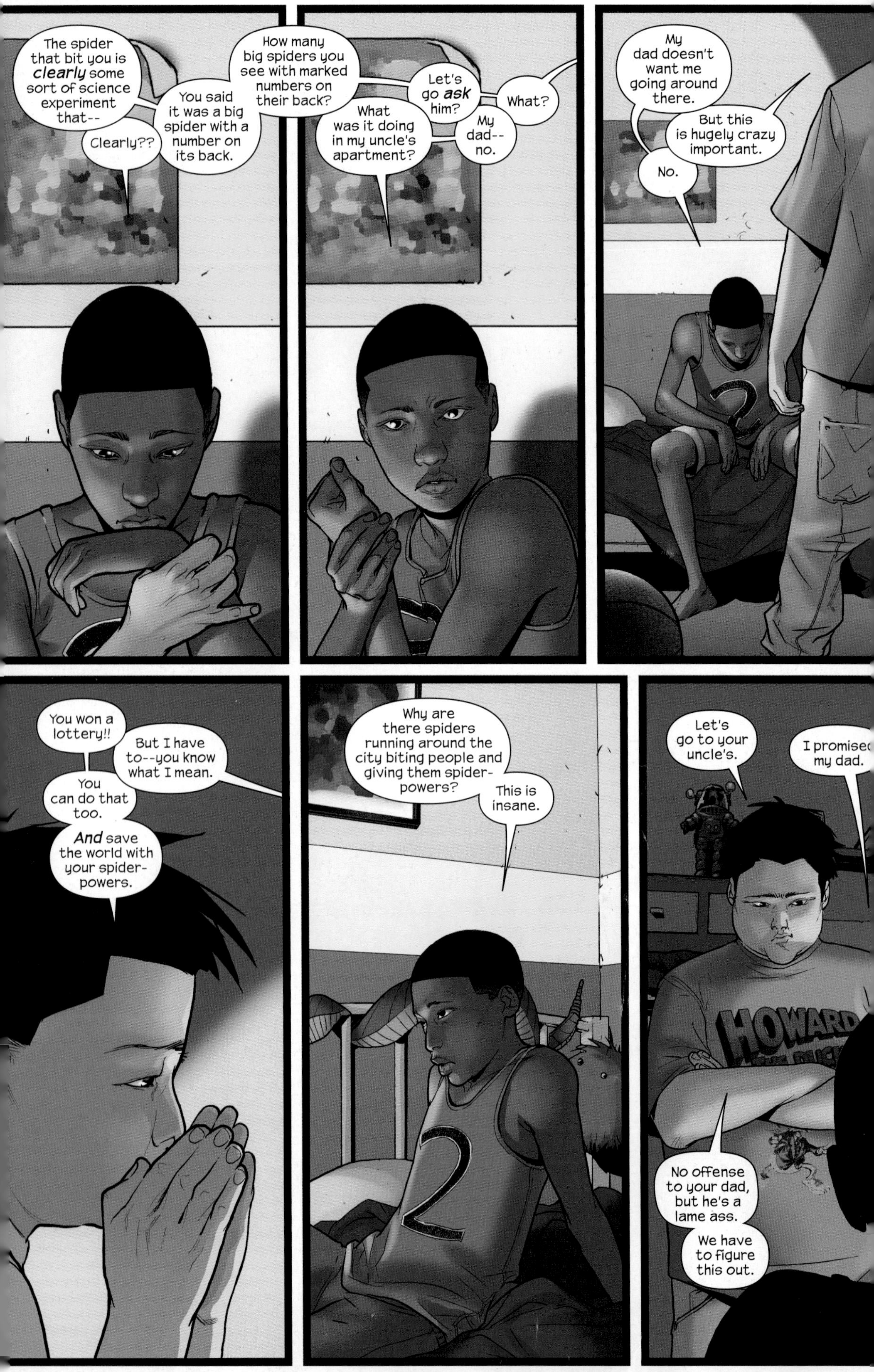
The spider that bit you is *clearly* some sort of science experiment that--
Clearly??
You said it was a big spider with a number on its back.
How many big spiders you see with marked numbers on their back?
What was it doing in my uncle's apartment?
Let's go *ask* him?
My dad-- no.
What?
My dad doesn't want me going around there.
But this is hugely crazy important.
No.
You won a lottery!!
But I have to--you know what I mean.
You can do that too.
And save the world with your spider-powers.
Why are there spiders running around the city biting people and giving them spider-powers?
This is insane.
Let's go to your uncle's.
I promised my dad.
HOWARD
No offense to your dad, but he's a lame ass.
We have to figure this out.

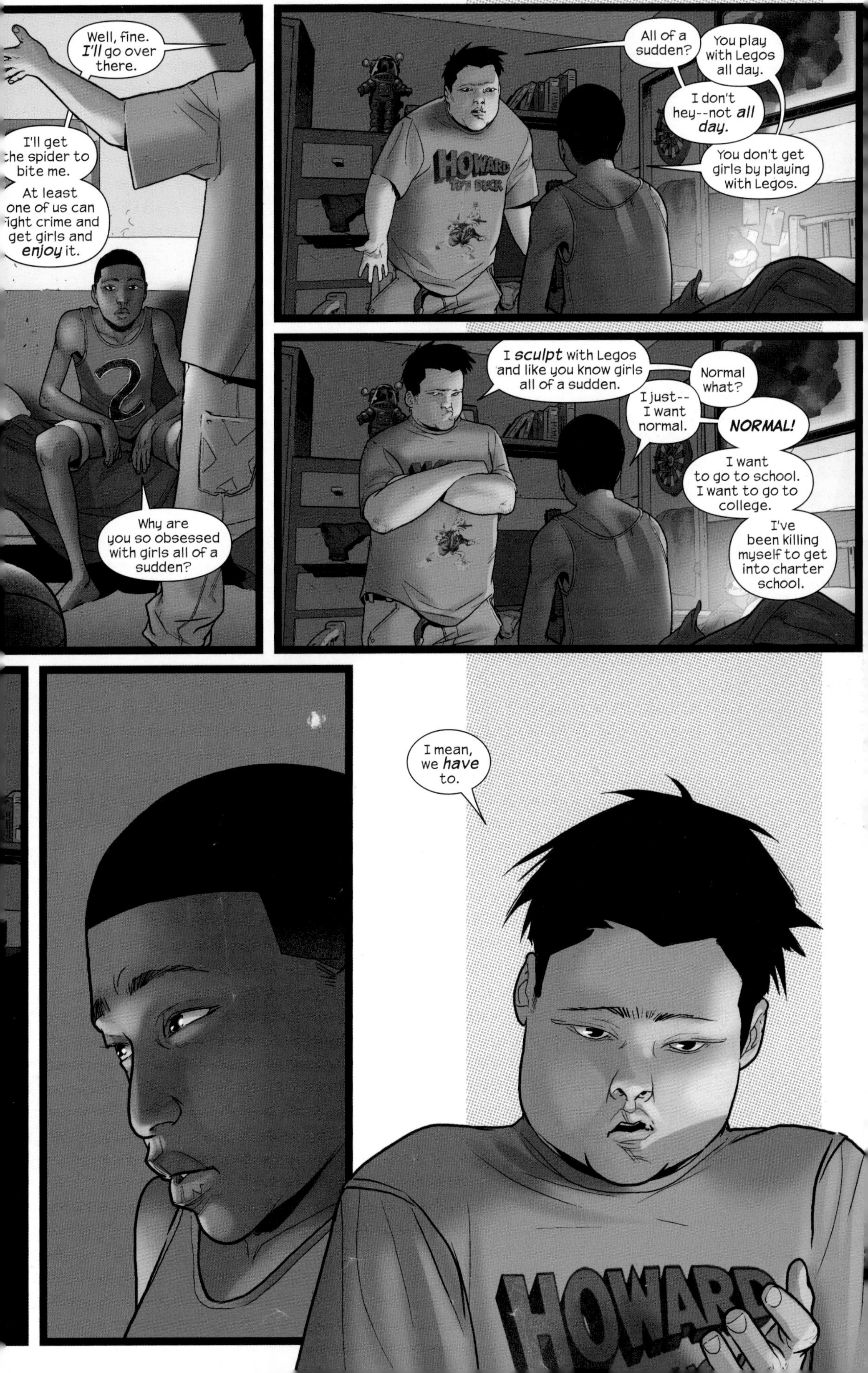

Well, fine. *I'll* go over there.
I'll get the spider to bite me.
At least one of us can fight crime and get girls and *enjoy* it.
Why are you so obsessed with girls all of a sudden?
All of a sudden?
You play with Legos all day.
I don't hey--not *all day.*
You don't get girls by playing with Legos.
HOWARD THE DUCK
I *sculpt* with Legos and like you know girls all of a sudden.
I just-- I want normal.
Normal what?
NORMAL!
I want to go to school. I want to go to college.
I've been killing myself to get into charter school.
I mean, we *have* to.
HOWARD

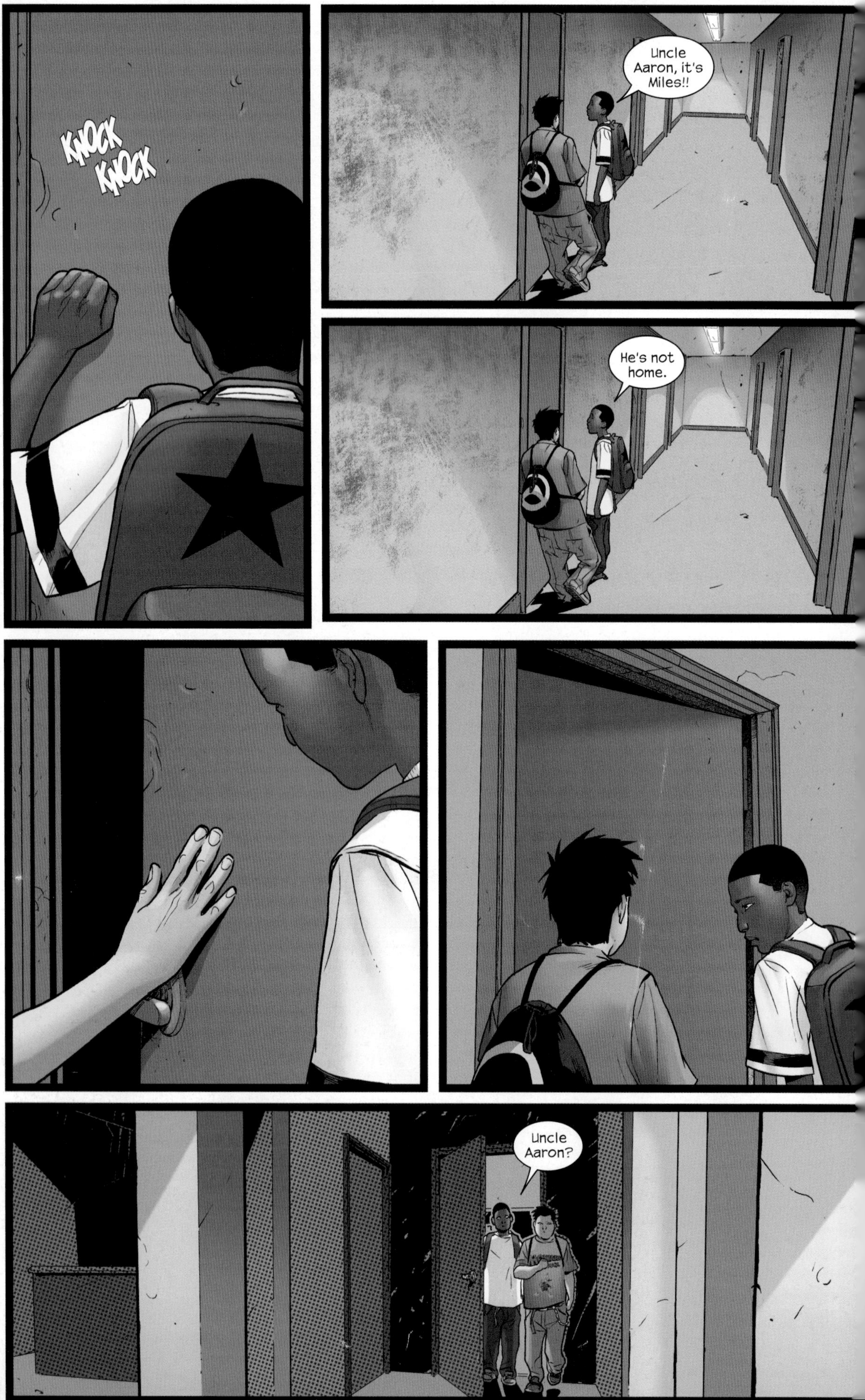
KNOCK KNOCK
Uncle Aaron, it's Miles!!
He's not home.
Uncle Aaron?

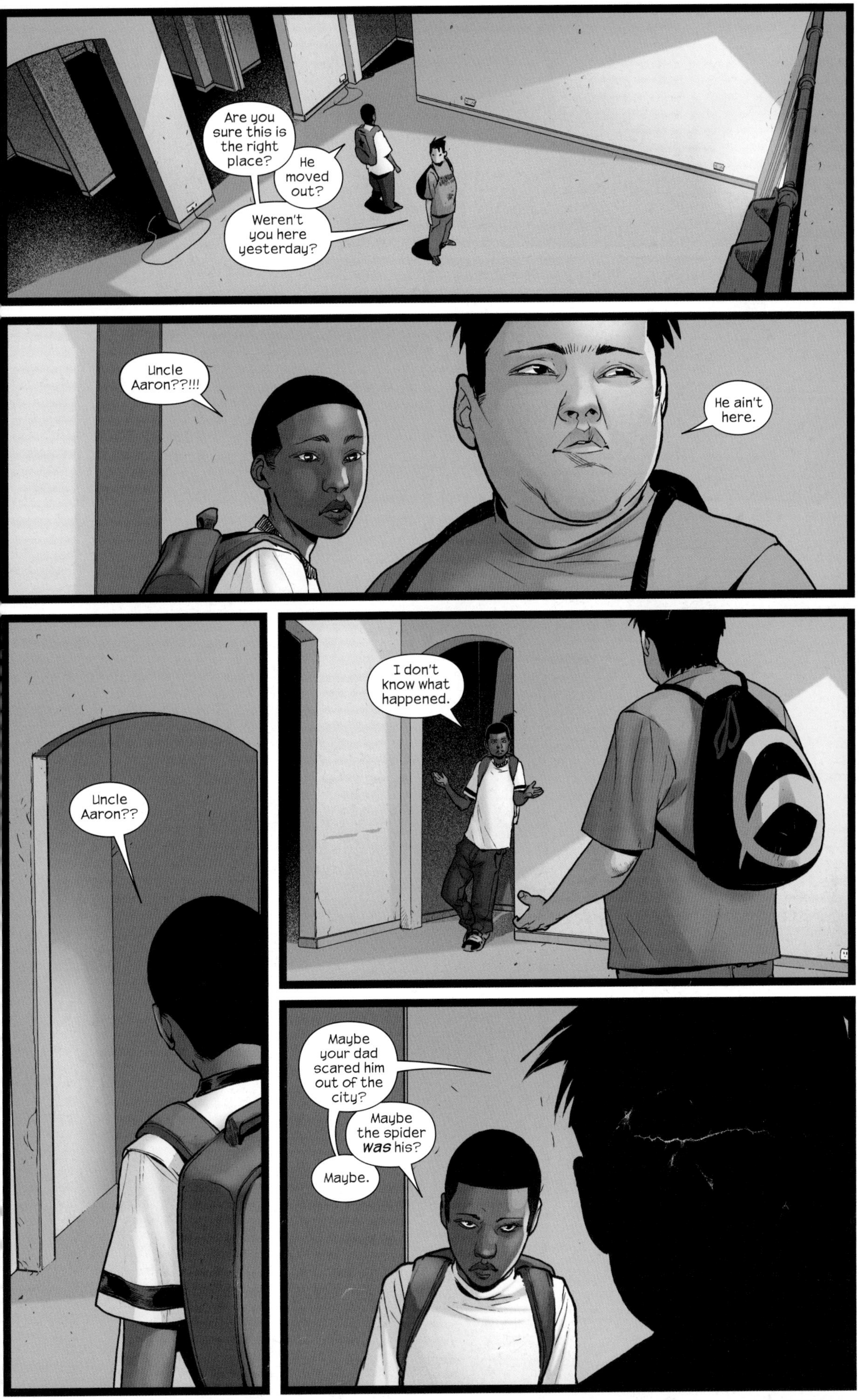

Are you sure this is the right place?
He moved out?
Weren't you here yesterday?
Uncle Aaron??!!!
He ain't here.
Uncle Aaron??
I don't know what happened.
Maybe your dad scared him out of the city?
Maybe the spider *was* his?
Maybe.

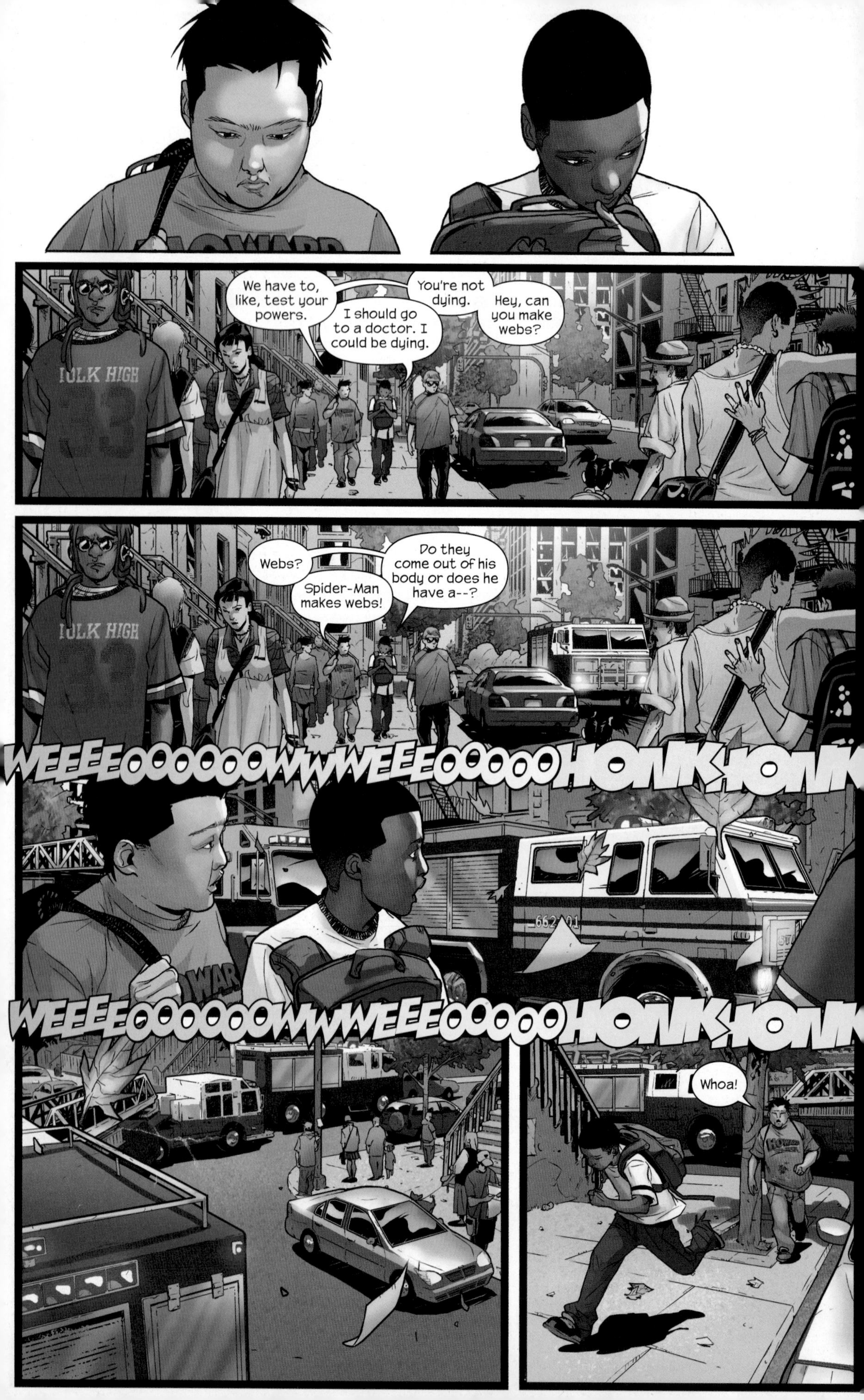
We have to, like, test your powers.
I should go to a doctor. I could be dying.
You're not dying.
Hey, can you make webs?
Webs?
Spider-Man makes webs!
Do they come out of his body or does he have a--?
WEEEEOOOOOOOWWWEEEEOOOOOOHONK HONK
WEEEEOOOOOOOWWWEEEEOOOOOOHONK HONK
Whoa!

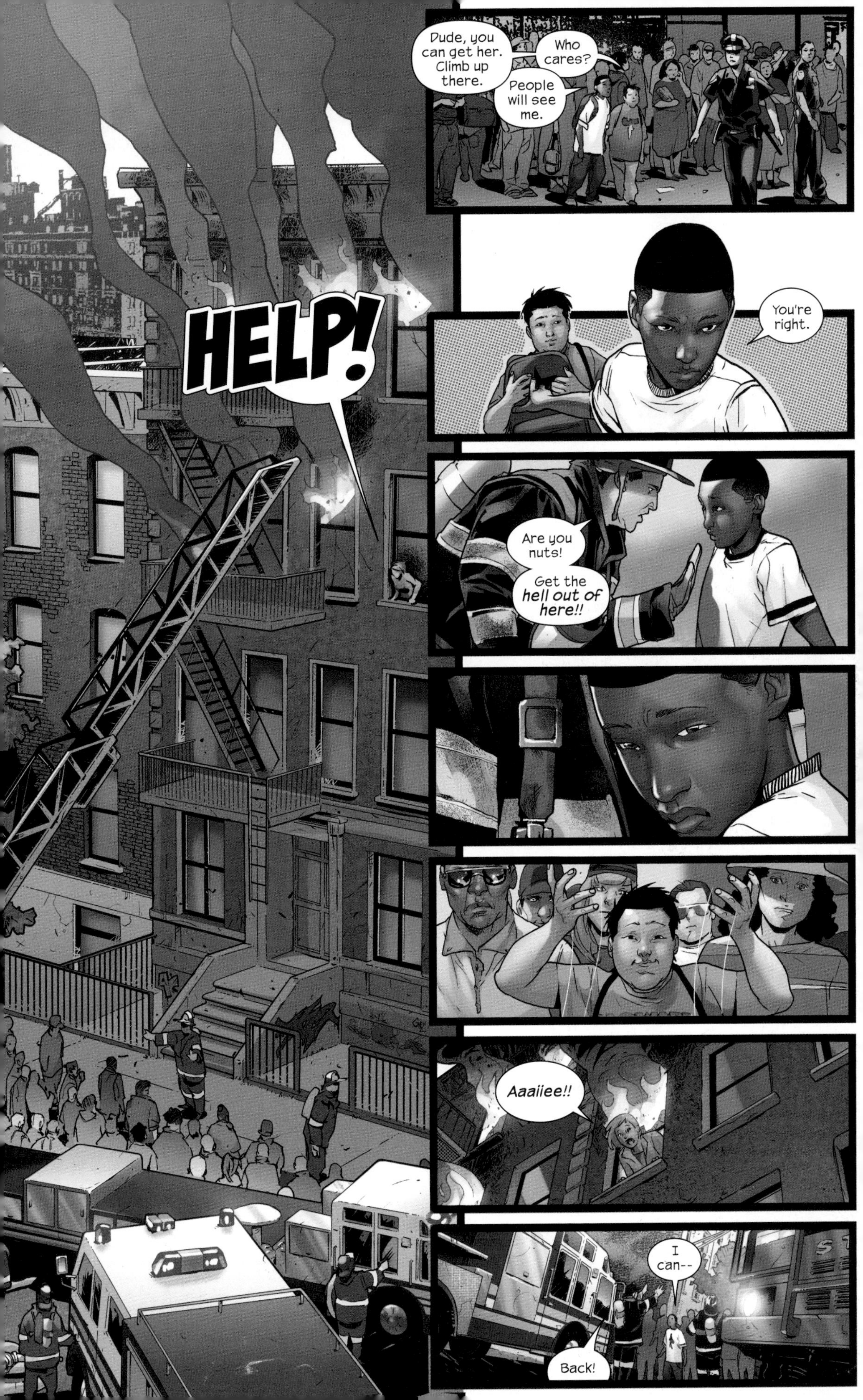
HELP!
Dude, you can get her. Climb up there.
Who cares?
People will see me.
You're right.
Are you nuts!
Get the hell out of here!!
Aaaiiee!!
I can--
Back!

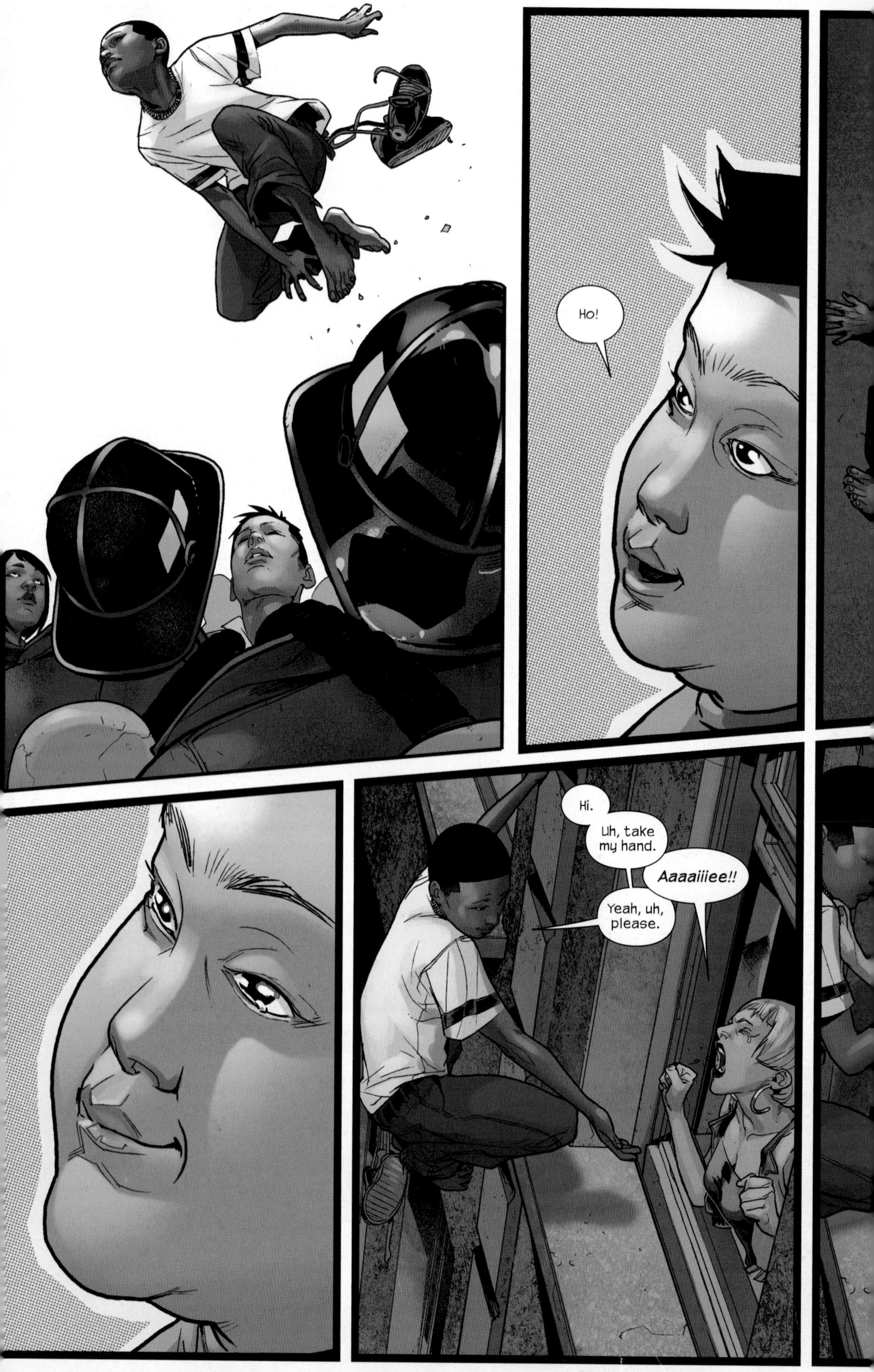
Ho!
Hi.
Uh, take my hand.
Aaaaiiiee!!
Yeah, uh, please.

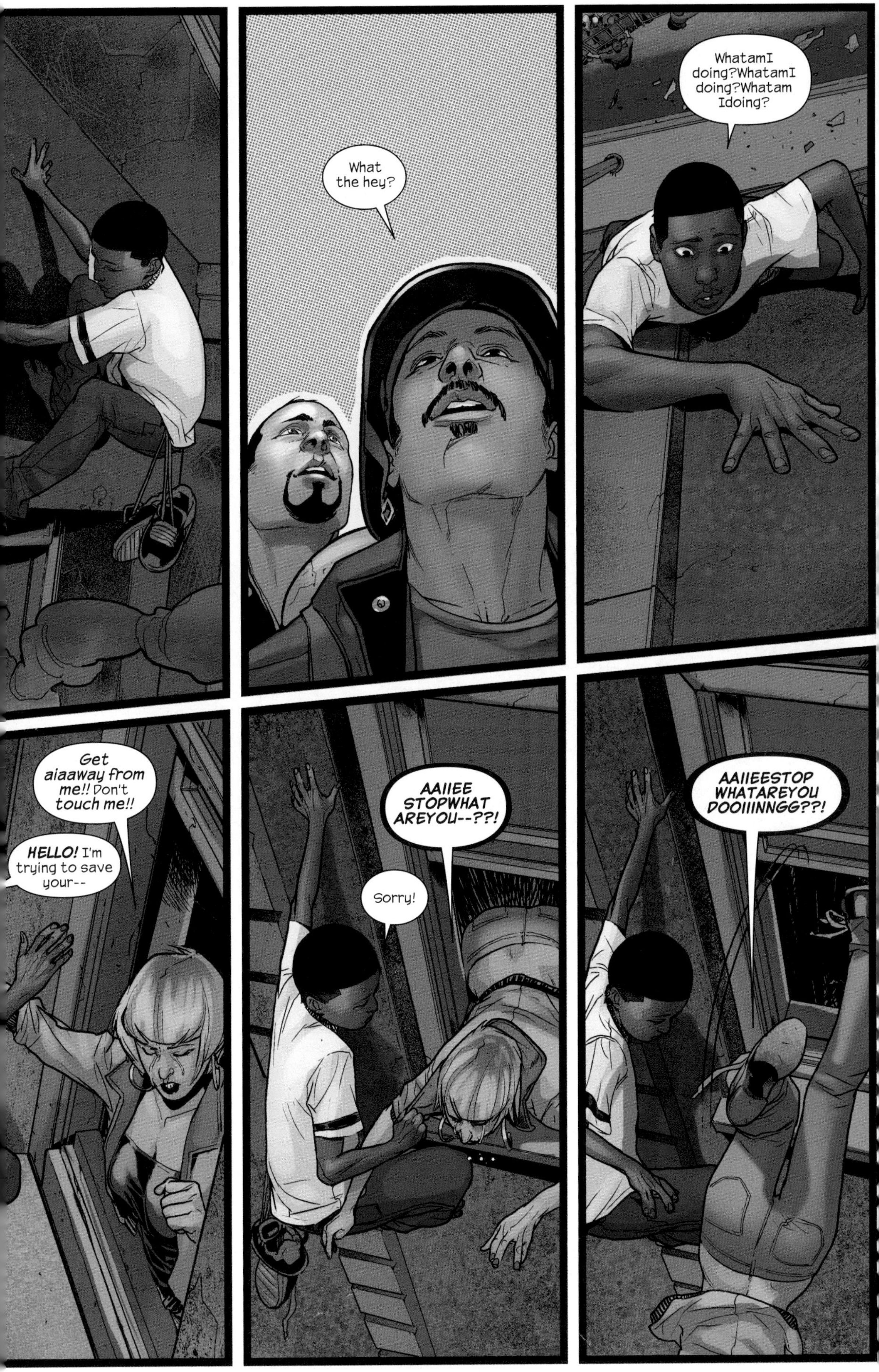
What the hey?
WhatamI doing?WhatamI doing?Whatam Idoing?
Get aiaaway from me!! Don't touch me!!
HELLO! I'm trying to save your--
AAIIEE STOPWHAT AREYOU--??!
Sorry!
AAIIEESTOP WHATAREYOU DOOIIINNGG??!

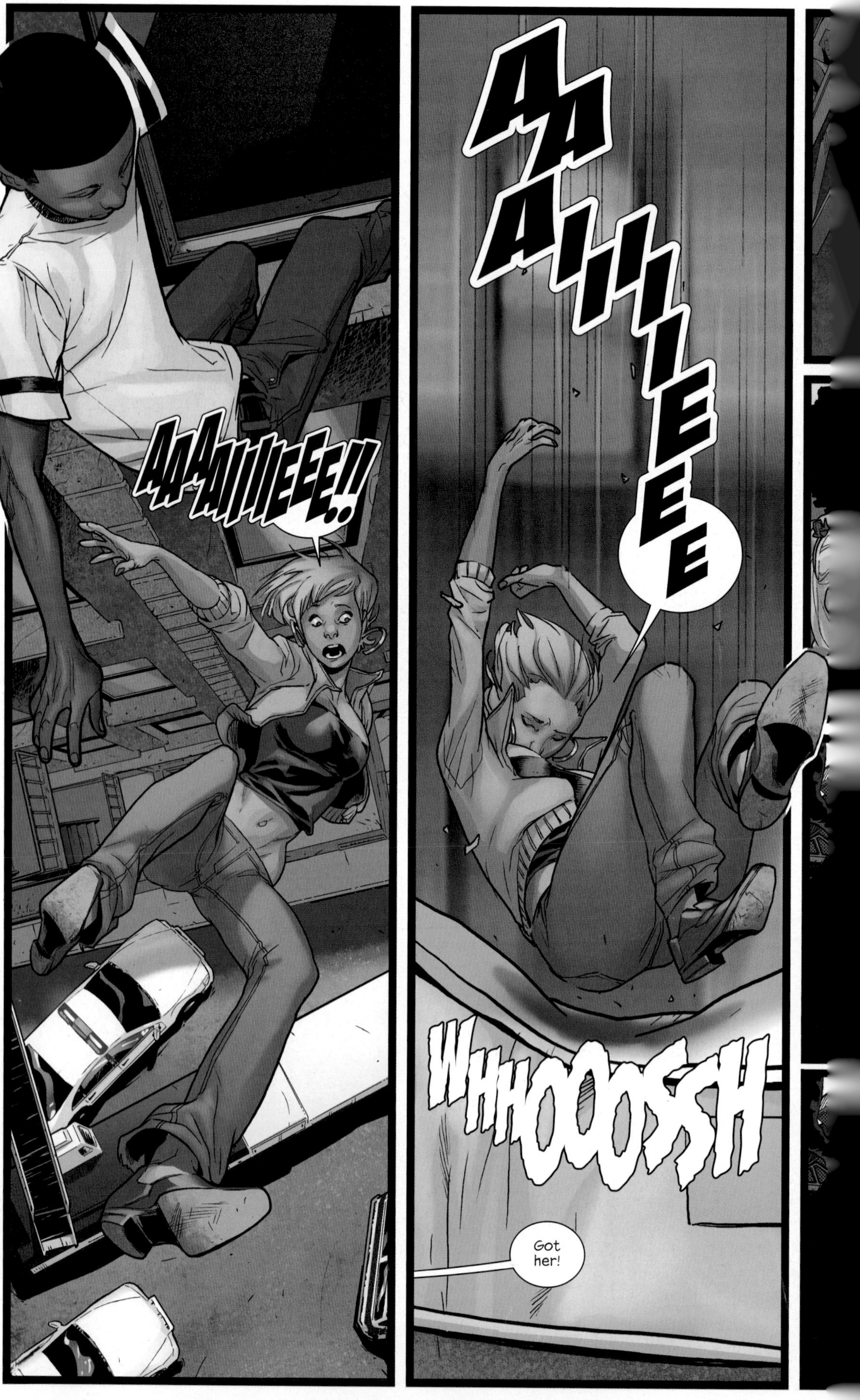
AAAAIIIIEEEE!!
AAAIIIIEEEE
WHHOOOOSSH
Got her!

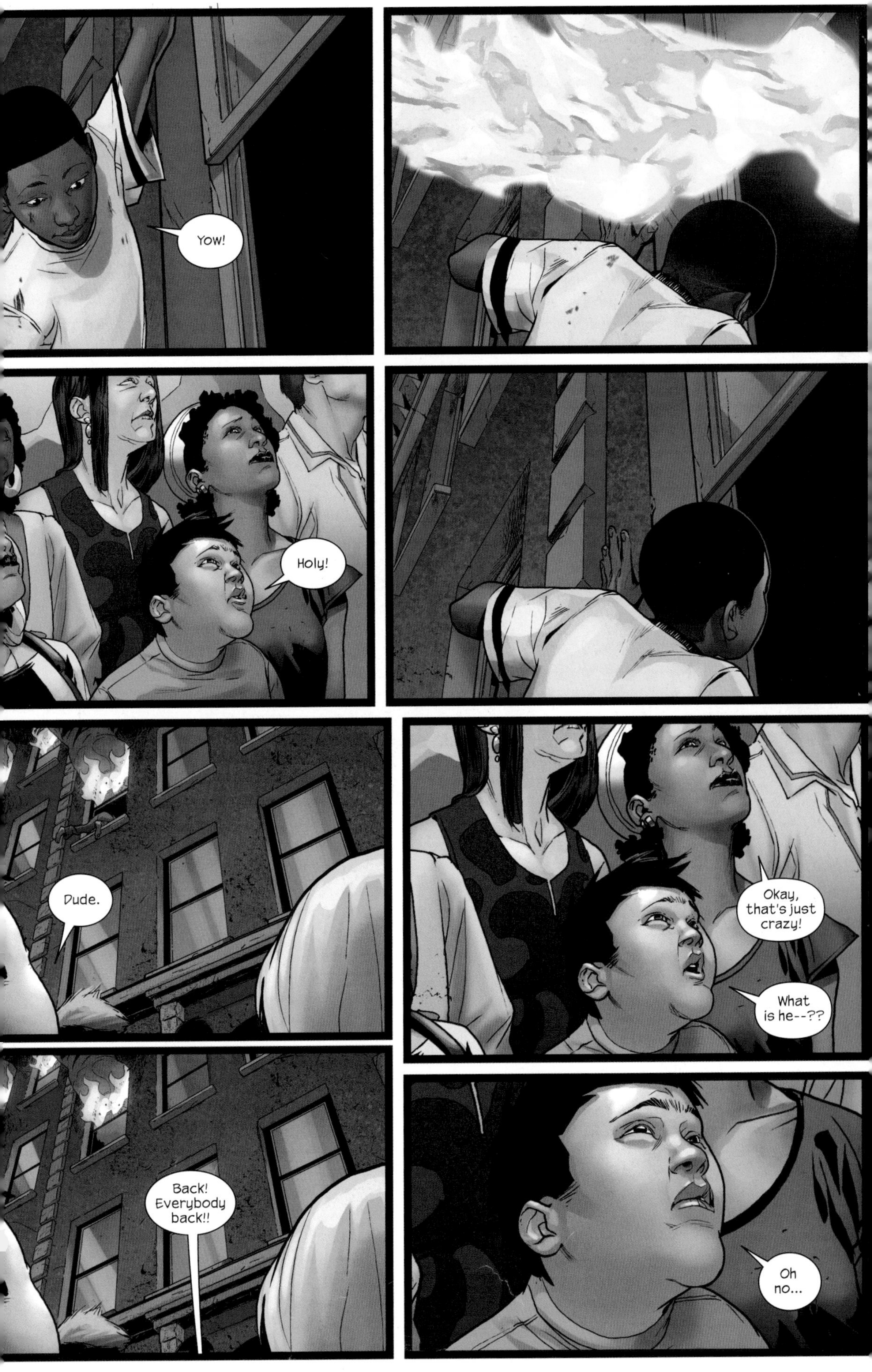
Yow!
Holy!
Dude.
Back! Everybody back!!
Okay, that's just crazy!
What is he--??
Oh no...

Woof!

Ruff!

FUMP

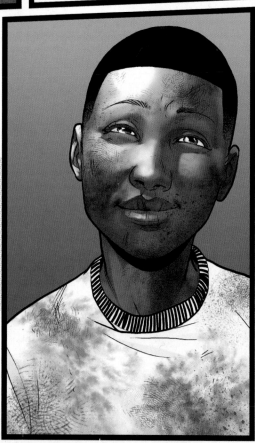

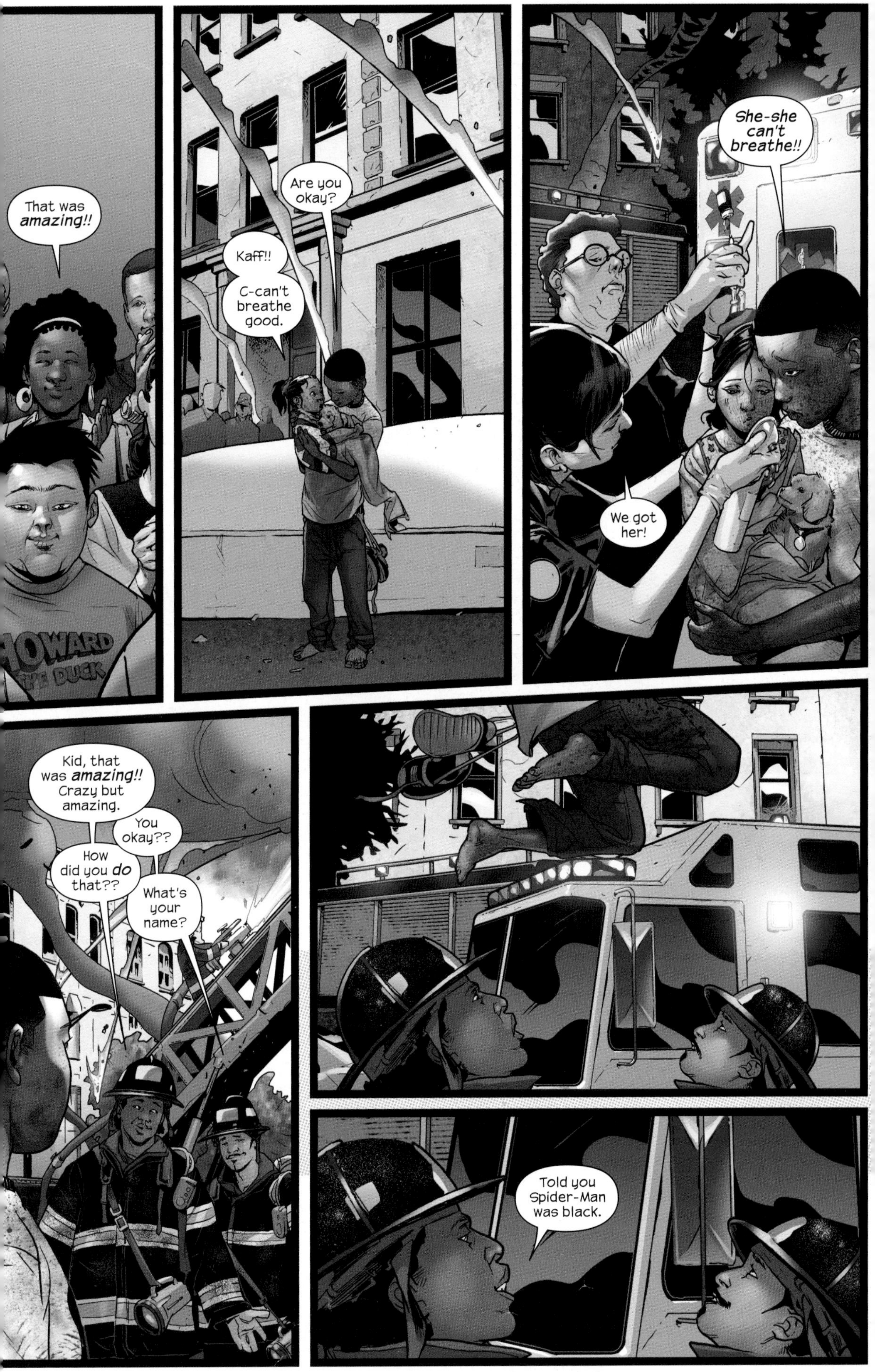
That was *amazing!!*
HOWARD THE DUCK
Are you okay?
Kaff!!
C-can't breathe good.
She-she can't breathe!!
We got her!
Kid, that was *amazing!!* Crazy but amazing.
You okay??
How did you *do* that??
What's your name?
Told you Spider-Man was black.

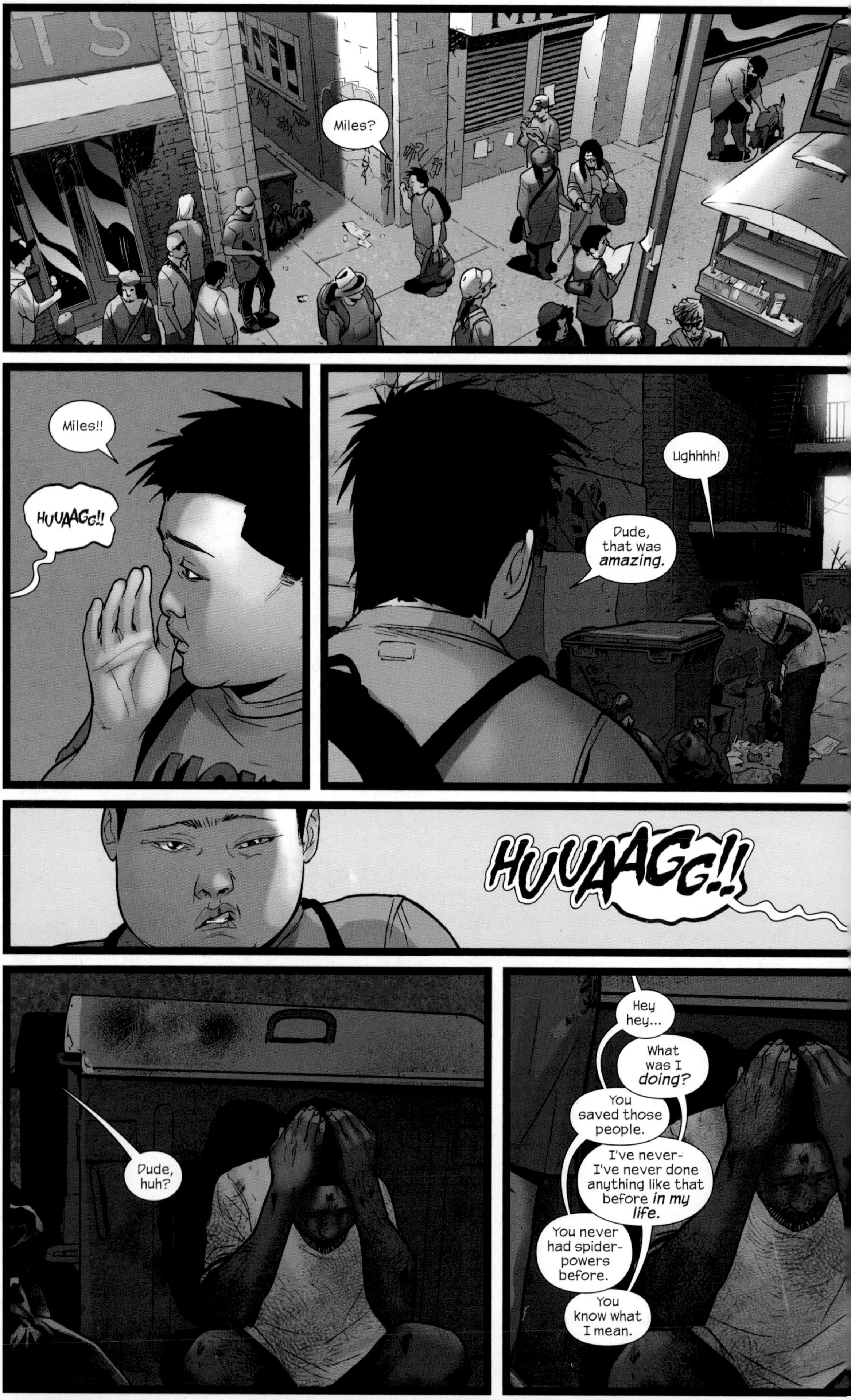
Miles?
Miles!!
HUUAAGG!!
Ughhhh!
Dude, that was *amazing.*
HUUAAGG!!
Dude, huh?
Hey hey...
What was I *doing?*
You saved those people.
I've never- I've never done anything like that before *in my life.*
You never had spider-powers before.
You know what I mean.

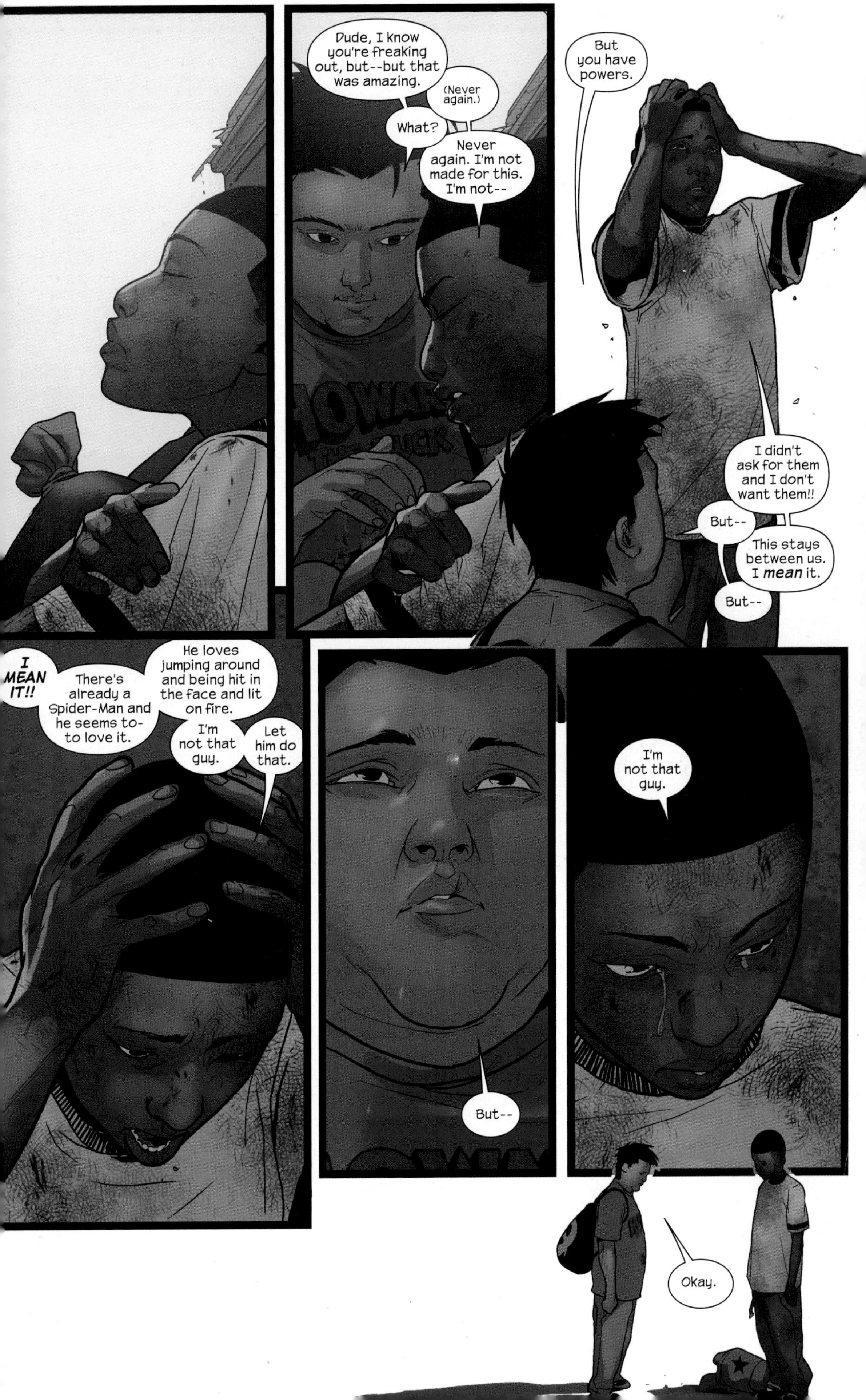
Dude, I know you're freaking out, but--but that was amazing.
(Never again.)
What?
Never again. I'm not made for this. I'm not--
But you have powers.
I didn't ask for them and I don't want them!!
But--
This stays between us. I *mean* it.
But--
I MEAN IT!!
There's already a Spider-Man and he seems to-to love it.
He loves jumping around and being hit in the face and lit on fire.
I'm not that guy.
Let him do that.
But--
I'm not that guy.
Okay.

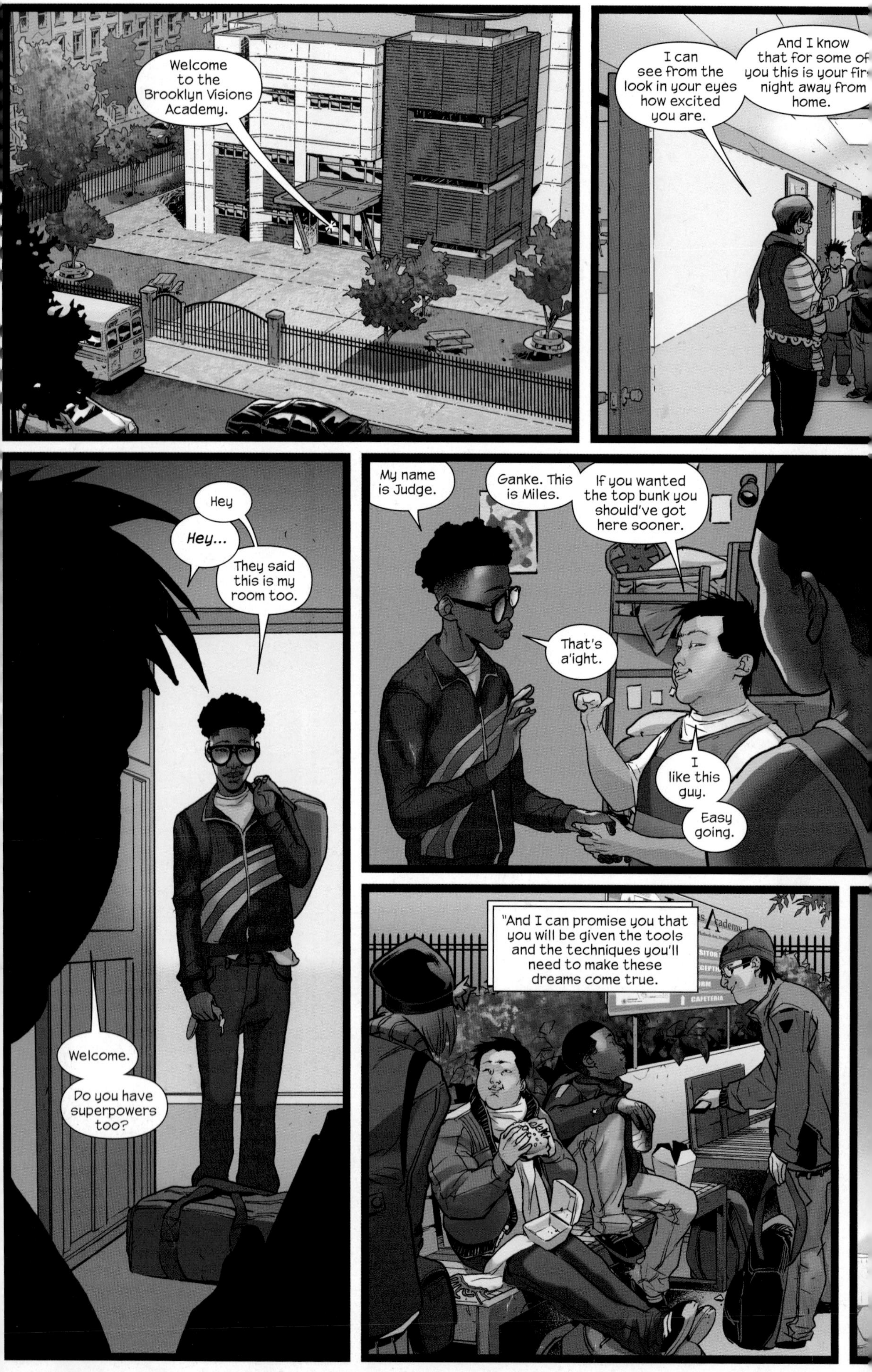

Welcome to the Brooklyn Visions Academy.
I can see from the look in your eyes how excited you are.
And I know that for some of you this is your fir night away from home.
Hey
Hey...
They said this is my room too.
Welcome.
Do you have superpowers too?
My name is Judge.
Ganke. This is Miles.
If you wanted the top bunk you should've got here sooner.
That's a'ight.
I like this guy.
Easy going.
"And I can promise you that you will be given the tools and the techniques you'll need to make these dreams come true.
CAFETERIA

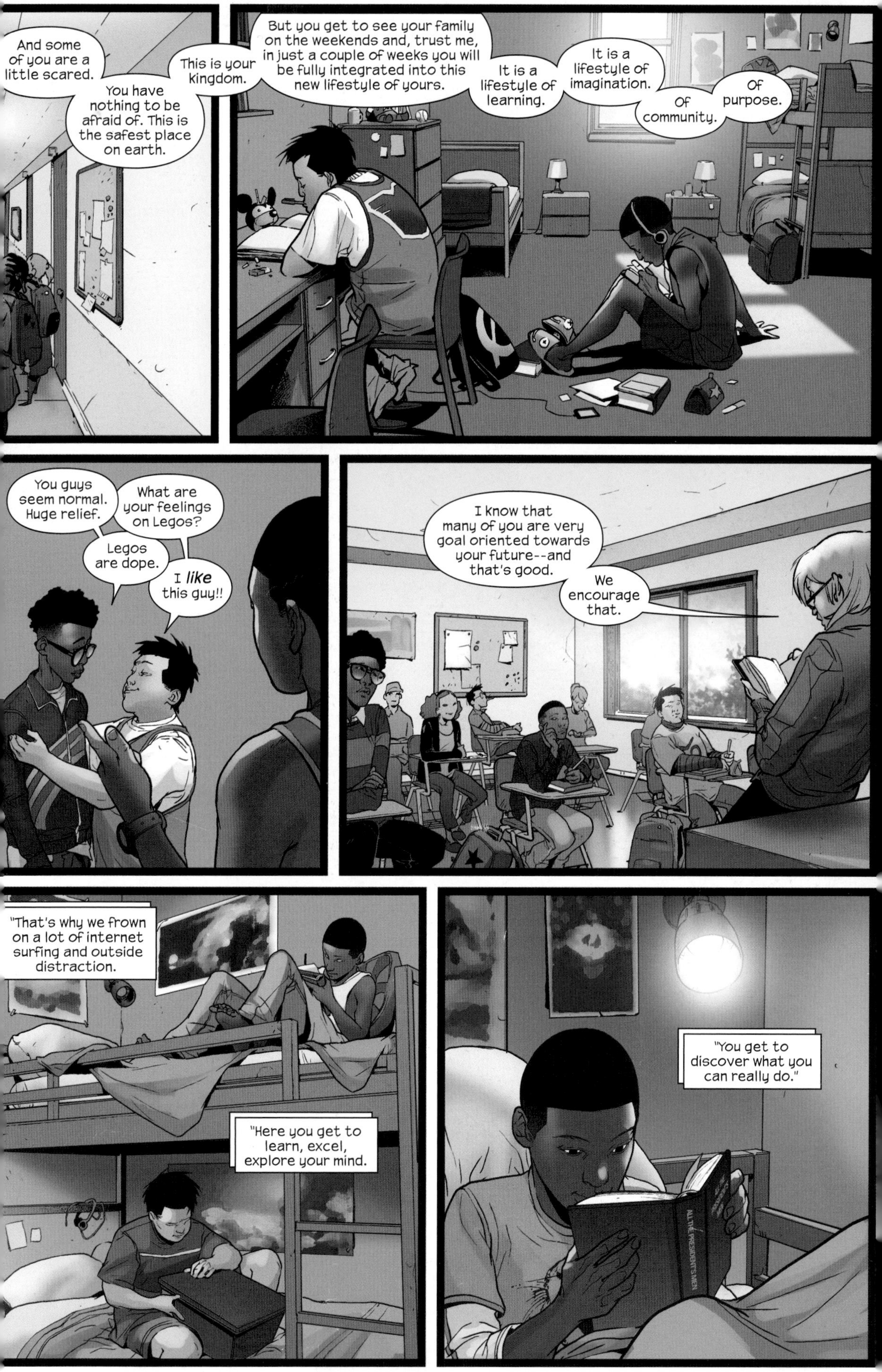

And some of you are a little scared.
You have nothing to be afraid of. This is the safest place on earth.
This is your kingdom.
But you get to see your family on the weekends and, trust me, in just a couple of weeks you will be fully integrated into this new lifestyle of yours.
It is a lifestyle of learning.
It is a lifestyle of imagination.
Of community.
Of purpose.
You guys seem normal. Huge relief.
What are your feelings on Legos?
Legos are dope.
I *like* this guy!!
I know that many of you are very goal oriented towards your future--and that's good.
We encourage that.
"That's why we frown on a lot of internet surfing and outside distraction.
"Here you get to learn, excel, explore your mind.
"You get to discover what you can really do."

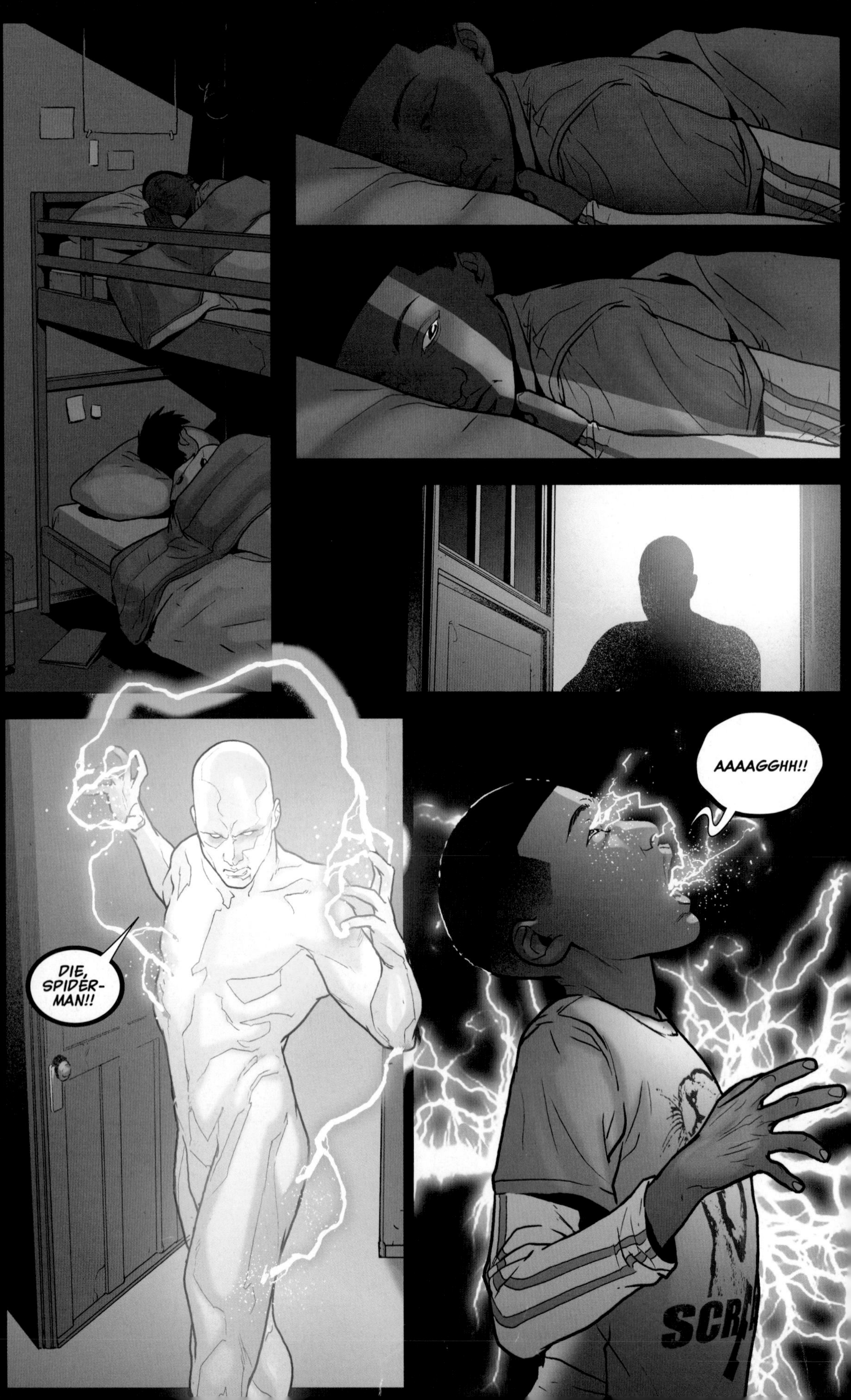
DIE, SPIDER-MAN!!
AAAAGGHH!!
SCR

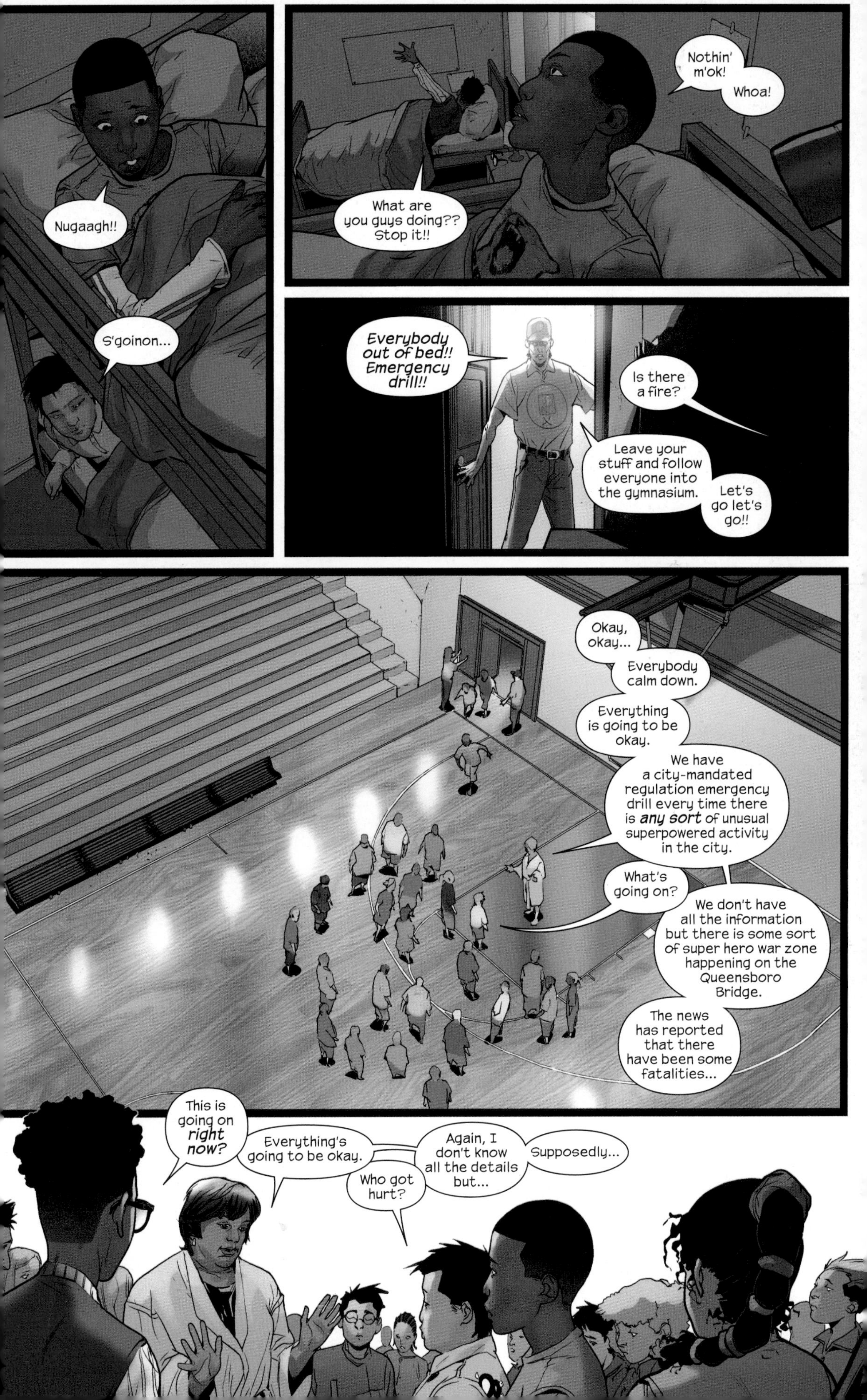
Nugaagh!!
S'goinon...
What are you guys doing?? Stop it!!
Nothin' m'ok!
Whoa!
Everybody out of bed!! Emergency drill!!
Is there a fire?
Leave your stuff and follow everyone into the gymnasium.
Let's go let's go!!
Okay, okay...
Everybody calm down.
Everything is going to be okay.
We have a city-mandated regulation emergency drill every time there is any sort of unusual superpowered activity in the city.
What's going on?
We don't have all the information but there is some sort of super hero war zone happening on the Queensboro Bridge.
The news has reported that there have been some fatalities...
This is going on right now?
Everything's going to be okay.
Who got hurt?
Again, I don't know all the details but...
Supposedly...

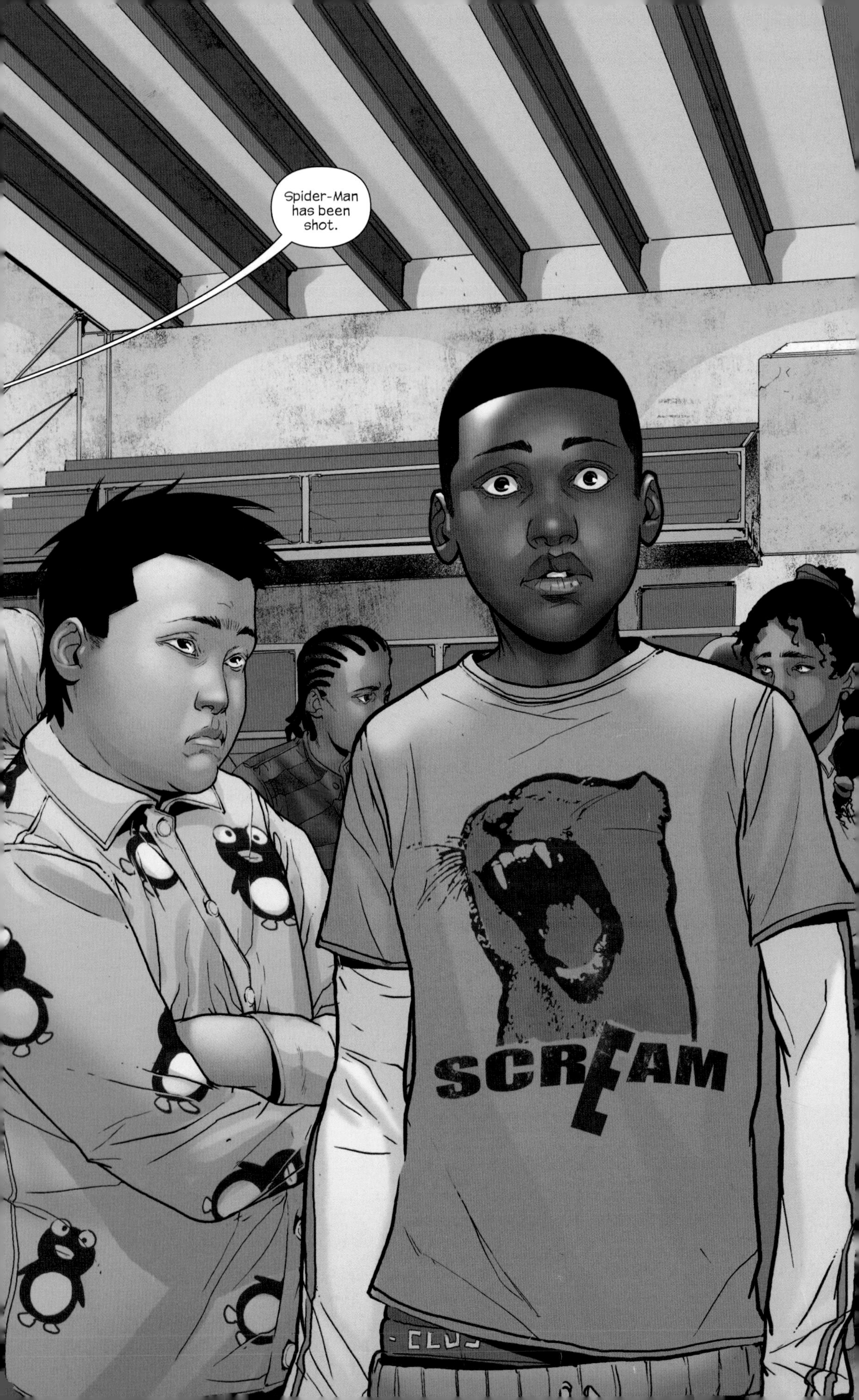
Spider-Man has been shot.
SCREAM

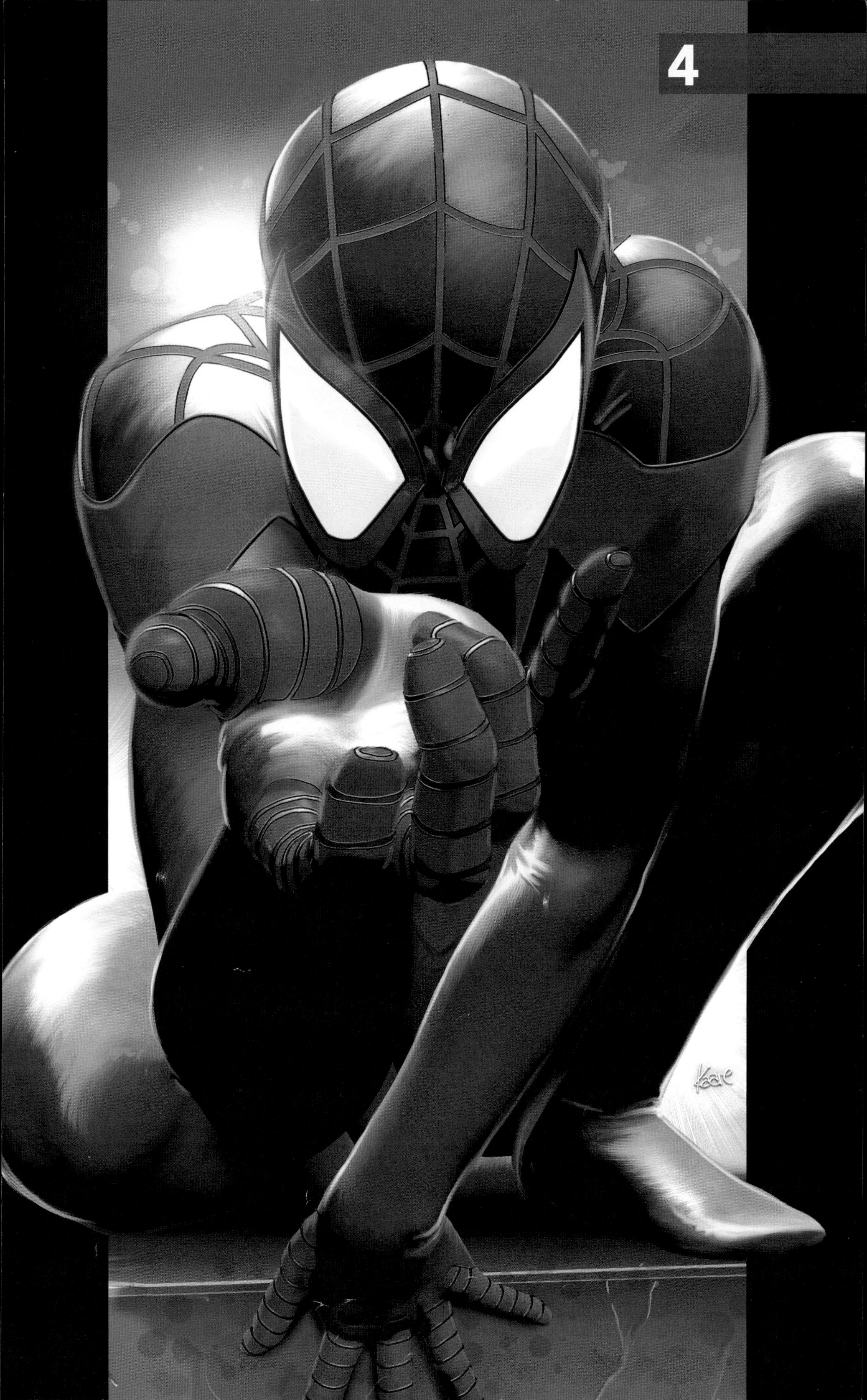
4

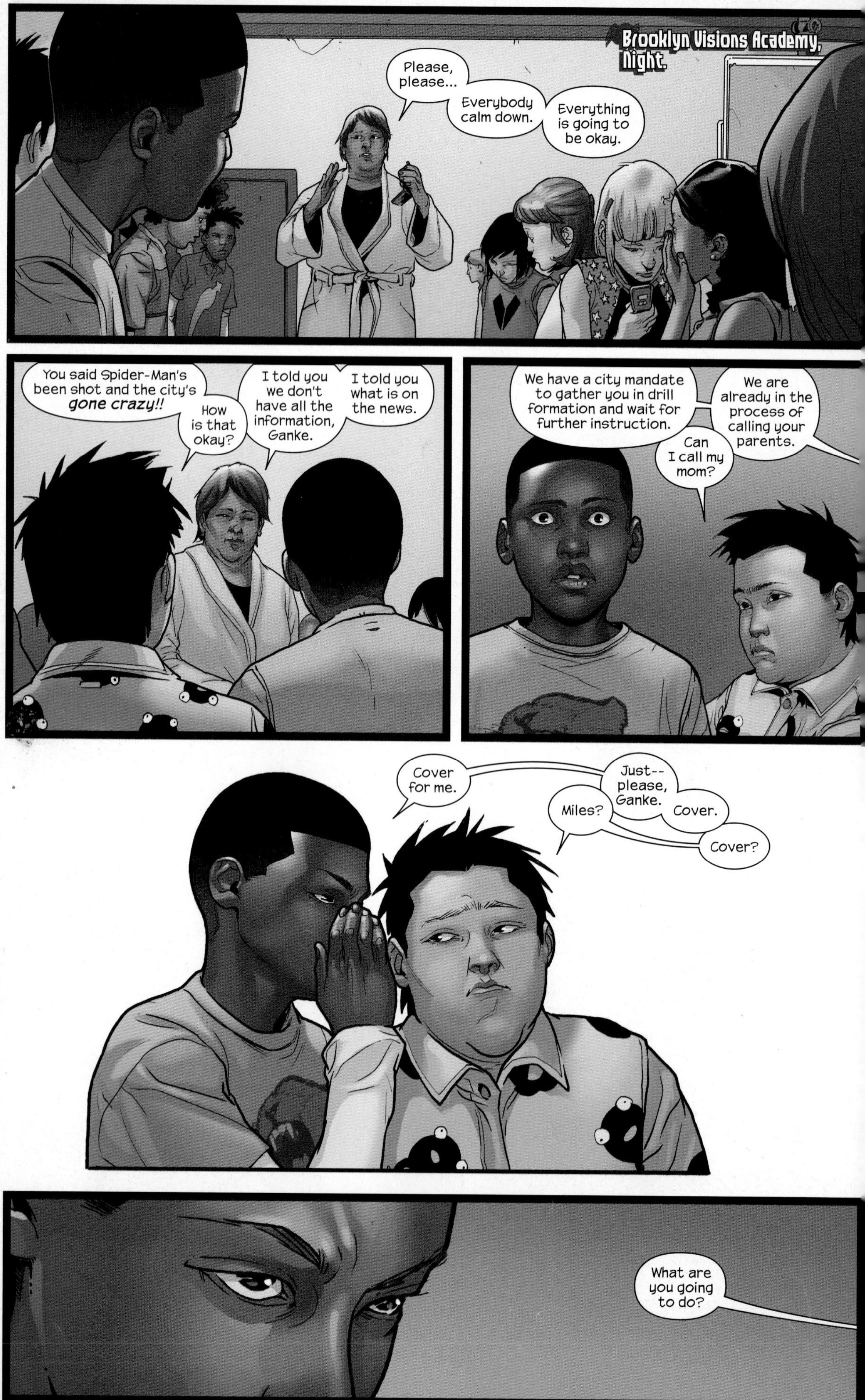
Brooklyn Visions Academy, Night.
Please, please...
Everybody calm down.
Everything is going to be okay.
You said Spider-Man's been shot and the city's gone crazy!!
How is that okay?
I told you we don't have all the information, Ganke.
I told you what is on the news.
We have a city mandate to gather you in drill formation and wait for further instruction.
We are already in the process of calling your parents.
Can I call my mom?
Cover for me.
Just-- please, Ganke.
Miles?
Cover.
Cover?
What are you going to do?

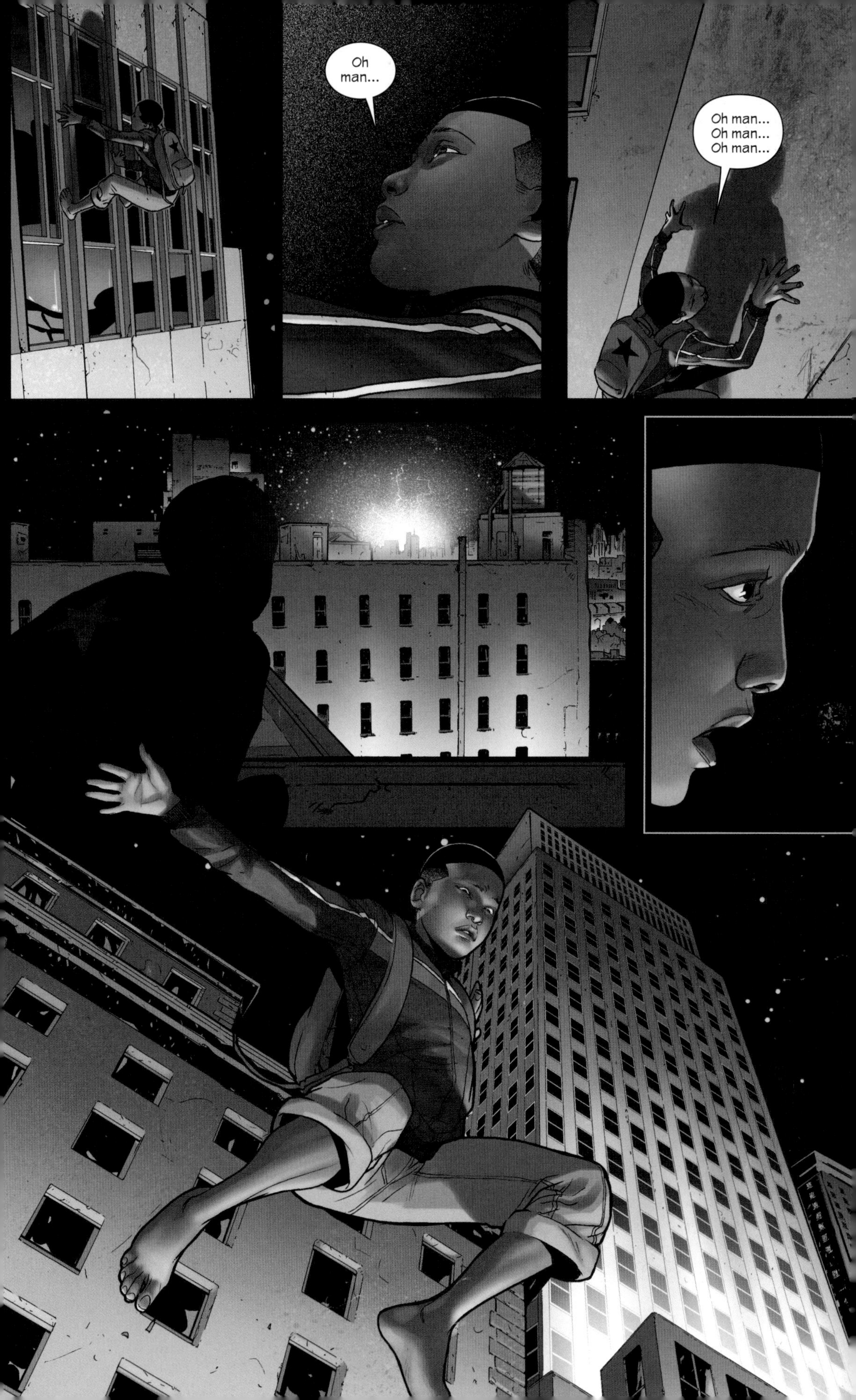
Oh man...
Oh man... Oh man... Oh man...

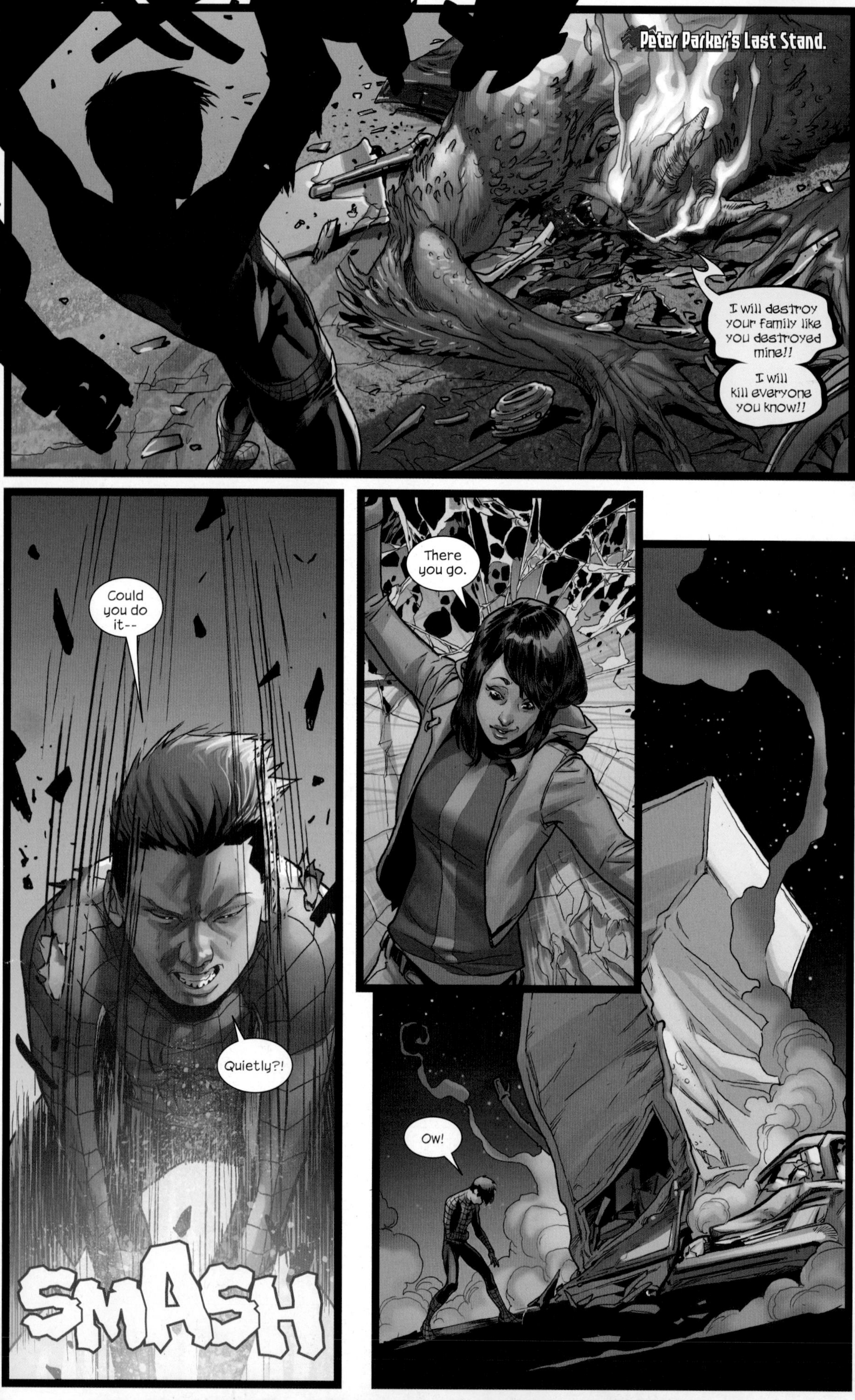
Peter Parker's Last Stand.
I will destroy your family like you destroyed mine!!
I will kill everyone you know!!
Could you do it--
Quietly?!
SMASH
There you go.
Ow!

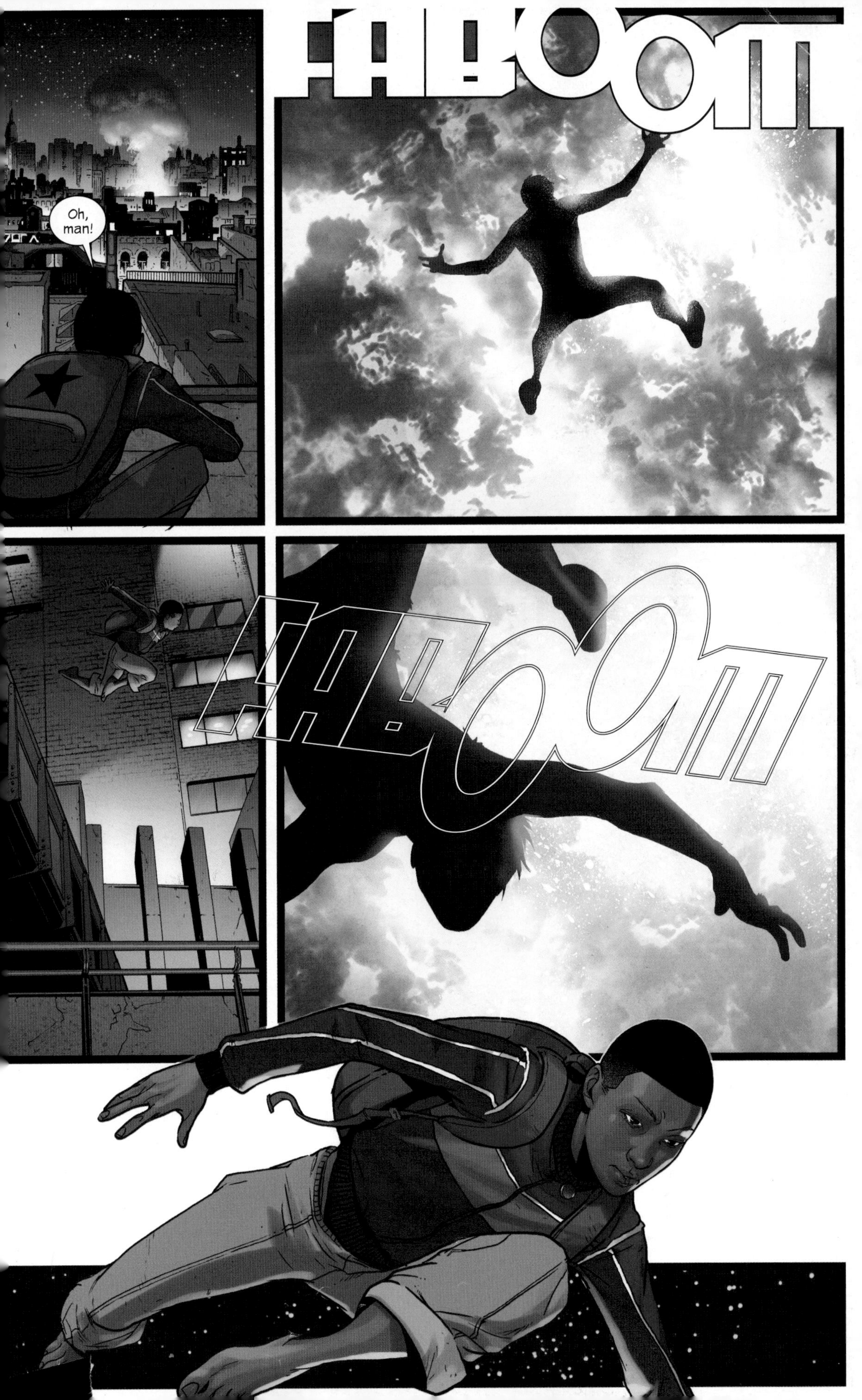
Oh, man!
KABOOM
KABOOM

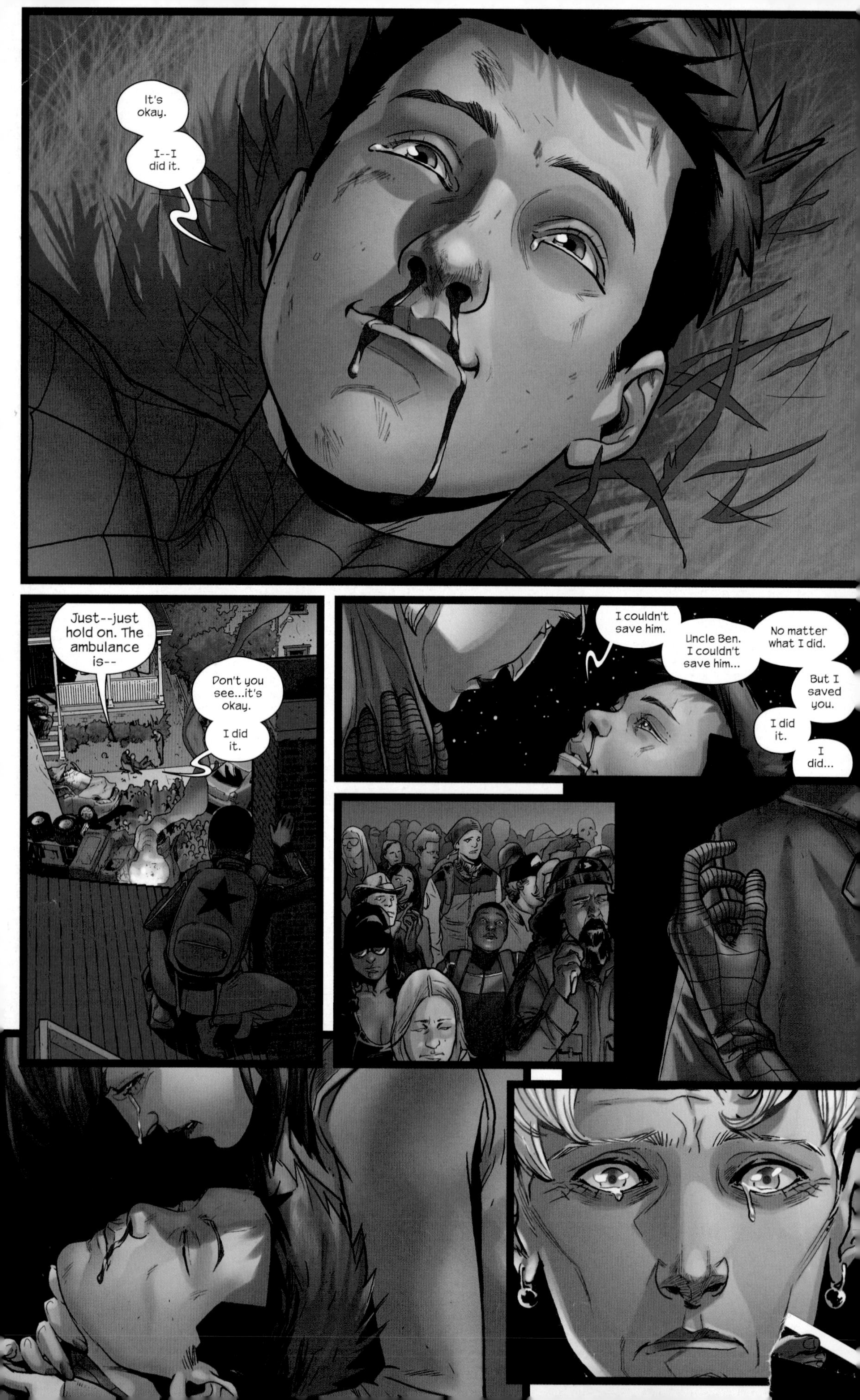
It's okay.
I--I did it.
Just--just hold on. The ambulance is--
Don't you see...it's okay.
I did it.
I couldn't save him.
Uncle Ben. I couldn't save him...
No matter what I did.
But I saved you.
I did it.
I did...

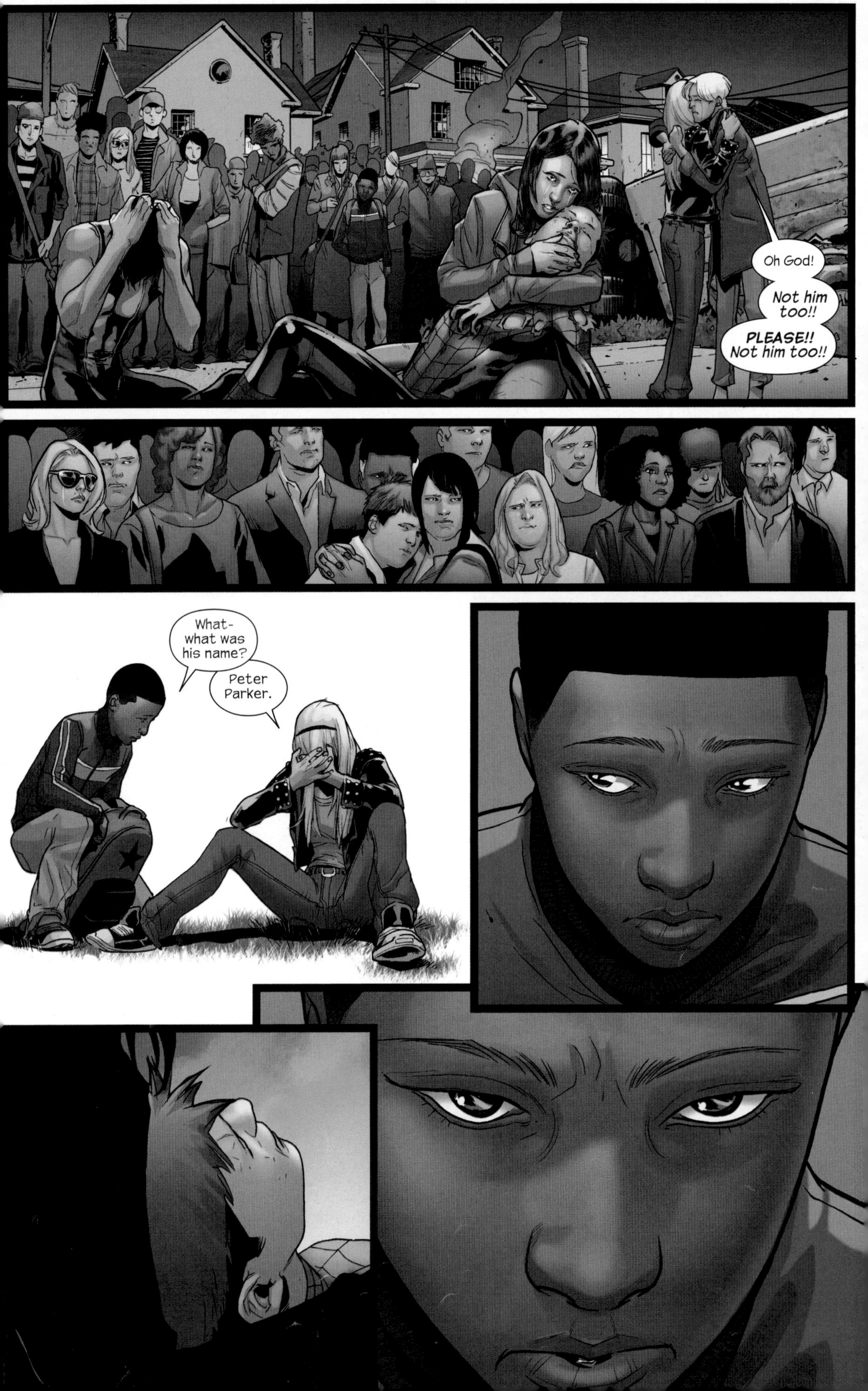
Oh God!
Not him too!!
PLEASE!! Not him too!!
What- what was his name?
Peter Parker.

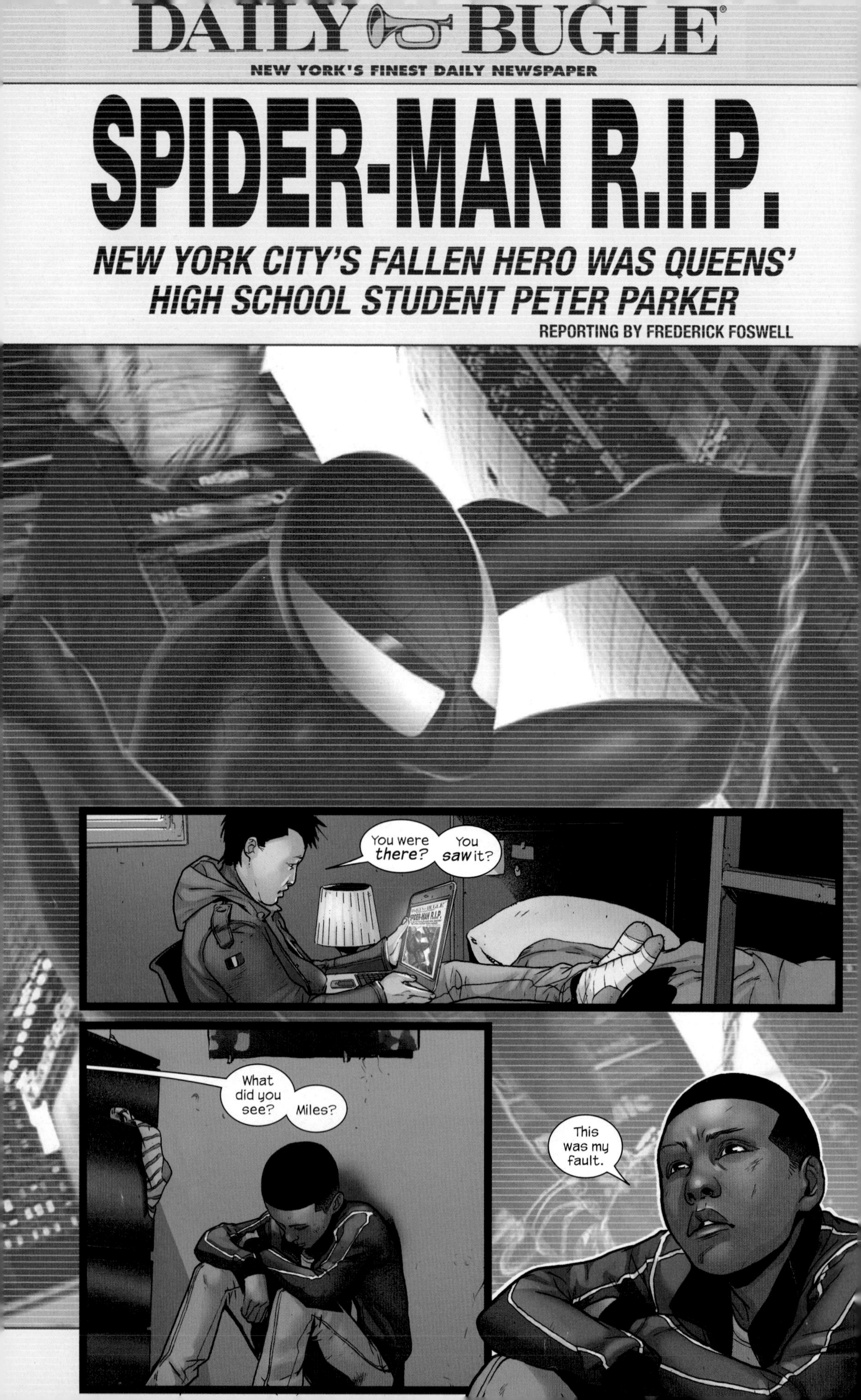
DAILY BUGLE
NEW YORK'S FINEST DAILY NEWSPAPER
SPIDER-MAN R.I.P.
NEW YORK CITY'S FALLEN HERO WAS QUEENS' HIGH SCHOOL STUDENT PETER PARKER
REPORTING BY FREDERICK FOSWELL
You were *there*?
You *saw* it?
What did you see?
Miles?
This was my fault.

What? How was this at all--??

Instead of being a coward.

You know I could have helped stop this.

If I would have used my powers when I first got them--

Like I was *supposed* to--

Like you *told* me to--

If I wouldn't have been *hiding* in this room...then by now my whole life would've been different.

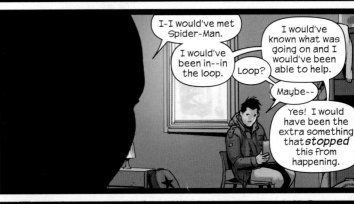

I-I would've met Spider-Man.

I would've been in--in the loop.

Loop?

I would've known what was going on and I would've been able to help.

Maybe--

Yes! I would have been the extra something that *stopped* this from happening.

Maybe.

Or maybe you would've gotten killed too.

I was given these powers for a reason.

You said it.

And I sit here...scared of my dad...

I'm scared of everything...

And now look at what's happened!!

Or Maybe-- Maybe *this* is what you were given the powers for. Maybe you're supposed to be Spider-Man now that we don't have one anymore.

Maybe you're the Spider-Man in the on-deck circle...and now it's your turn.

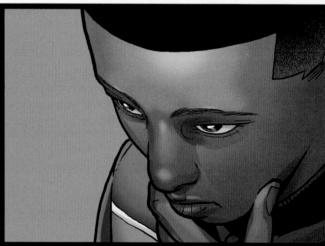

This is crazy. All the bridges are closed. You think we'll get the day off school?

What?

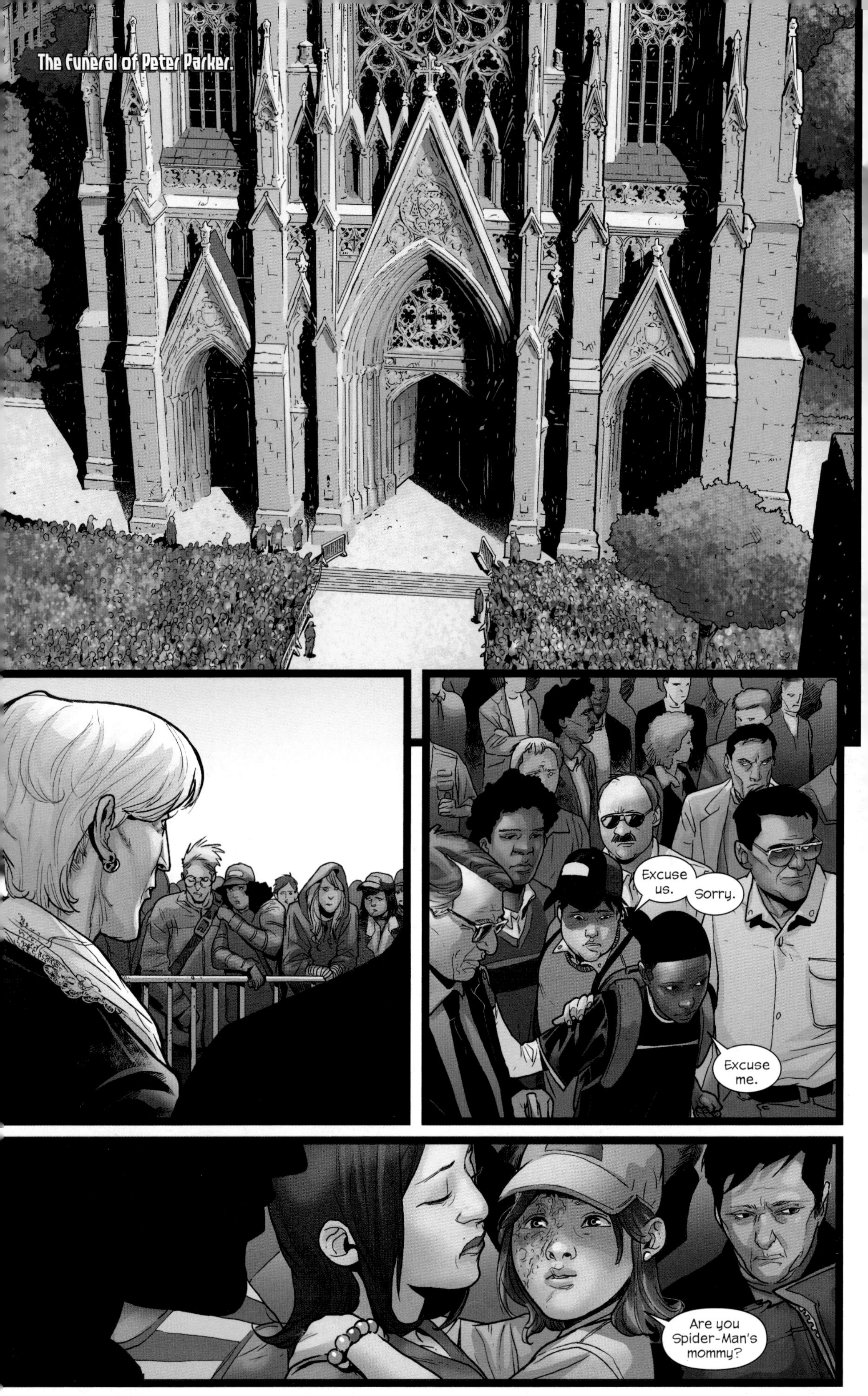
The Funeral of Peter Parker.
Excuse us.
Sorry.
Excuse me.
Are you Spider-Man's mommy?

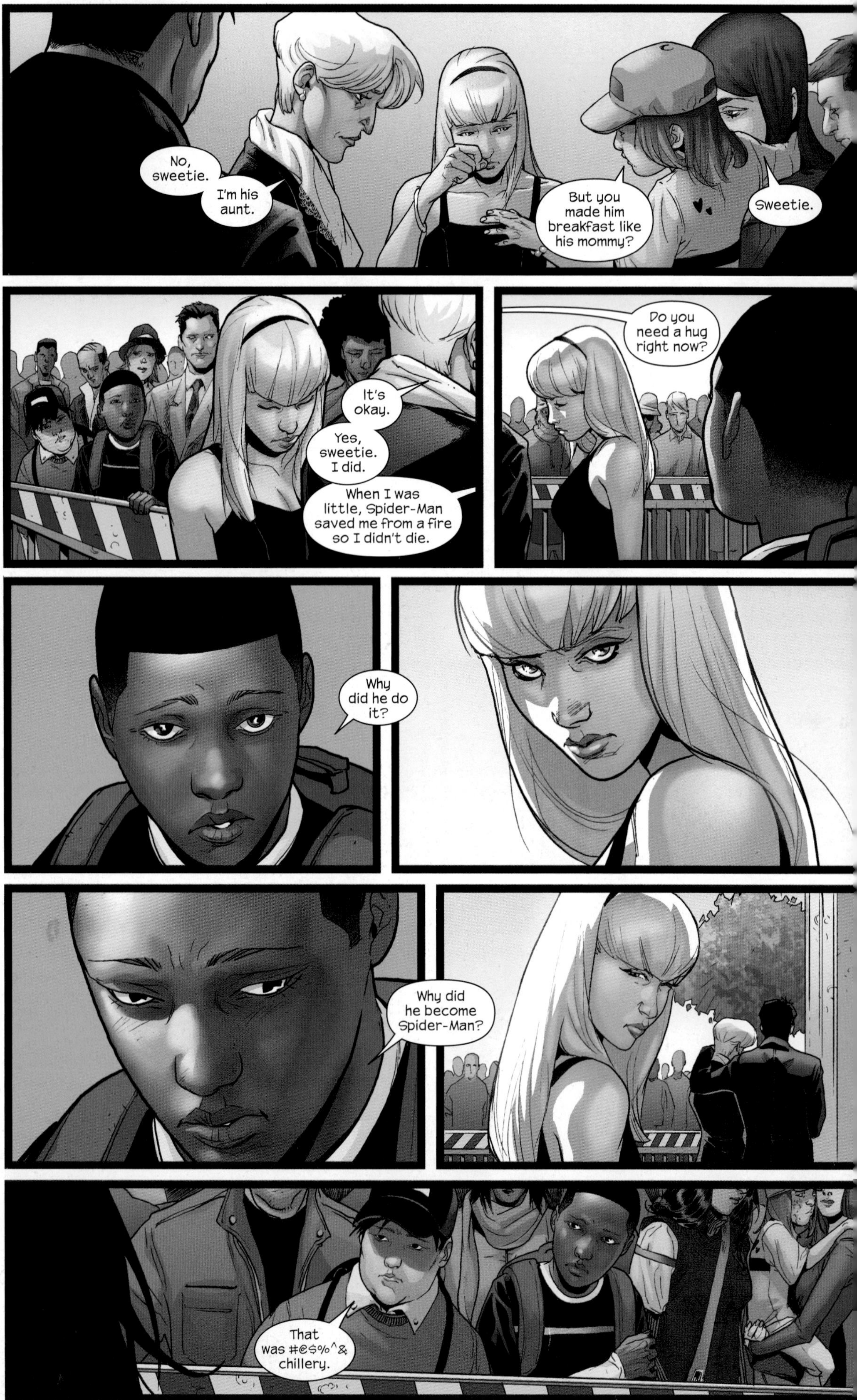
No, sweetie.
I'm his aunt.
But you made him breakfast like his mommy?
Sweetie.
It's okay.
Yes, sweetie. I did.
When I was little, Spider-Man saved me from a fire so I didn't die.
Do you need a hug right now?
Why did he do it?
Why did he become Spider-Man?
That was #@$%^& chillery.

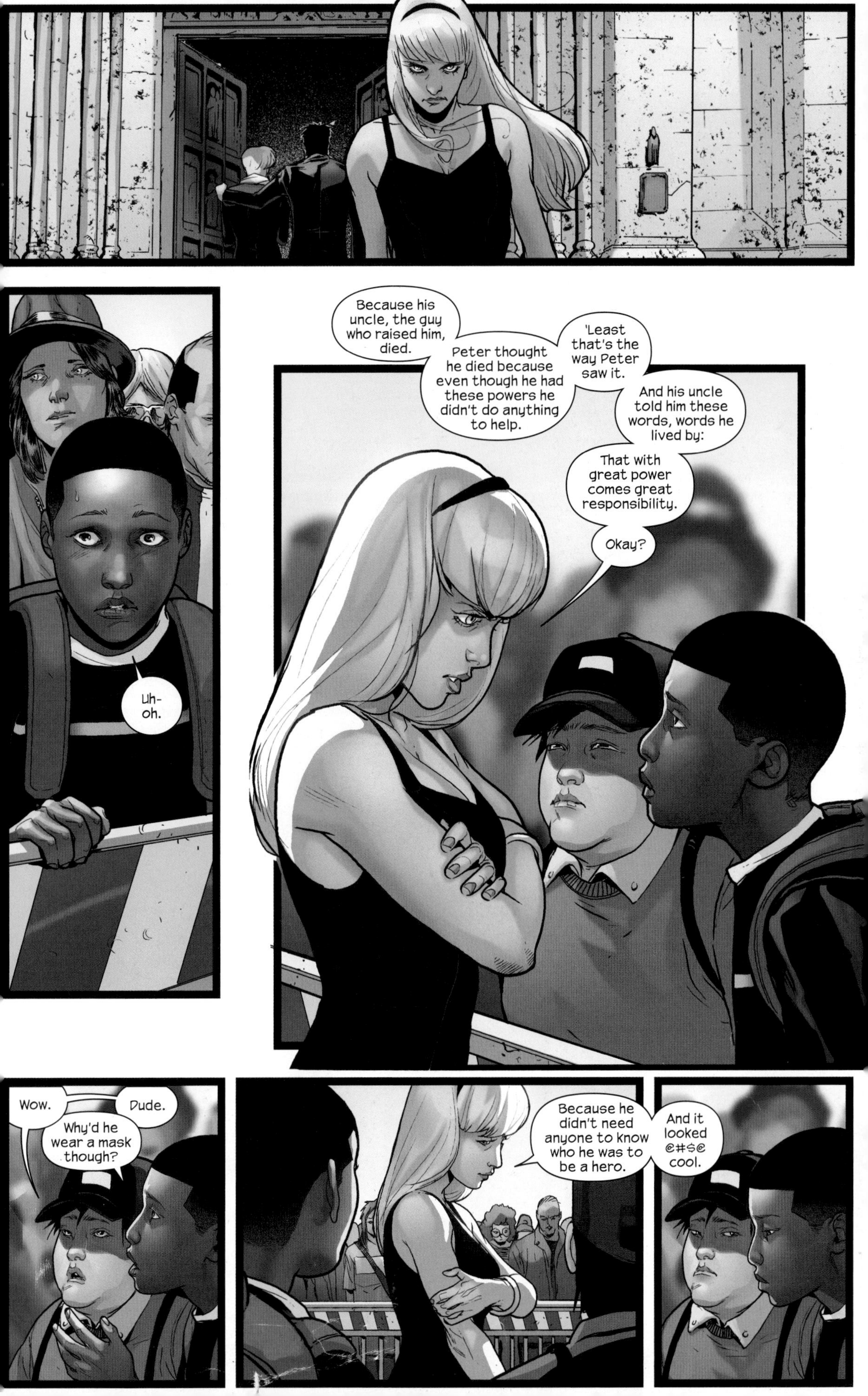
Uh-oh.
Because his uncle, the guy who raised him, died.
Peter thought he died because even though he had these powers he didn't do anything to help.
'Least that's the way Peter saw it.
And his uncle told him these words, words he lived by:
That with great power comes great responsibility.
Okay?
Wow.
Dude.
Why'd he wear a mask though?
Because he didn't need anyone to know who he was to be a hero.
And it looked @#$@ cool.

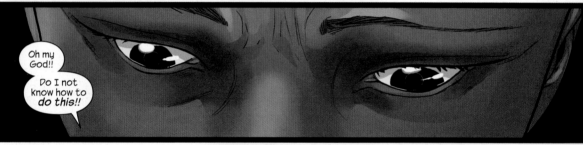

Oh my God!!

Do I not know how to *do this!!*

Say thank you.

What did you do?

No.

You say thank you because I just made your life insanely easy.

SPIDER-MAN
costume & mask

Halloween exclusive

You've got to be kidding me.

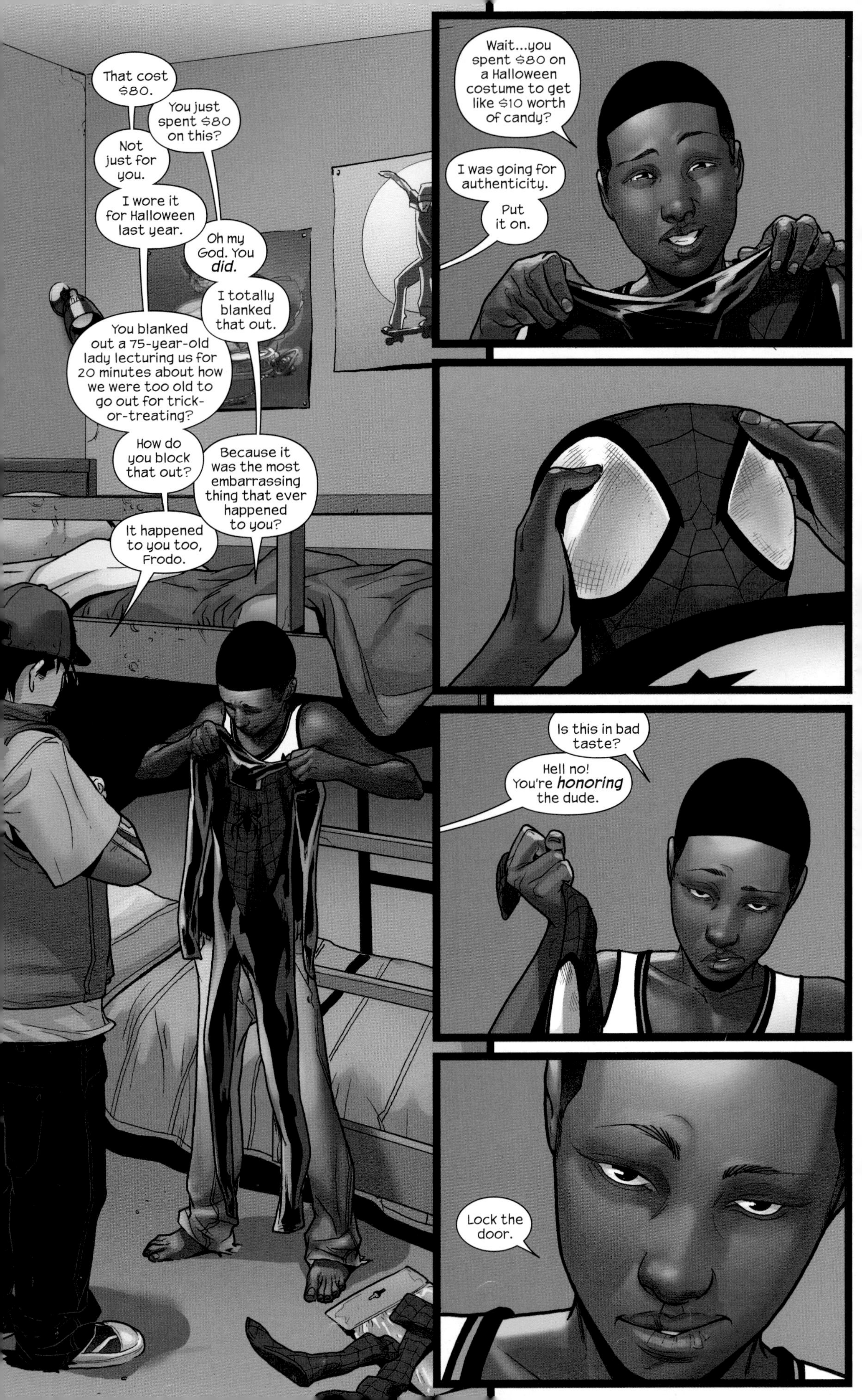
That cost $80.
You just spent $80 on this?
Not just for you.
I wore it for Halloween last year.
Oh my God. You *did.*
I totally blanked that out.
You blanked out a 75-year-old lady lecturing us for 20 minutes about how we were too old to go out for trick-or-treating?
How do you block that out?
Because it was the most embarrassing thing that ever happened to you?
It happened to you too, Frodo.
Wait...you spent $80 on a Halloween costume to get like $10 worth of candy?
I was going for authenticity.
Put it on.
Is this in bad taste?
Hell no! You're ***honoring*** the dude.
Lock the door.

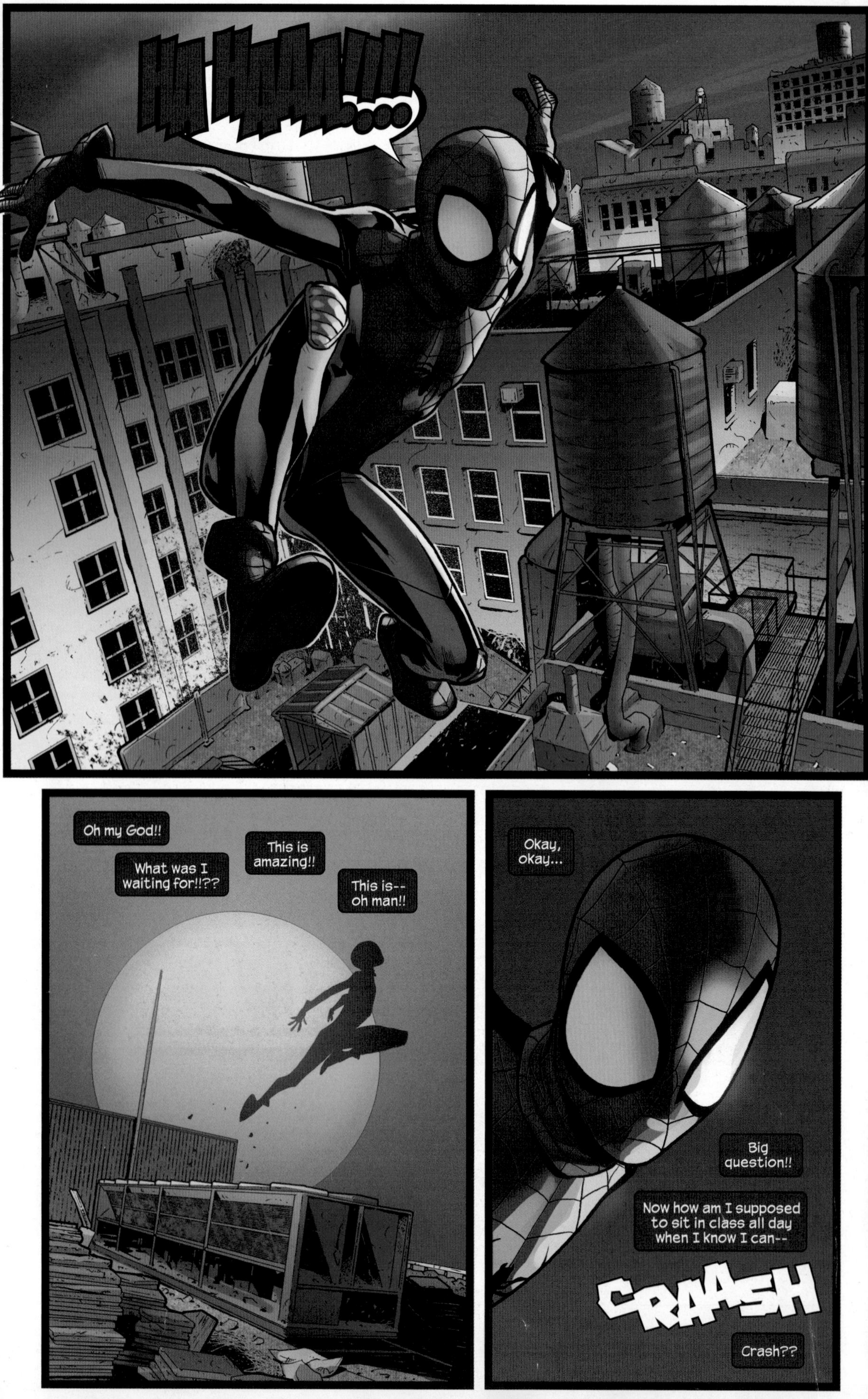
HA HAAA!!!...
Oh my God!!
What was I waiting for!!??
This is amazing!!
This is-- oh man!!
Okay, okay...
Big question!!
Now how am I supposed to sit in class all day when I know I can--
CRAASH
Crash??

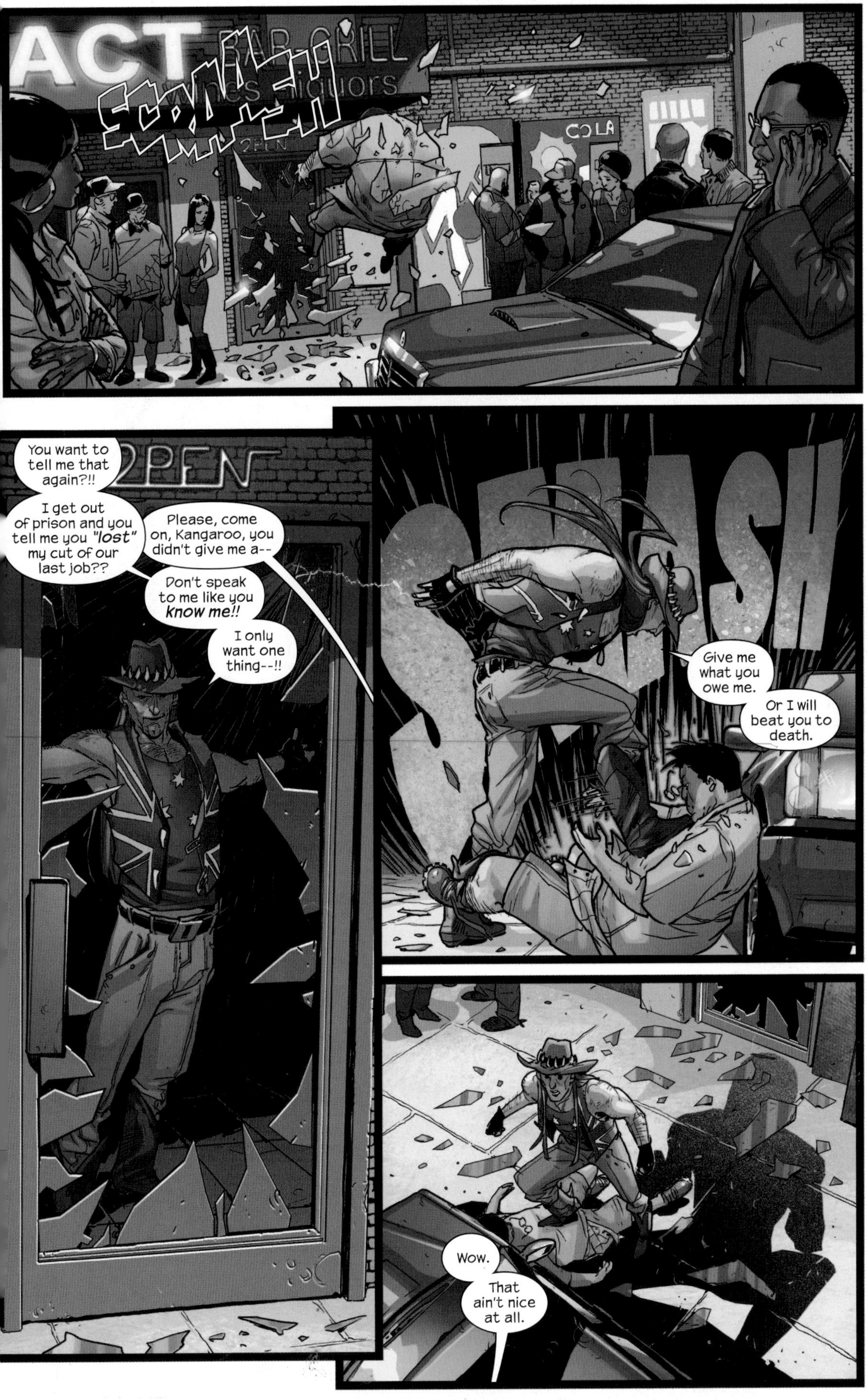

You want to tell me that again?!!
I get out of prison and you tell me you *"lost"* my cut of our last job??
Please, come on, Kangaroo, you didn't give me a--
Don't speak to me like you ***know me!!***
I only want one thing--!!
Give me what you owe me.
Or I will beat you to death.
Wow.
That ain't nice at all.

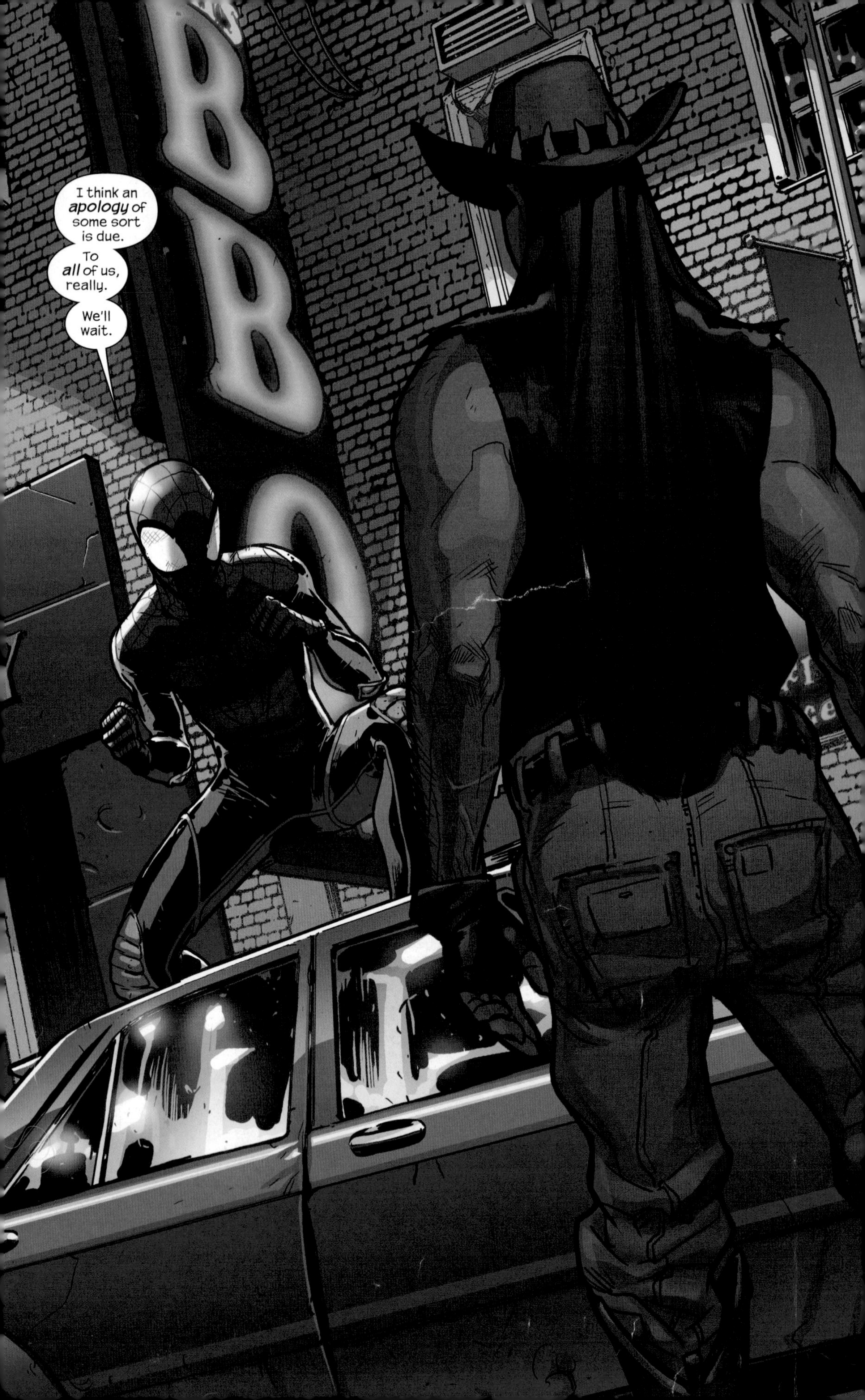
I think an *apology* of some sort is due.
To *all* of us, really.
We'll wait.

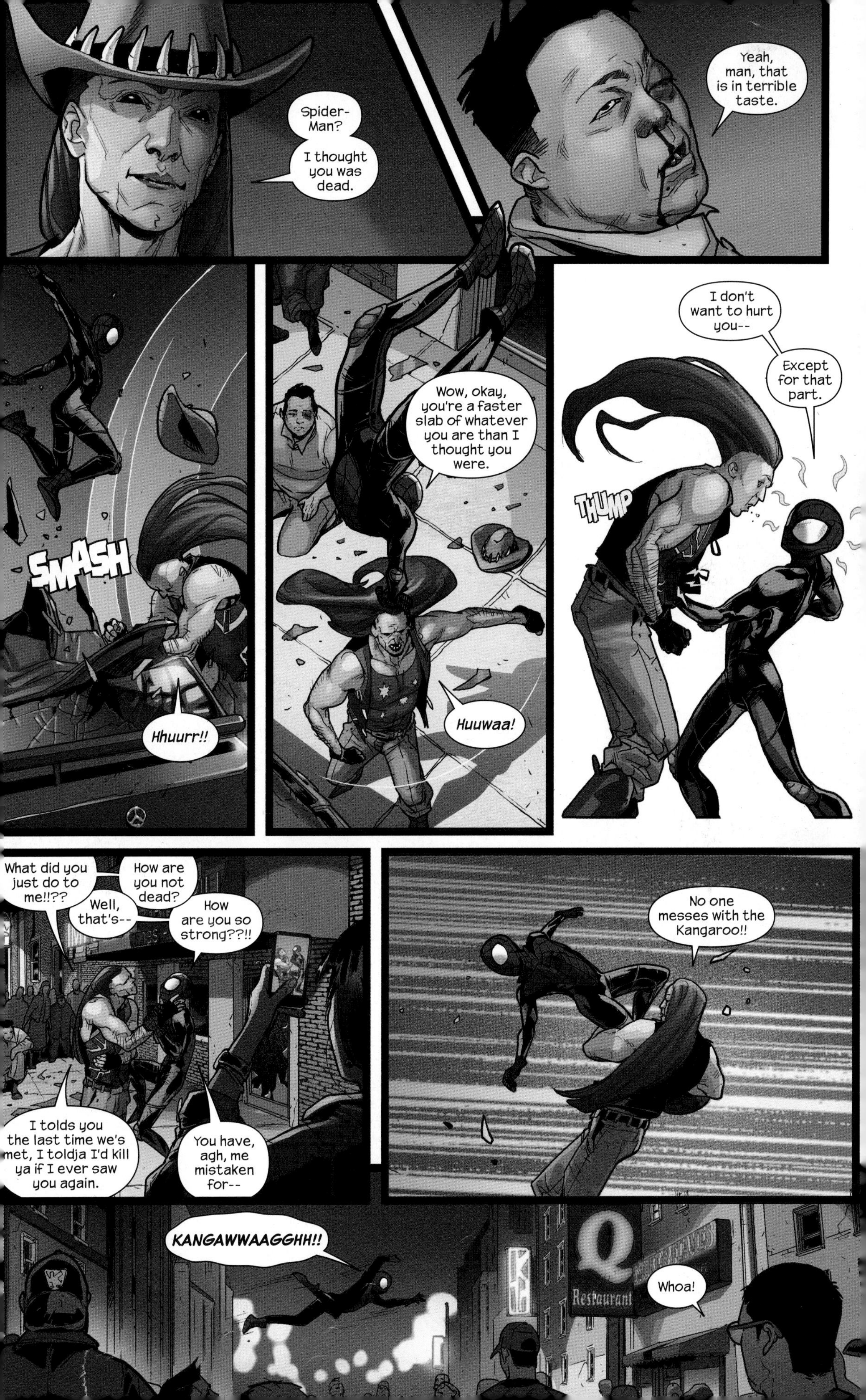

Spider-Man?
I thought you was dead.
Yeah, man, that is in terrible taste.
SMASH
Hhuurr!!
Wow, okay, you're a faster slab of whatever you are than I thought you were.
Huuwaa!
I don't want to hurt you--
Except for that part.
THUMP
What did you just do to me!!??
How are you not dead?
Well, that's--
How are you so strong??!!
I tolds you the last time we's met, I toldja I'd kill ya if I ever saw you again.
You have, agh, me mistaken for--
No one messes with the Kangaroo!!
KANGAWWAAGGHH!!
Restaurant
Whoa!

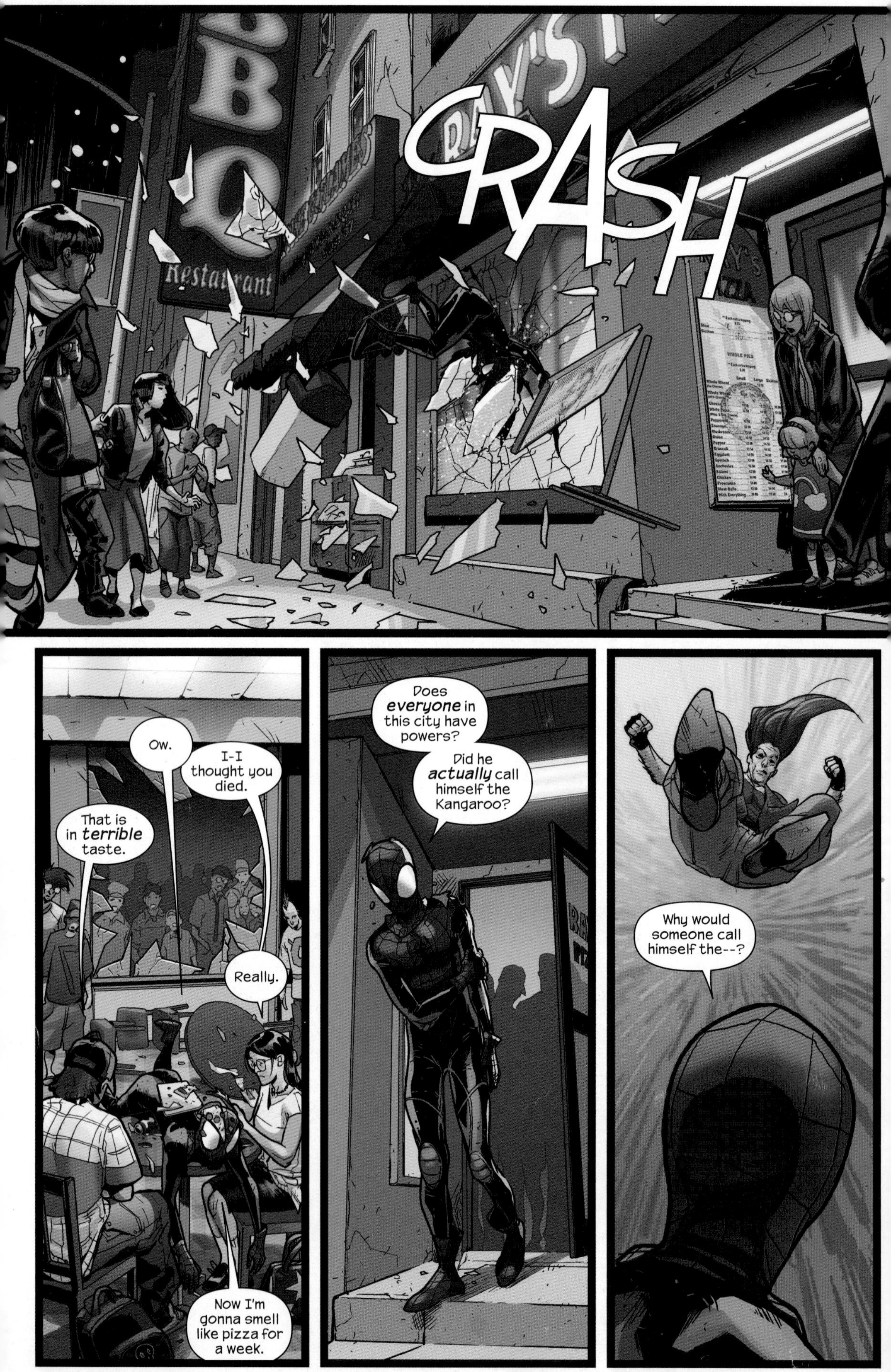

Restaurant
CRASH
Ow.
I-I thought you died.
That is in *terrible* taste.
Really.
Now I'm gonna smell like pizza for a week.
Does *everyone* in this city have powers?
Did he *actually* call himself the Kangaroo?
Why would someone call himself the--?

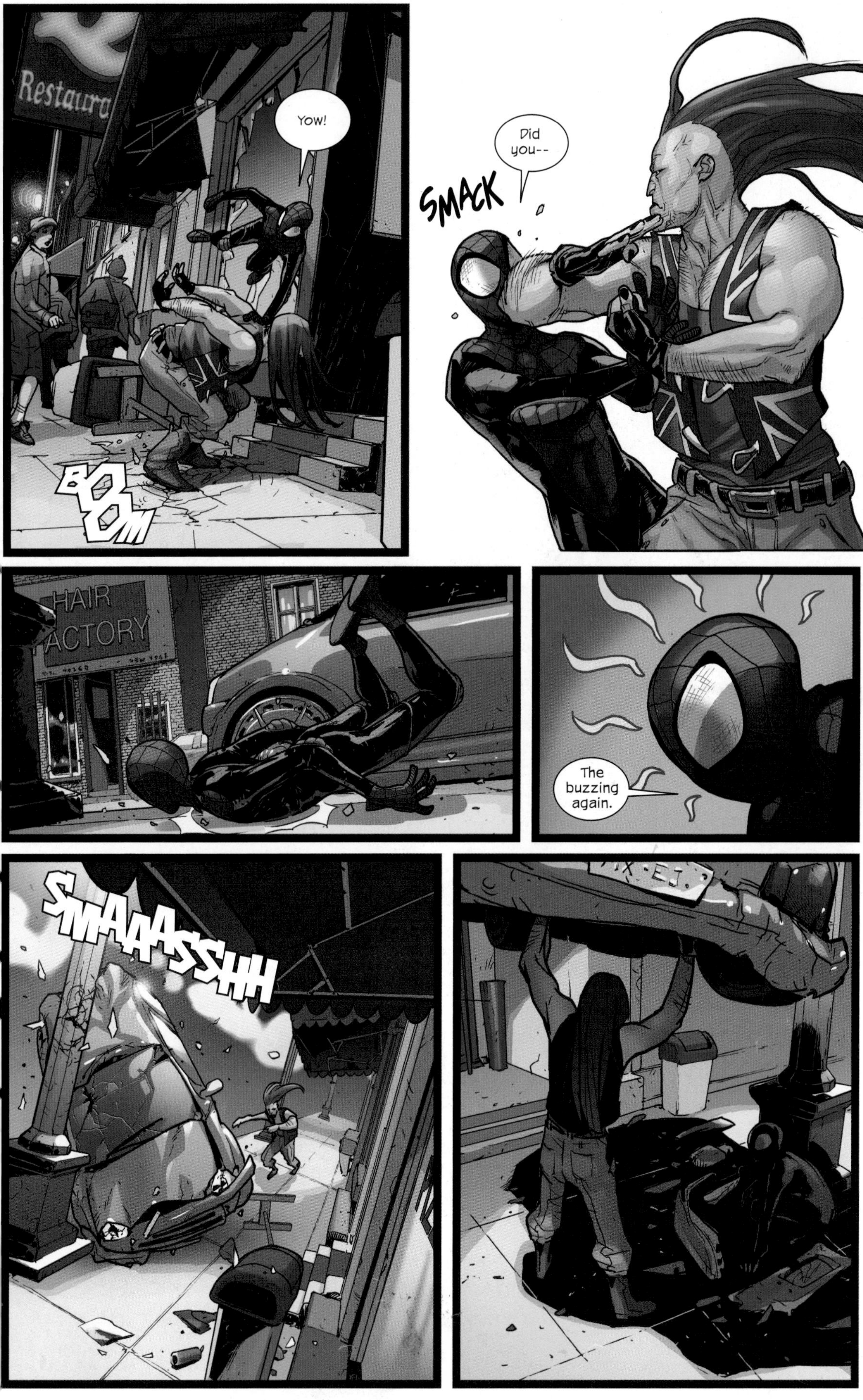
Restaura
Yow!
BOOM
Did you--
SMACK
HAIR FACTORY
The buzzing again.
SMAAASSHH

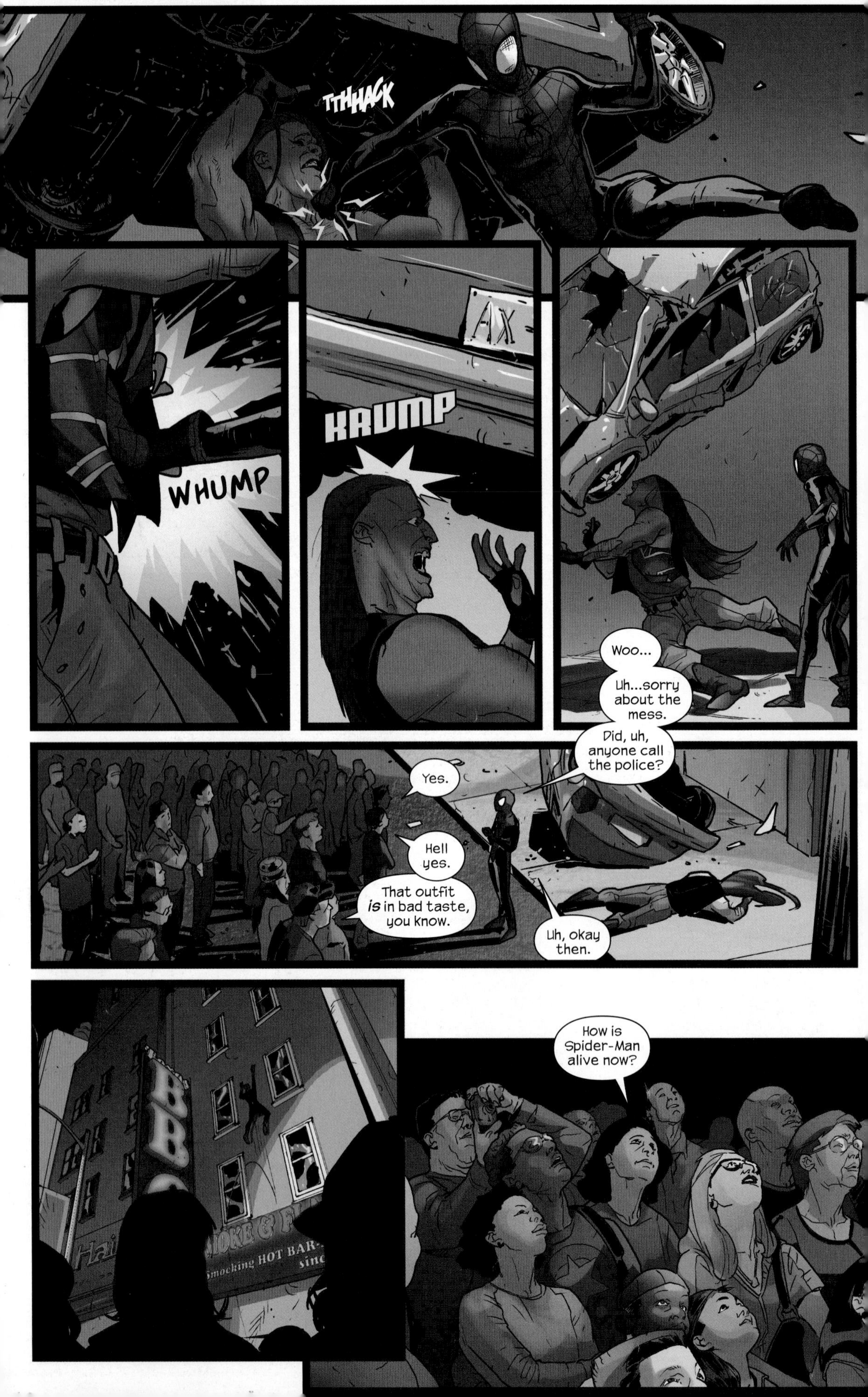
TTHHACK
WHUMP
KRUMP
Woo...
Uh...sorry about the mess.
Did, uh, anyone call the police?
Yes.
Hell yes.
That outfit *is* in bad taste, you know.
Uh, okay then.
How is Spider-Man alive now?

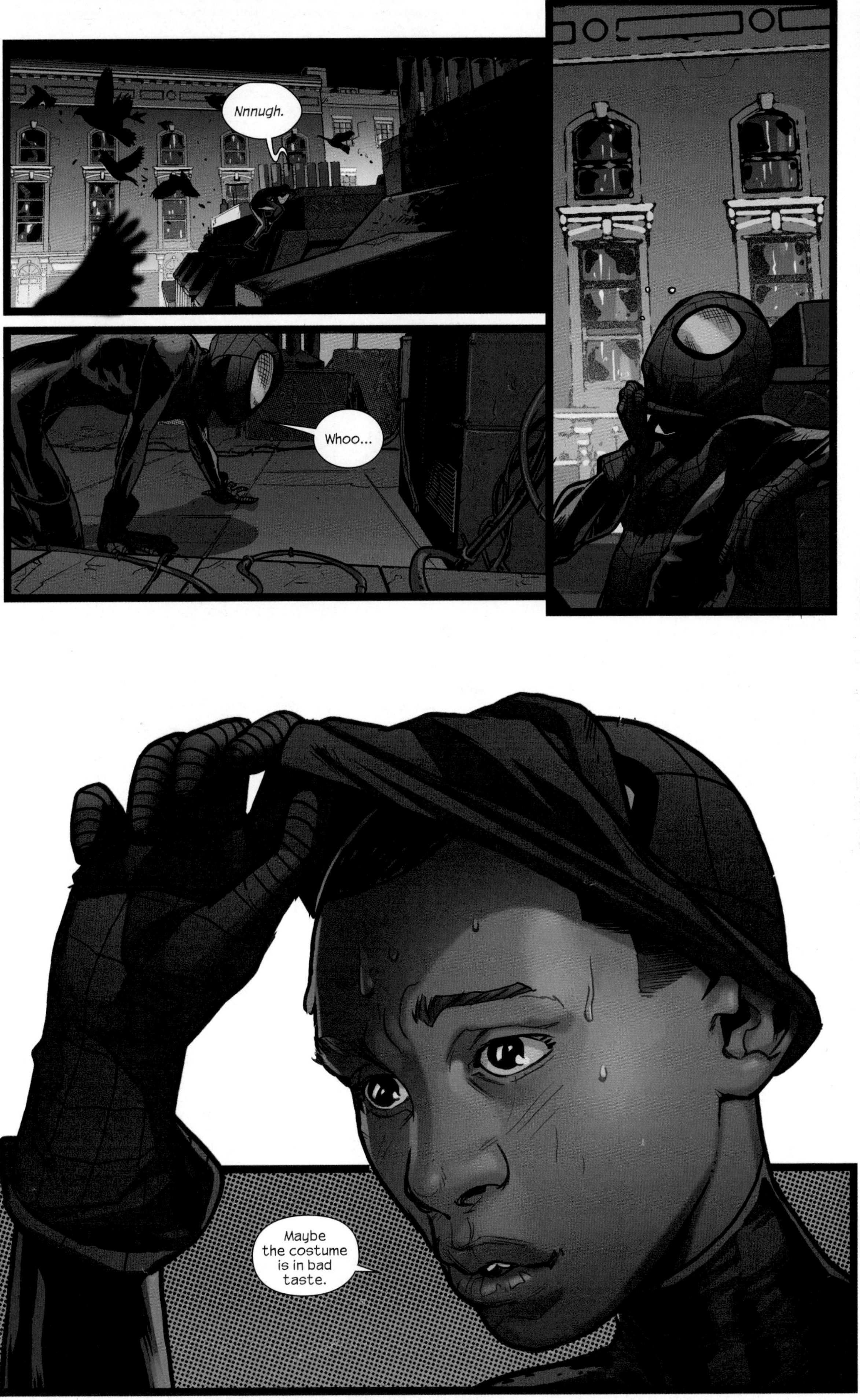
Nnnugh.
Whoo...
Maybe the costume is in bad taste.

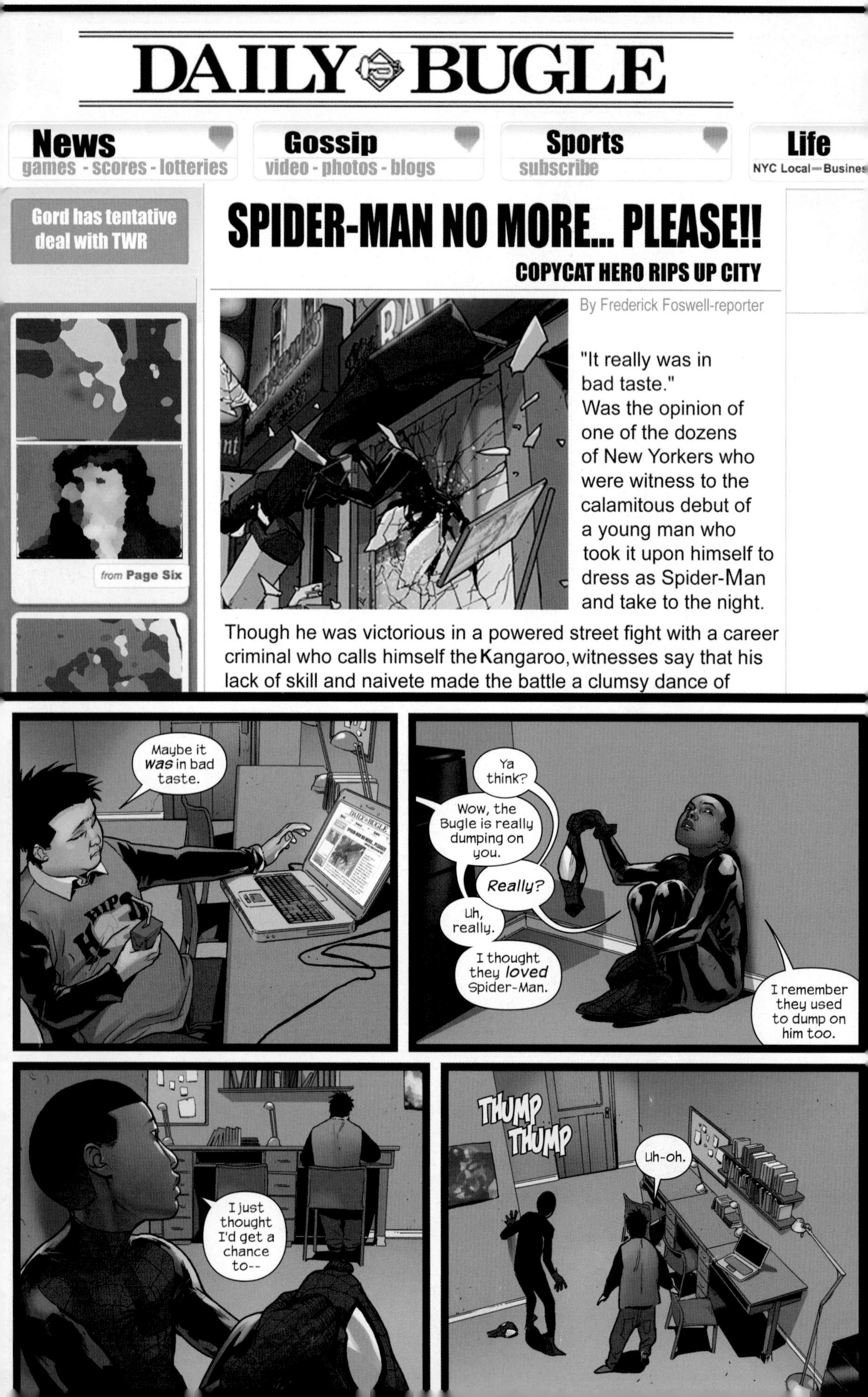

DAILY BUGLE
News
games - scores - lotteries
Gossip
video - photos - blogs
Sports
subscribe
Life
NYC Local—Busines
Gord has tentative deal with TWR
from Page Six
SPIDER-MAN NO MORE... PLEASE!!
COPYCAT HERO RIPS UP CITY
By Frederick Foswell-reporter
"It really was in bad taste." Was the opinion of one of the dozens of New Yorkers who were witness to the calamitous debut of a young man who took it upon himself to dress as Spider-Man and take to the night.
Though he was victorious in a powered street fight with a career criminal who calls himself the Kangaroo, witnesses say that his lack of skill and naivete made the battle a clumsy dance of
Maybe it *was* in bad taste.
Ya think?
Wow, the Bugle is really dumping on you.
Really?
Uh, really.
I thought they *loved* Spider-Man.
I remember they used to dump on him too.
I just thought I'd get a chance to--
THUMP THUMP
Uh-oh.

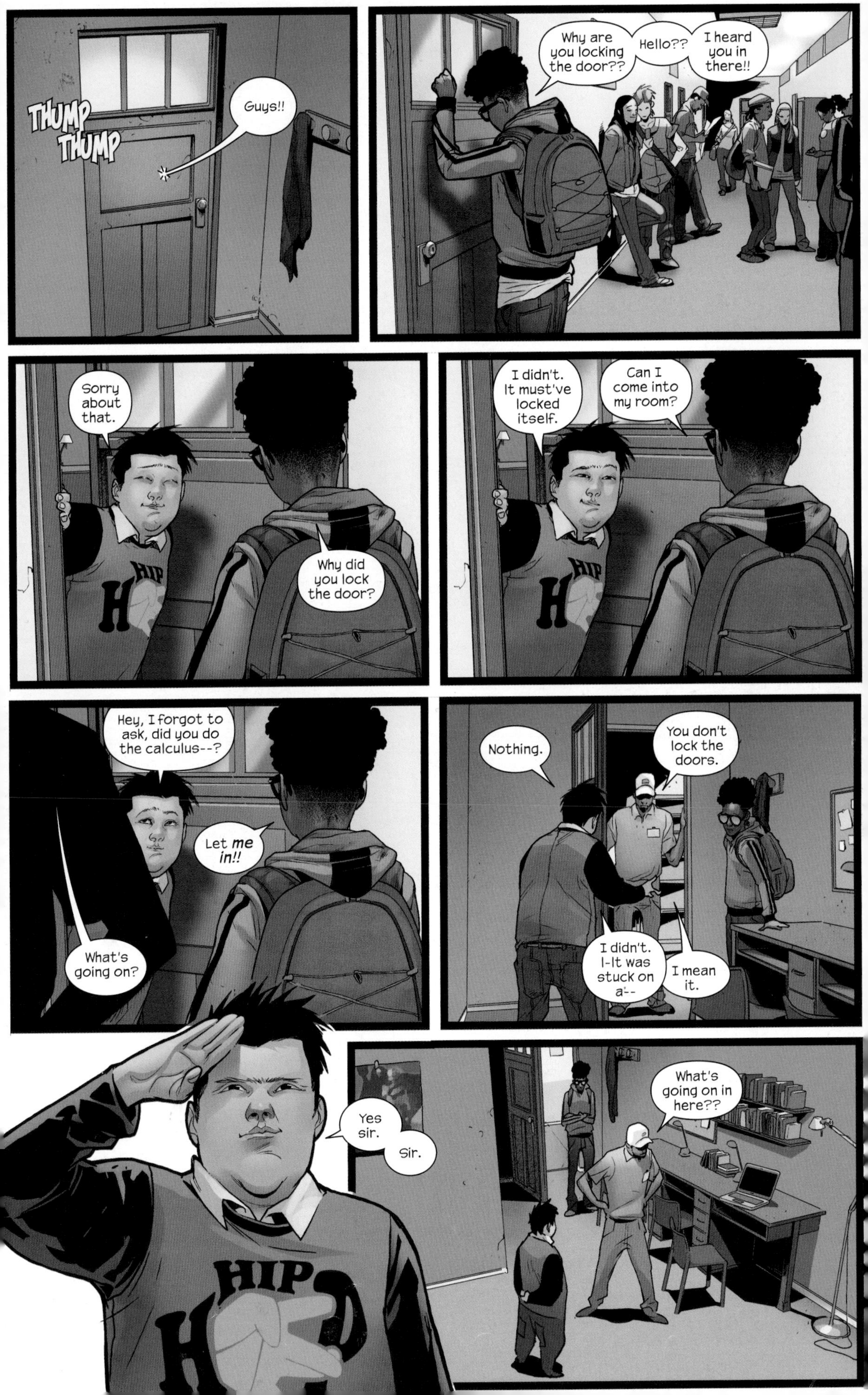
THUMP THUMP
Guys!!
Why are you locking the door??
Hello??
I heard you in there!!
Sorry about that.
Why did you lock the door?
I didn't. It must've locked itself.
Can I come into my room?
Hey, I forgot to ask, did you do the calculus--?
Let me in!!
What's going on?
Nothing.
You don't lock the doors.
I didn't. I-It was stuck on a--
I mean it.
Yes sir.
Sir.
What's going on in here??

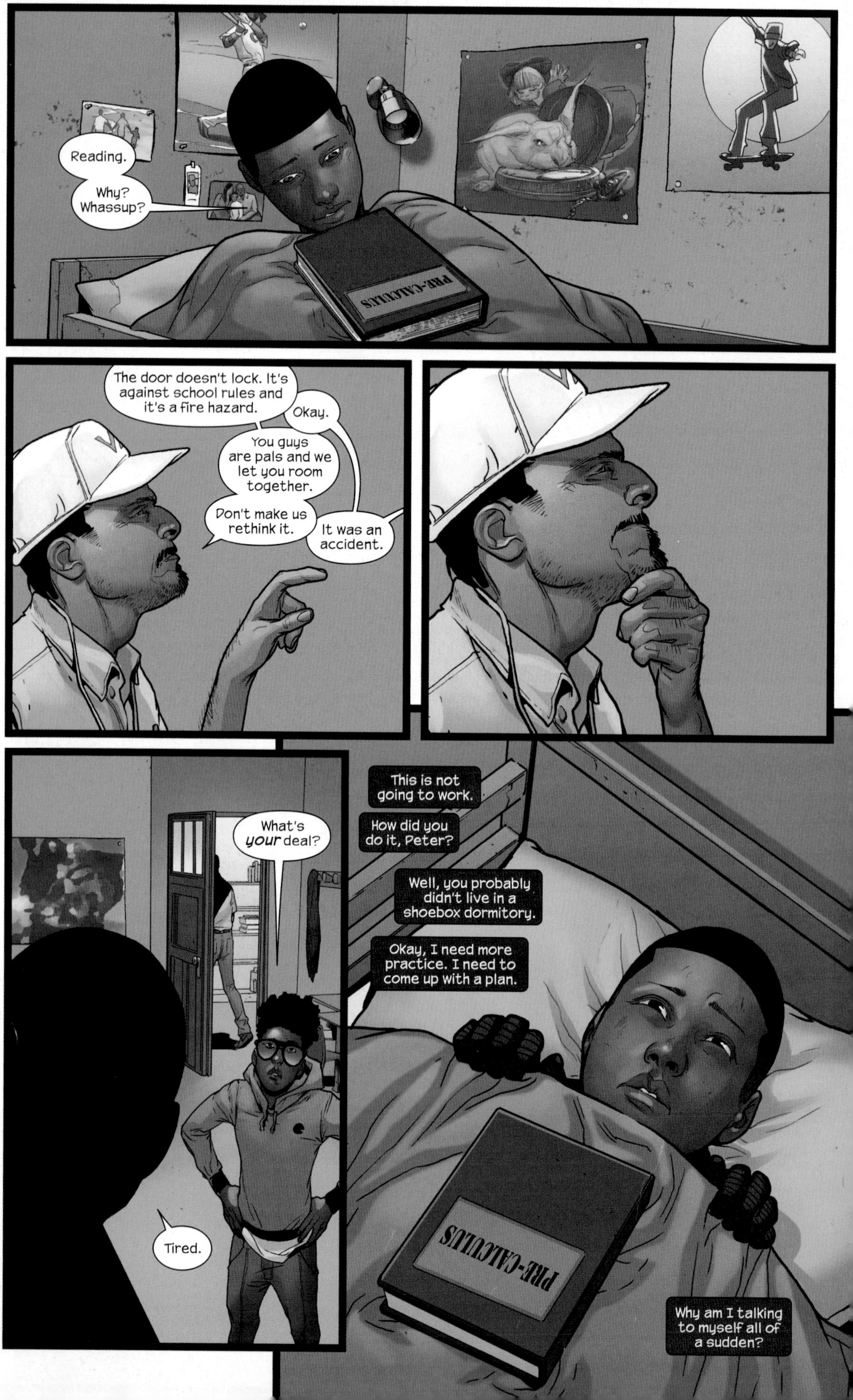
Reading.
Why? Whassup?
PRE-CALCULUS
The door doesn't lock. It's against school rules and it's a fire hazard.
Okay.
You guys are pals and we let you room together.
Don't make us rethink it.
It was an accident.
What's *your* deal?
Tired.
This is not going to work.
How did you do it, Peter?
Well, you probably didn't live in a shoebox dormitory.
Okay, I need more practice. I need to come up with a plan.
PRE-CALCULUS
Why am I talking to myself all of a sudden?

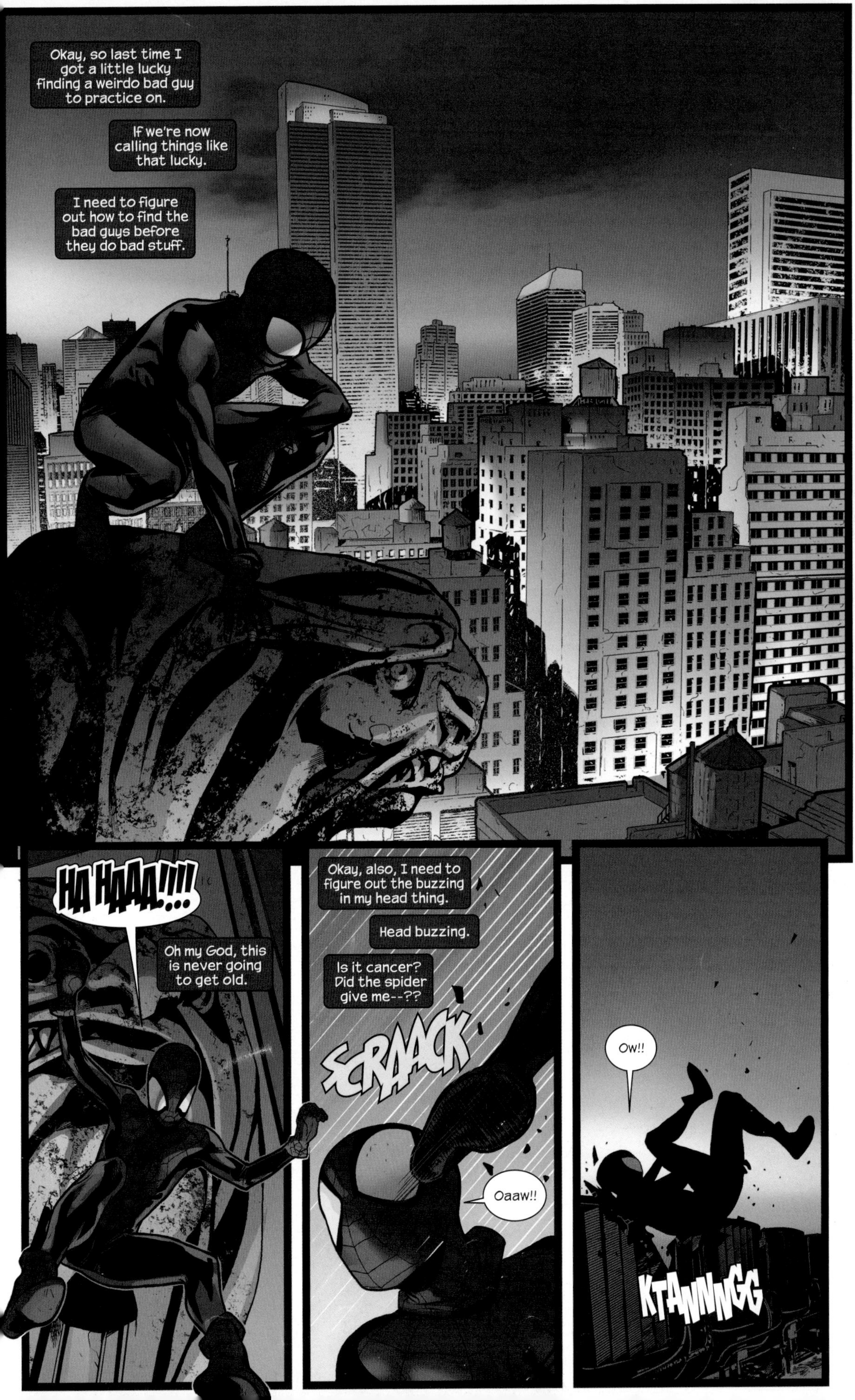
Okay, so last time I got a little lucky finding a weirdo bad guy to practice on.
If we're now calling things like that lucky.
I need to figure out how to find the bad guys before they do bad stuff.
HA HAAA!!!!!...
Oh my God, this is never going to get old.
Okay, also, I need to figure out the buzzing in my head thing.
Head buzzing.
Is it cancer? Did the spider give me--??
SCRAACK
Oaaw!!
Ow!!
KTANNNGG

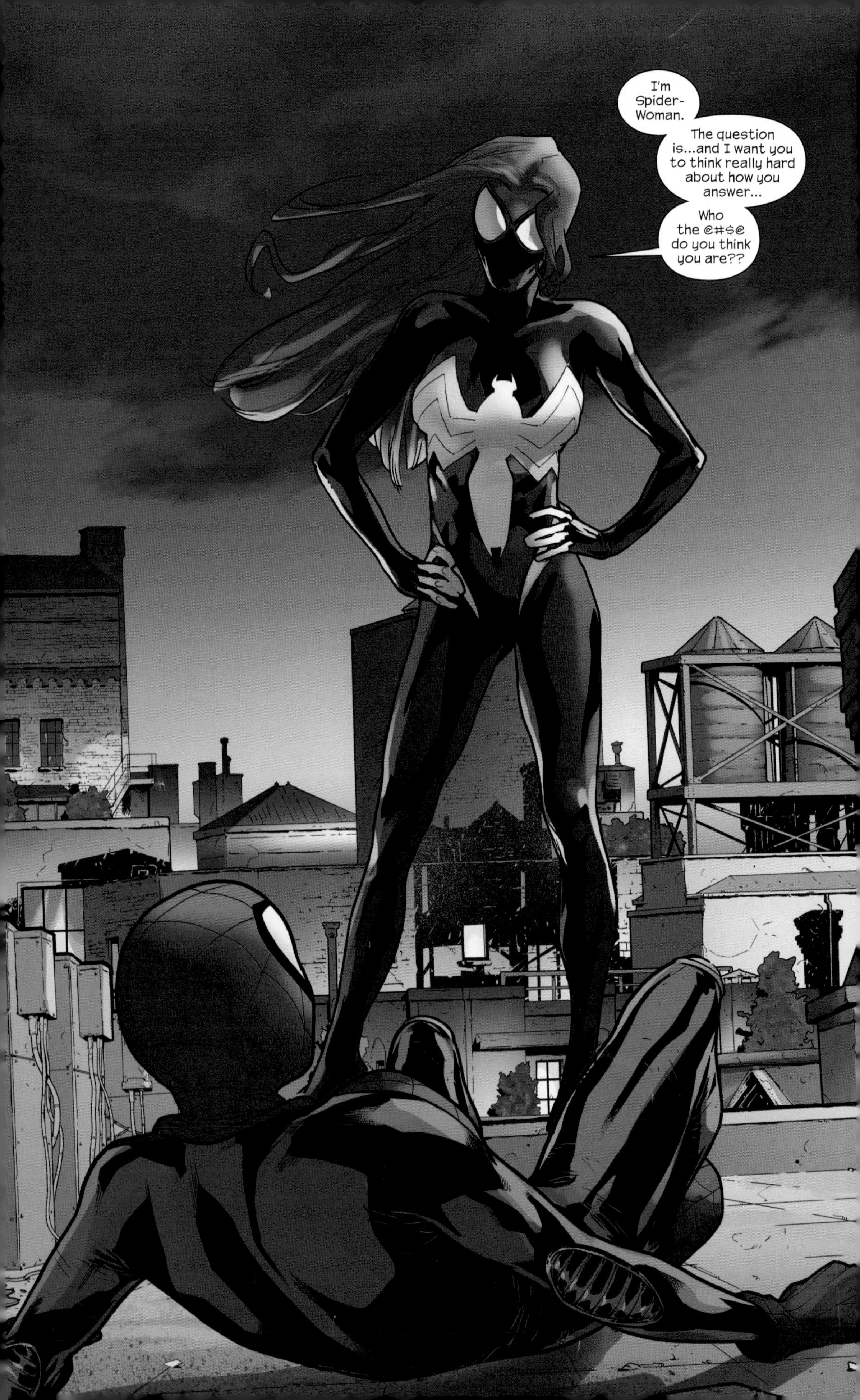
I'm Spider-Woman.
The question is...and I want you to think really hard about how you answer...
Who the @#$@ do you think you are??

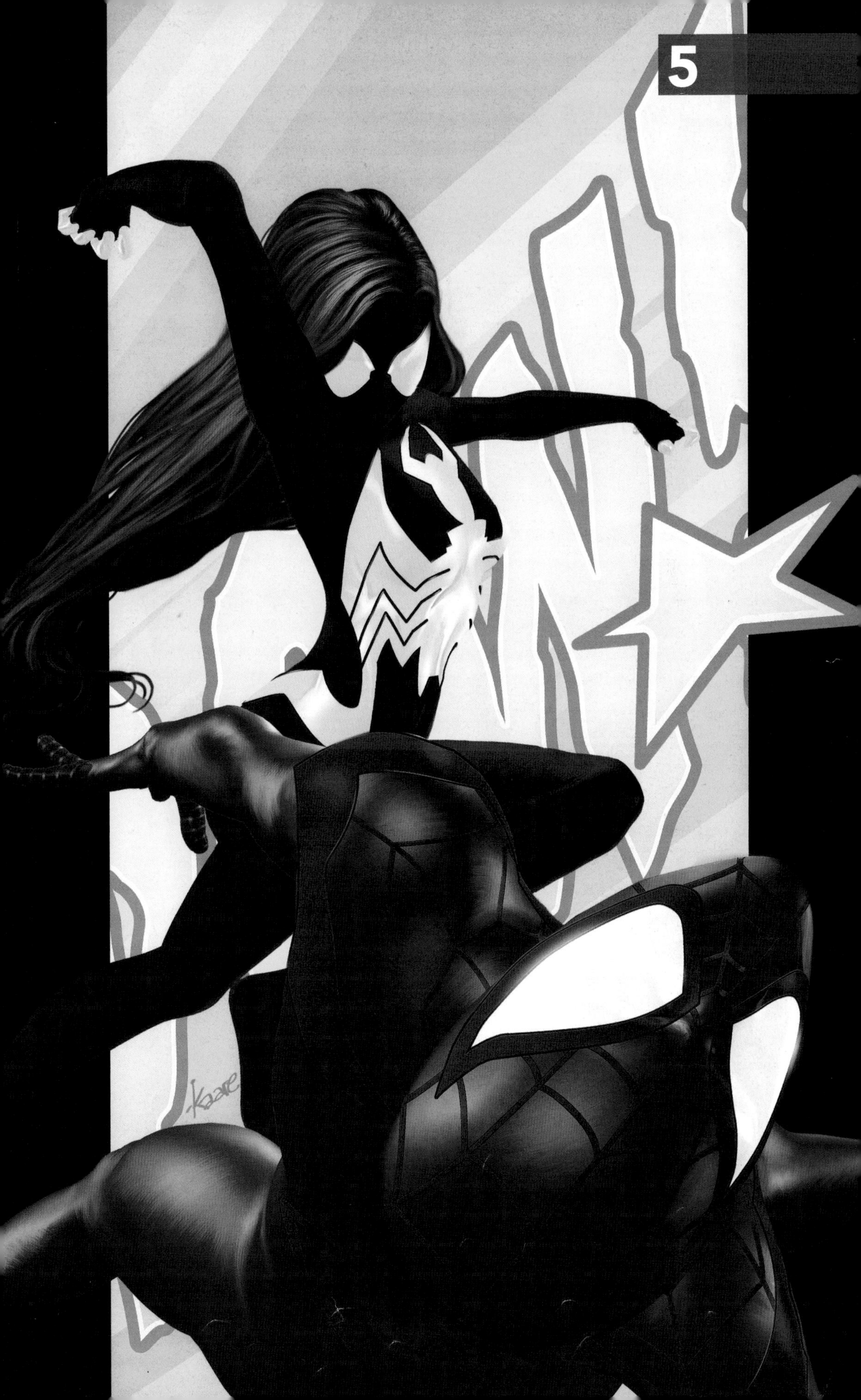
5

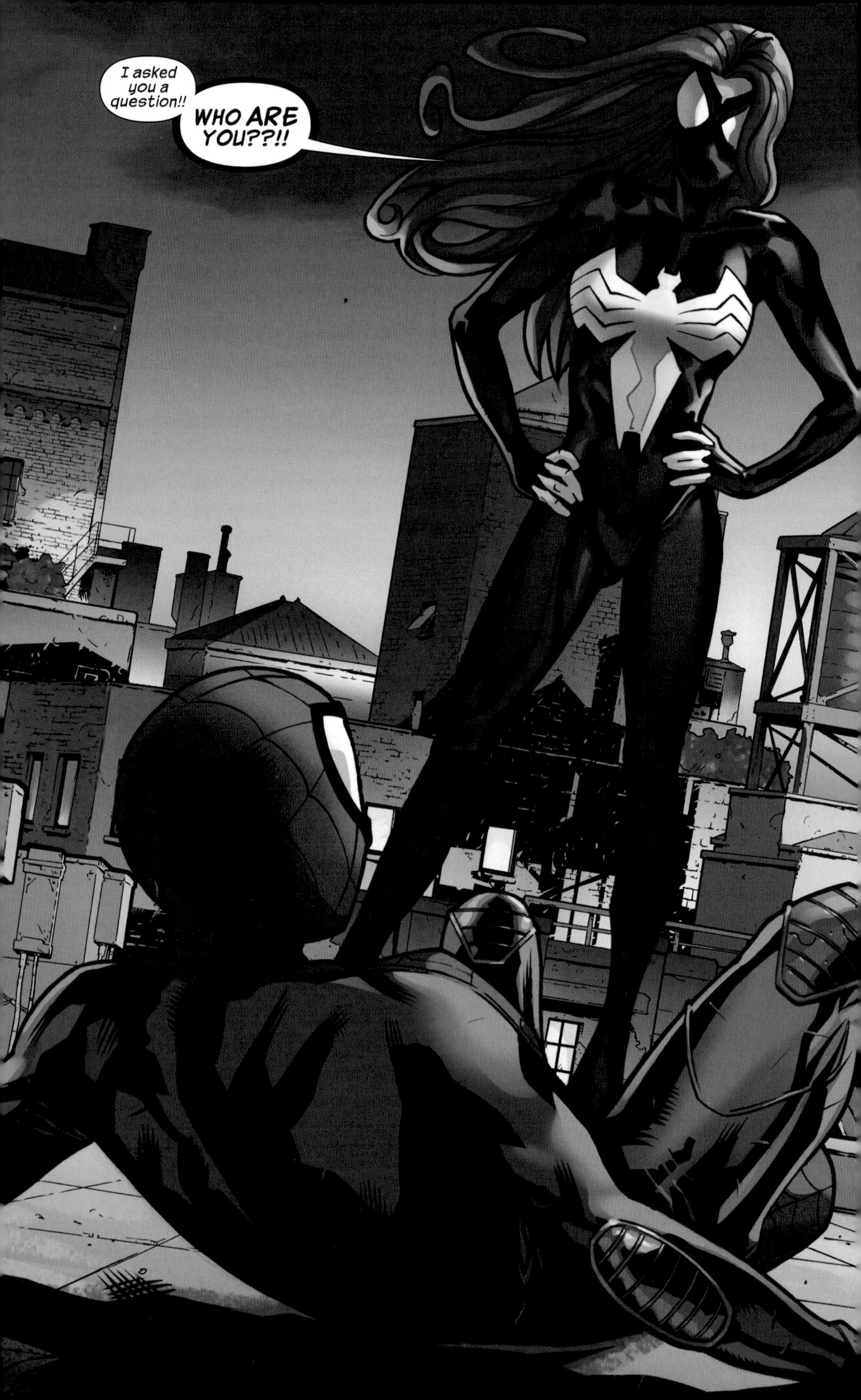
I asked you a question!!
WHO ARE YOU??!!

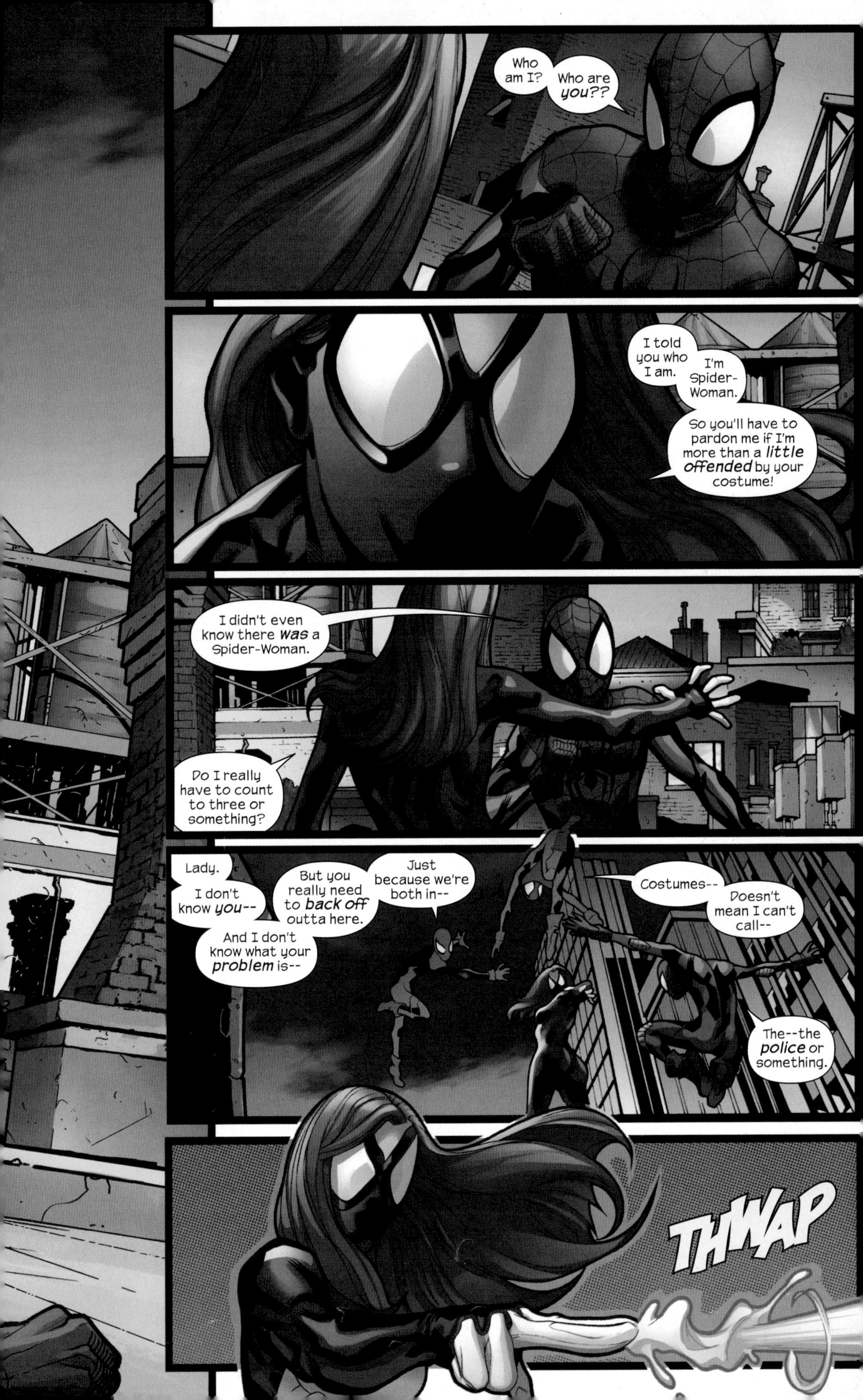
Who am I?
Who are *you??*
I told you who I am.
I'm Spider-Woman.
So you'll have to pardon me if I'm more than a *little offended* by your costume!
I didn't even know there *was* a Spider-Woman.
Do I really have to count to three or something?
Lady.
I don't know *you--*
And I don't know what your *problem* is--
But you really need to *back off* outta here.
Just because we're both in--
Costumes--
Doesn't mean I can't call--
The--the *police* or something.
THWAP

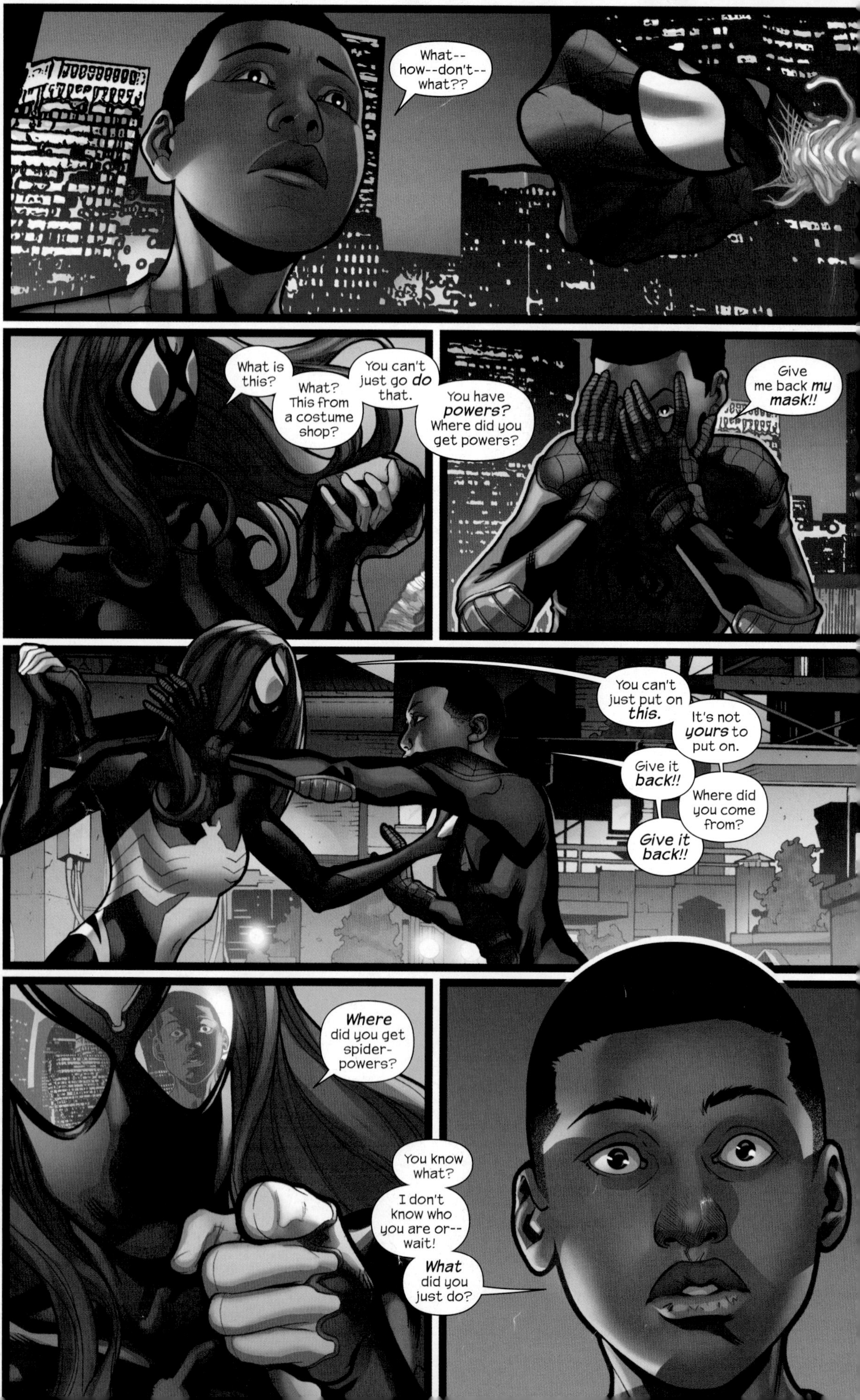
What--
how--don't--
what??
What is
this?
What?
This from
a costume
shop?
You can't
just go do
that.
You have
powers?
Where did you
get powers?
Give
me back my
mask!!
You can't
just put on
this.
It's not
yours to
put on.
Give it
back!!
Where did
you come
from?
Give it
back!!
Where
did you get
spider-
powers?
You know
what?
I don't
know who
you are or--
wait!
What
did you
just do?

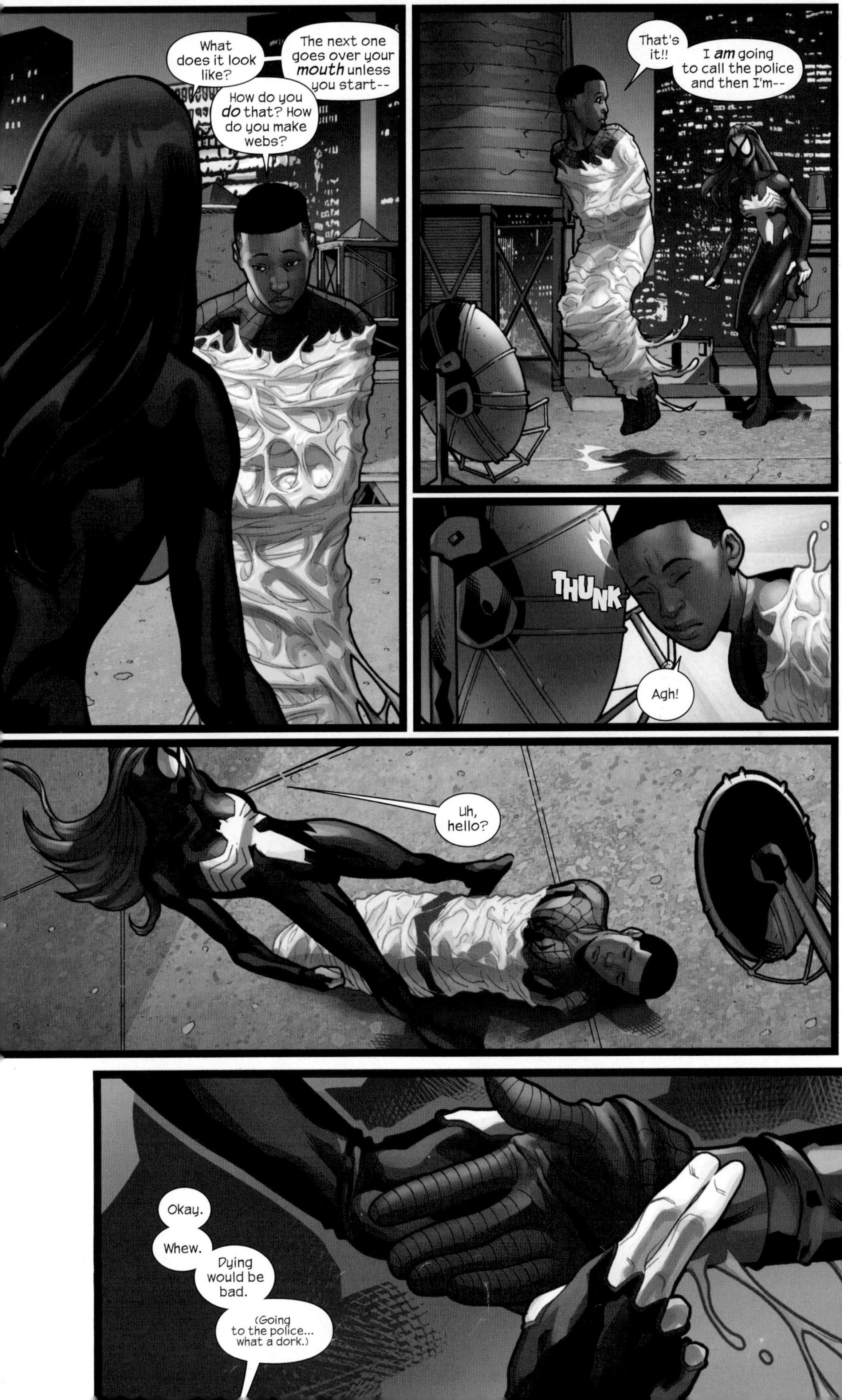
What does it look like?
The next one goes over your *mouth* unless you start--
How do you *do* that? How do you make webs?
That's it!!
I *am* going to call the police and then I'm--
THUNK
Agh!
Uh, hello?
Okay.
Whew.
Dying would be bad.
(Going to the police... what a dork.)

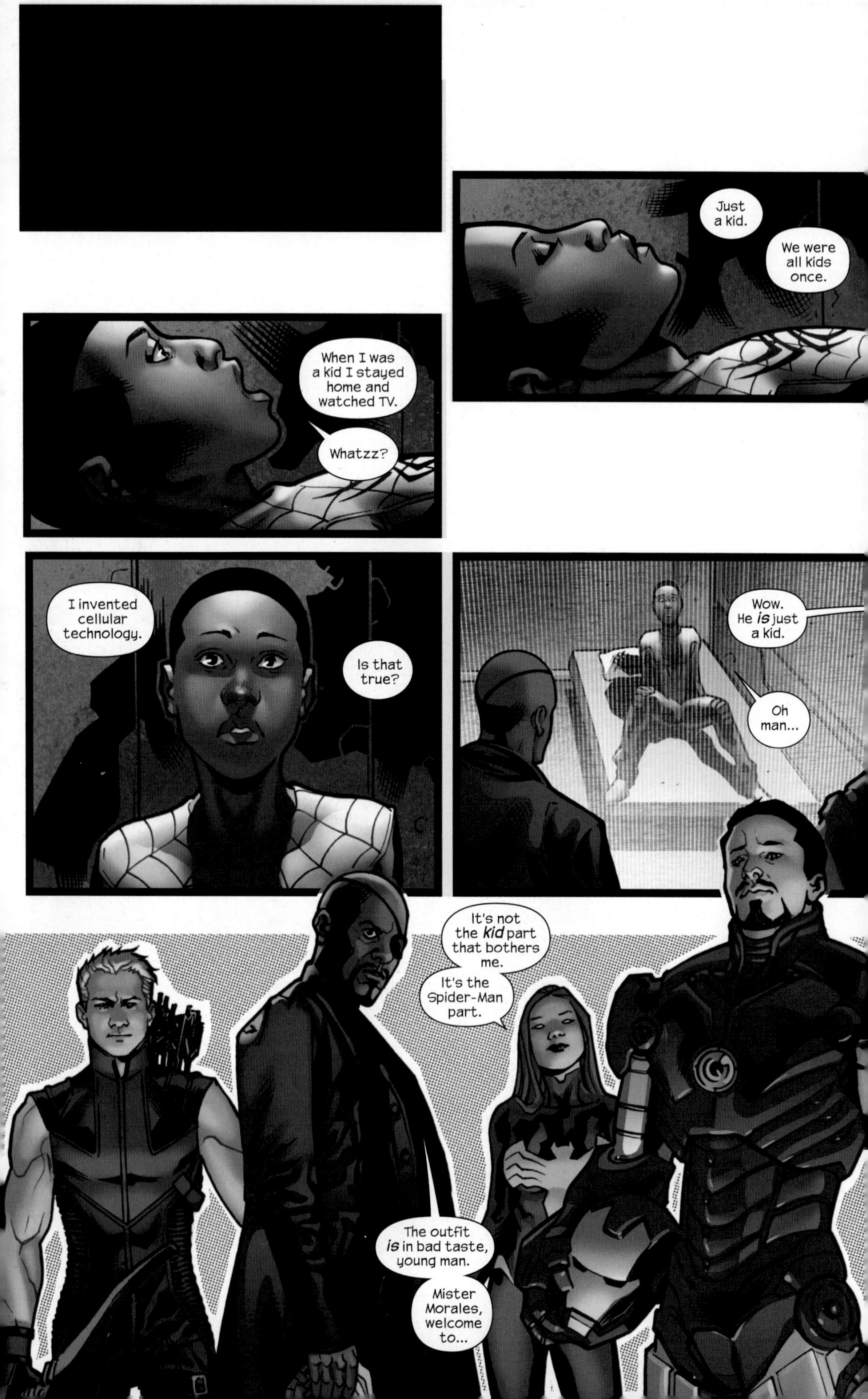
Just a kid.
We were all kids once.
When I was a kid I stayed home and watched TV.
Whatzz?
I invented cellular technology.
Is that true?
Wow. He *is* just a kid.
Oh man...
It's not the *kid* part that bothers me.
It's the Spider-Man part.
The outfit *is* in bad taste, young man.
Mister Morales, welcome to...

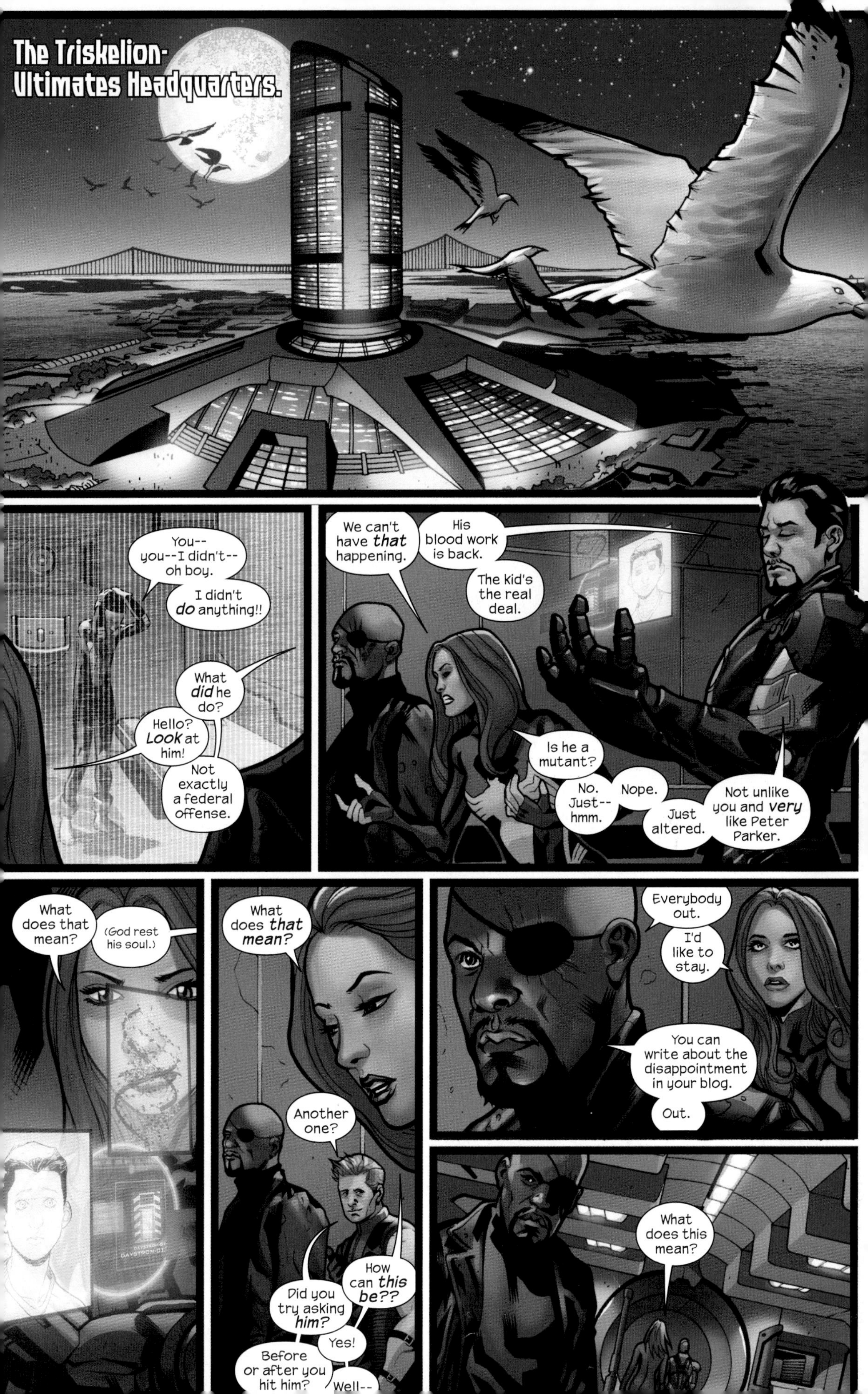

The Triskelion-
Ultimates Headquarters.
You-- you--I didn't-- oh boy.
I didn't *do* anything!!
What *did* he do?
Hello? *Look* at him!
Not exactly a federal offense.
We can't have *that* happening.
His blood work is back.
The kid's the real deal.
Is he a mutant?
No. Just-- hmm.
Nope.
Just altered.
Not unlike you and *very* like Peter Parker.
What does that mean?
(God rest his soul.)
What does *that mean?*
Another one?
How can *this be??*
Did you try asking *him?*
Yes!
Before or after you hit him?
Well--
Everybody out.
I'd like to stay.
You can write about the disappointment in your blog.
Out.
What does this mean?

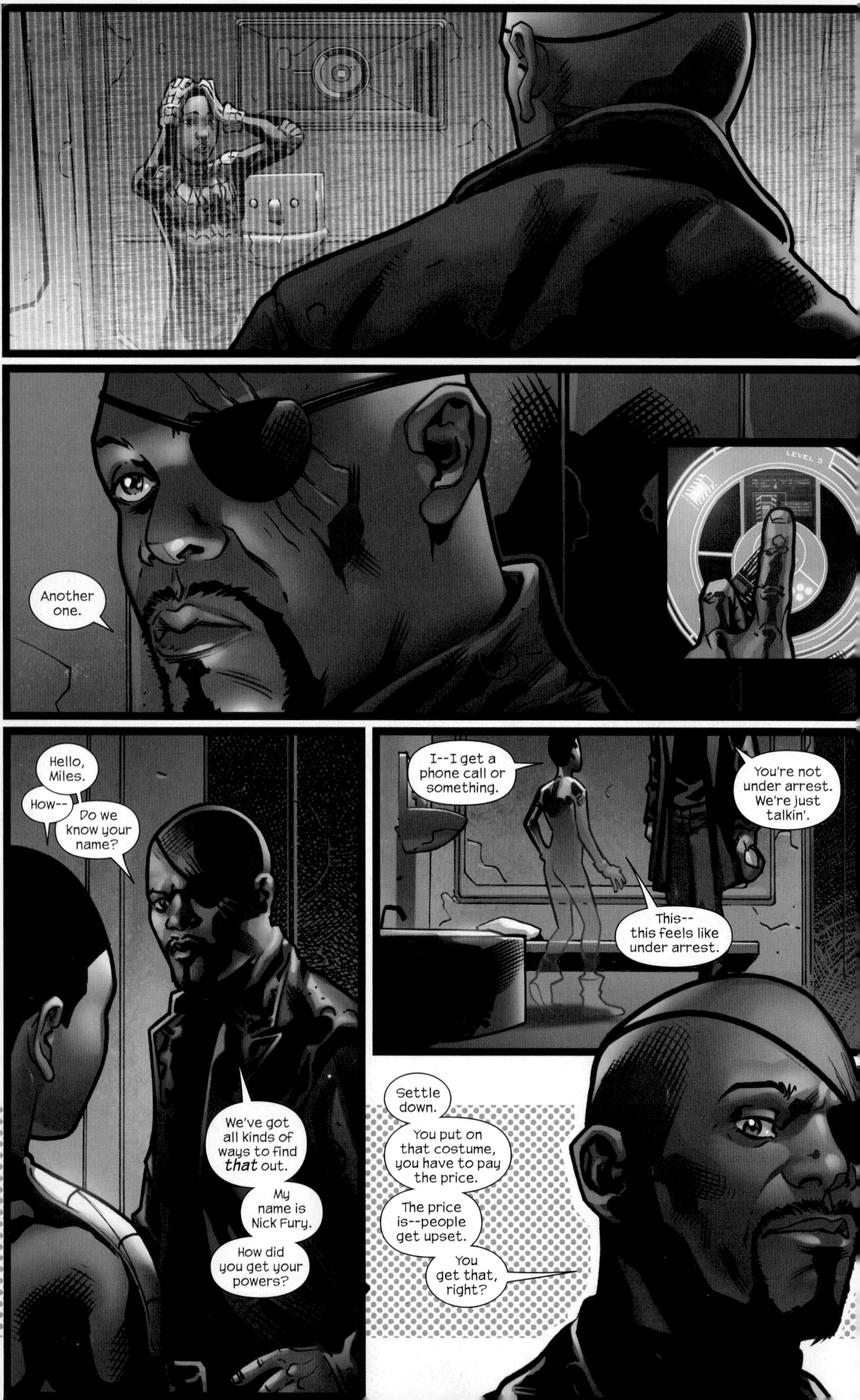
LEVEL 3
Another one.
Hello, Miles.
How--
Do we know your name?
We've got all kinds of ways to find *that* out.
My name is Nick Fury.
How did you get your powers?
I--I get a phone call or something.
You're not under arrest. We're just talkin'.
This--this feels like under arrest.
Settle down.
You put on that costume, you have to pay the price.
The price is--people get upset.
You get that, right?

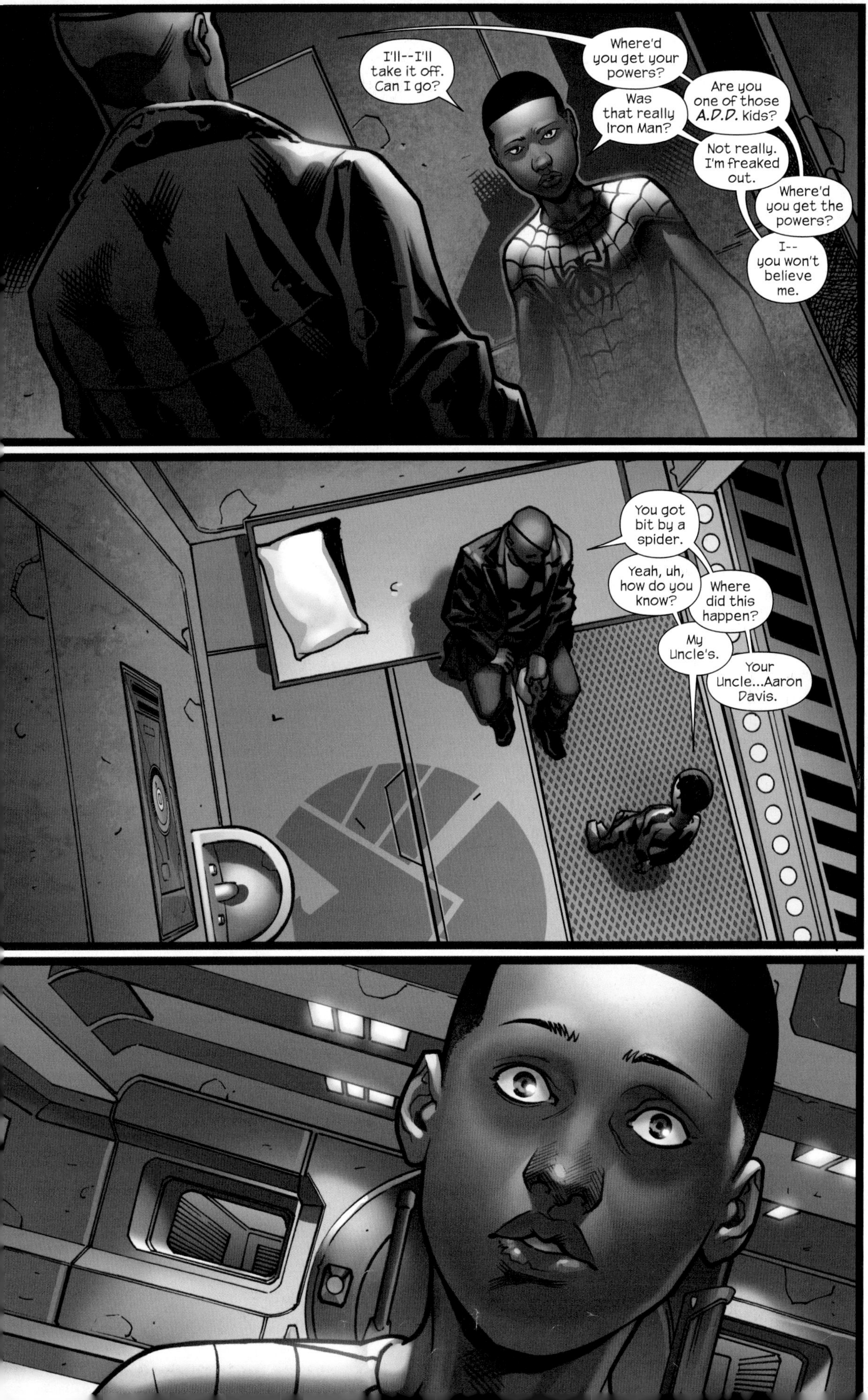
I'll--I'll take it off. Can I go?
Where'd you get your powers?
Was that really Iron Man?
Are you one of those A.D.D. kids?
Not really. I'm freaked out.
Where'd you get the powers?
I-- you won't believe me.
You got bit by a spider.
Yeah, uh, how do you know?
Where did this happen?
My Uncle's.
Your Uncle...Aaron Davis.

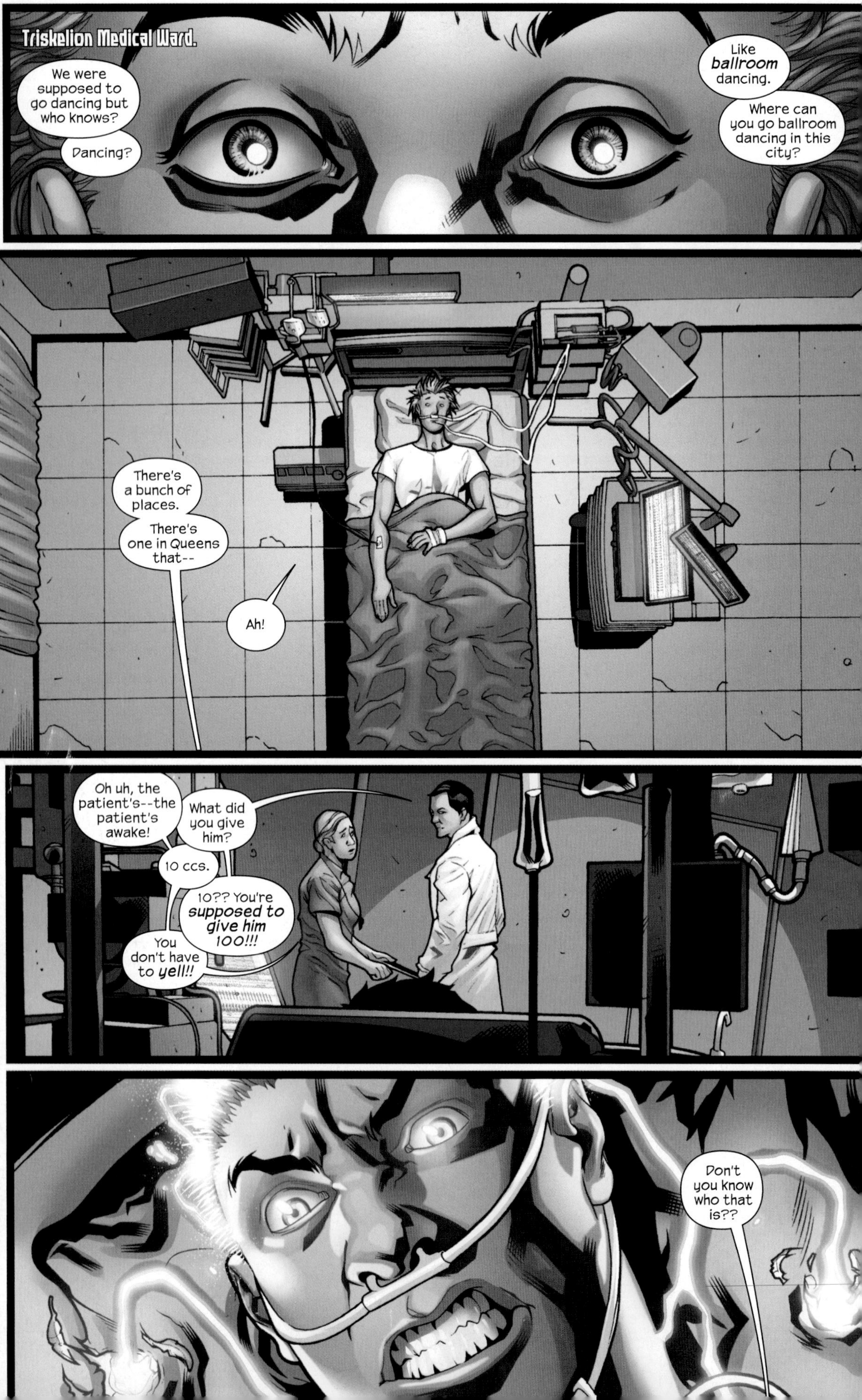
Triskelion Medical Ward.
We were supposed to go dancing but who knows?
Dancing?
Like ballroom dancing.
Where can you go ballroom dancing in this city?
There's a bunch of places.
There's one in Queens that--
Ah!
Oh uh, the patient's--the patient's awake!
What did you give him?
10 ccs.
10?? You're supposed to give him 100!!!
You don't have to yell!!
Don't you know who that is??

Quite a rap sheet on that uncle of yours.

The FBI calls him *The Prowler*.

(I didn't know that.)

I didn't think so.

Do your parents know about your... spiderness?

No.

And you don't want them to?

No-- no, not yet.

ZZZZZT!

Why the costume?

The other one--the other Spider-Man died.

I thought--

I felt--

That with great power.

Comes-- yeah.

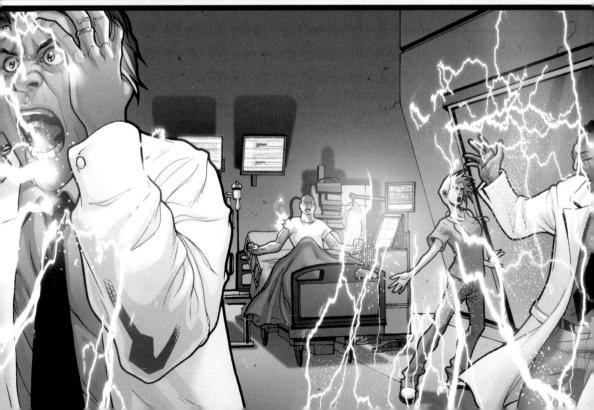

How many times have you gone out and done this?

Uh, twice.

Three times.

Third time and *here* you are.

Yeah, I, maybe I need more practice.

And a new costume.

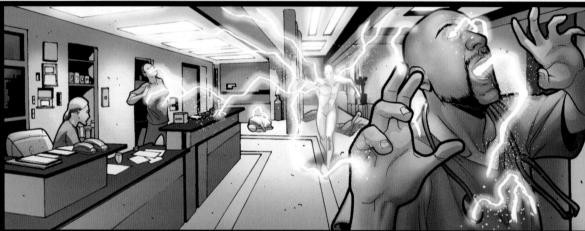

I didn't *mean* any disrespect.

I didn't think so--

I was just trying to--to honor the--the--

Uh...

Is this-- normal?

@#$@#!

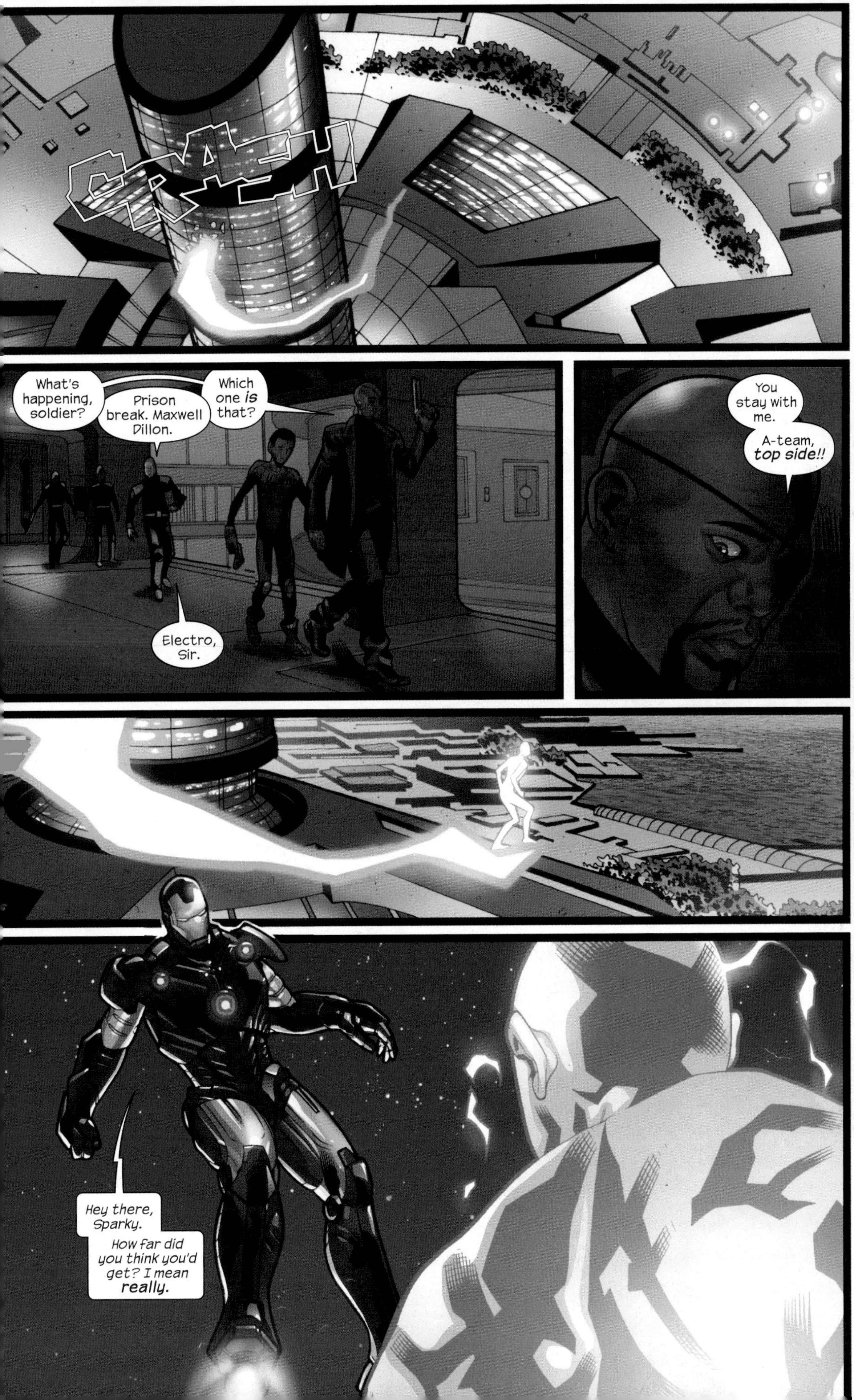
CRASH
What's happening, soldier?
Prison break. Maxwell Dillon.
Which one *is* that?
Electro, Sir.
You stay with me.
A-team, *top side!!*
Hey there, Sparky.
How far did you think you'd get? I mean **really.**

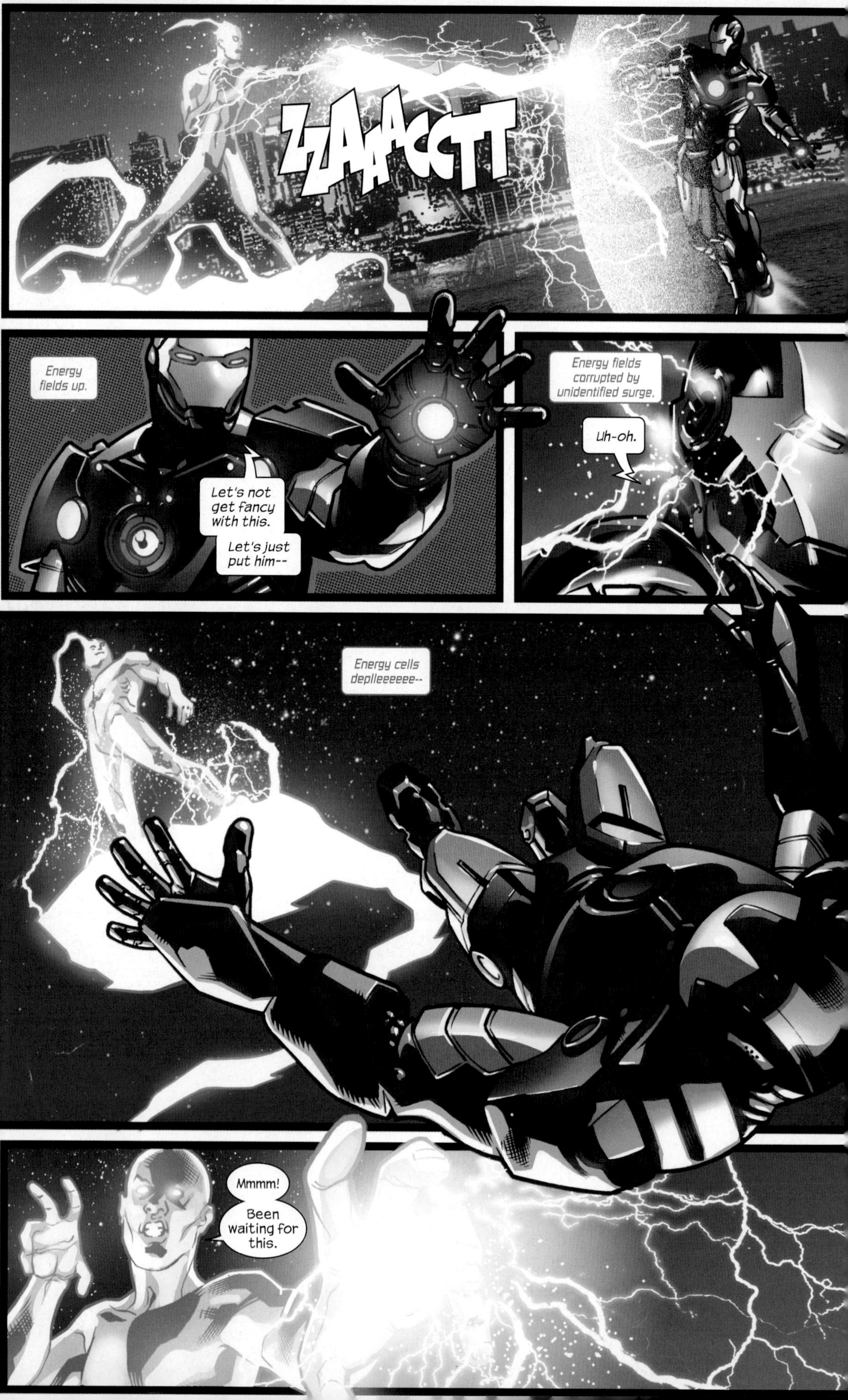
ZZAAACCTT
Energy fields up.
Let's not get fancy with this.
Let's just put him--
Energy fields corrupted by unidentified surge.
Uh-oh.
Energy cells deplleeeeee--
Mmmm!
Been waiting for this.

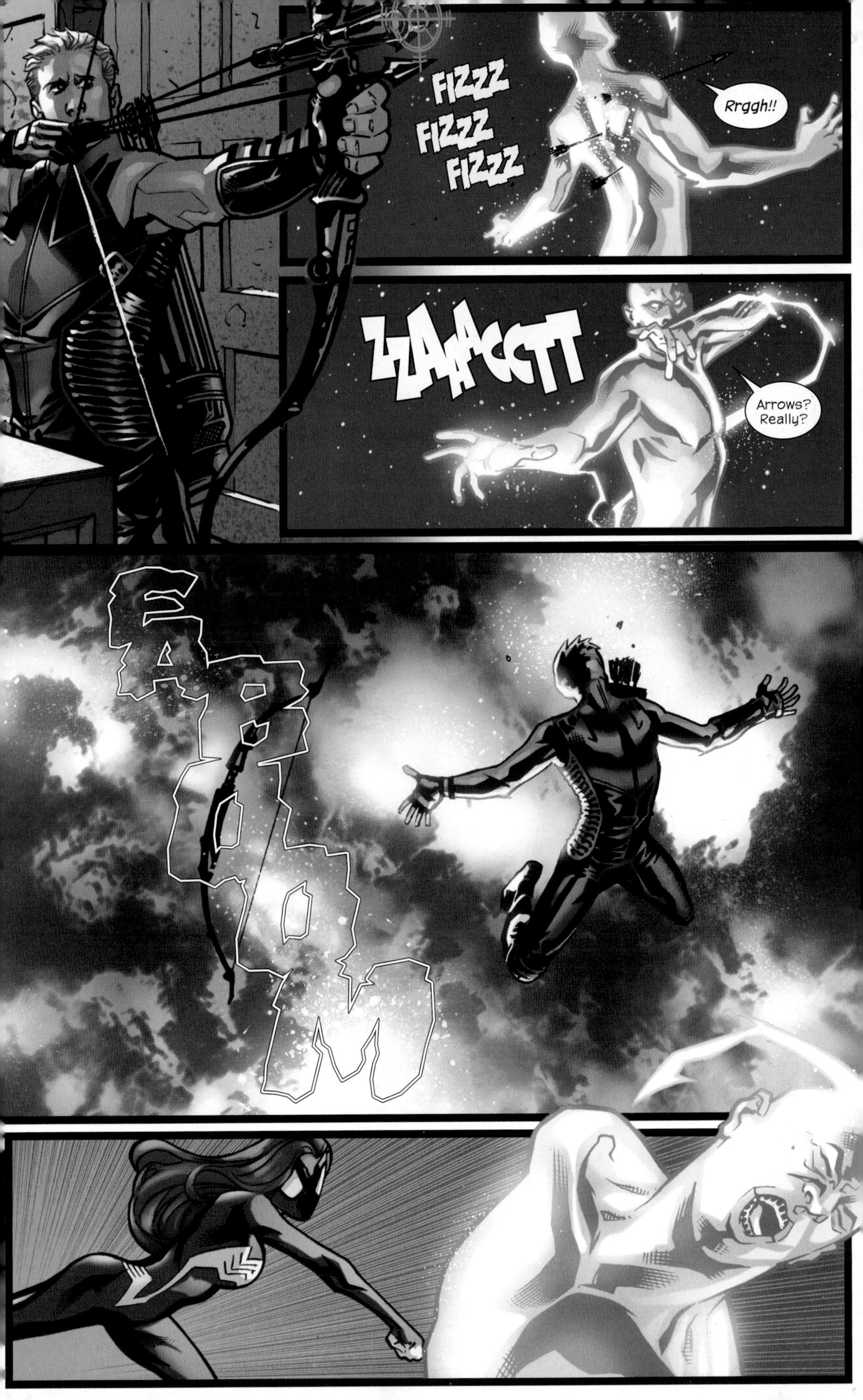
FIZZZ
FIZZZ
FIZZZ
Rrggh!!
ZZZAAACCTT
Arrows? Really?
BABOOM

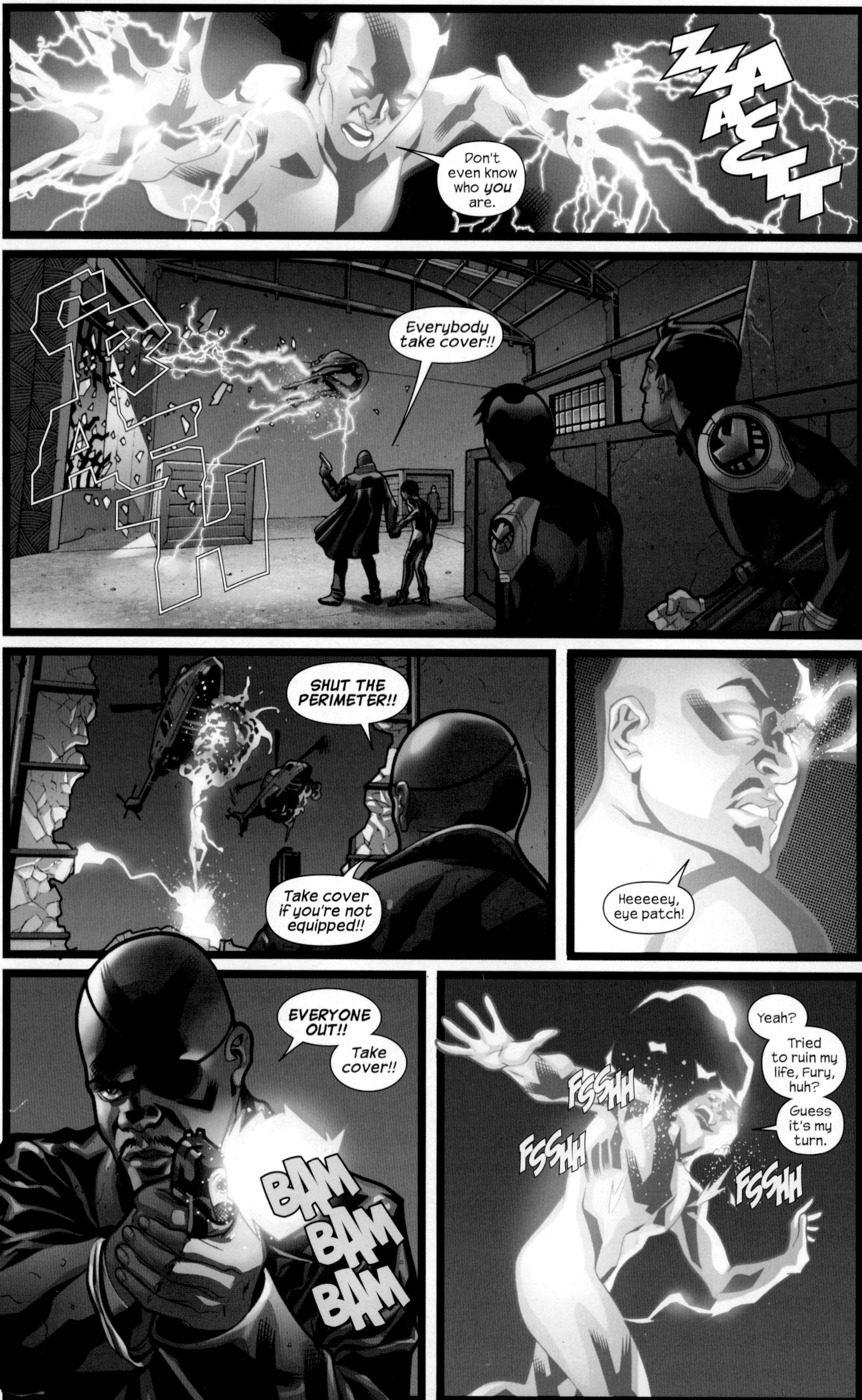

Don't even know who *you* are.
ZZAACKT
Everybody take cover!!
SHUT THE PERIMETER!!
Take cover if you're not equipped!!
Heeeeey, eye patch!
EVERYONE OUT!!
Take cover!!
BAM
BAM
BAM
Yeah?
Tried to ruin my life, Fury, huh?
Guess it's my turn.
FSSHH
FSSHH
FSSHH

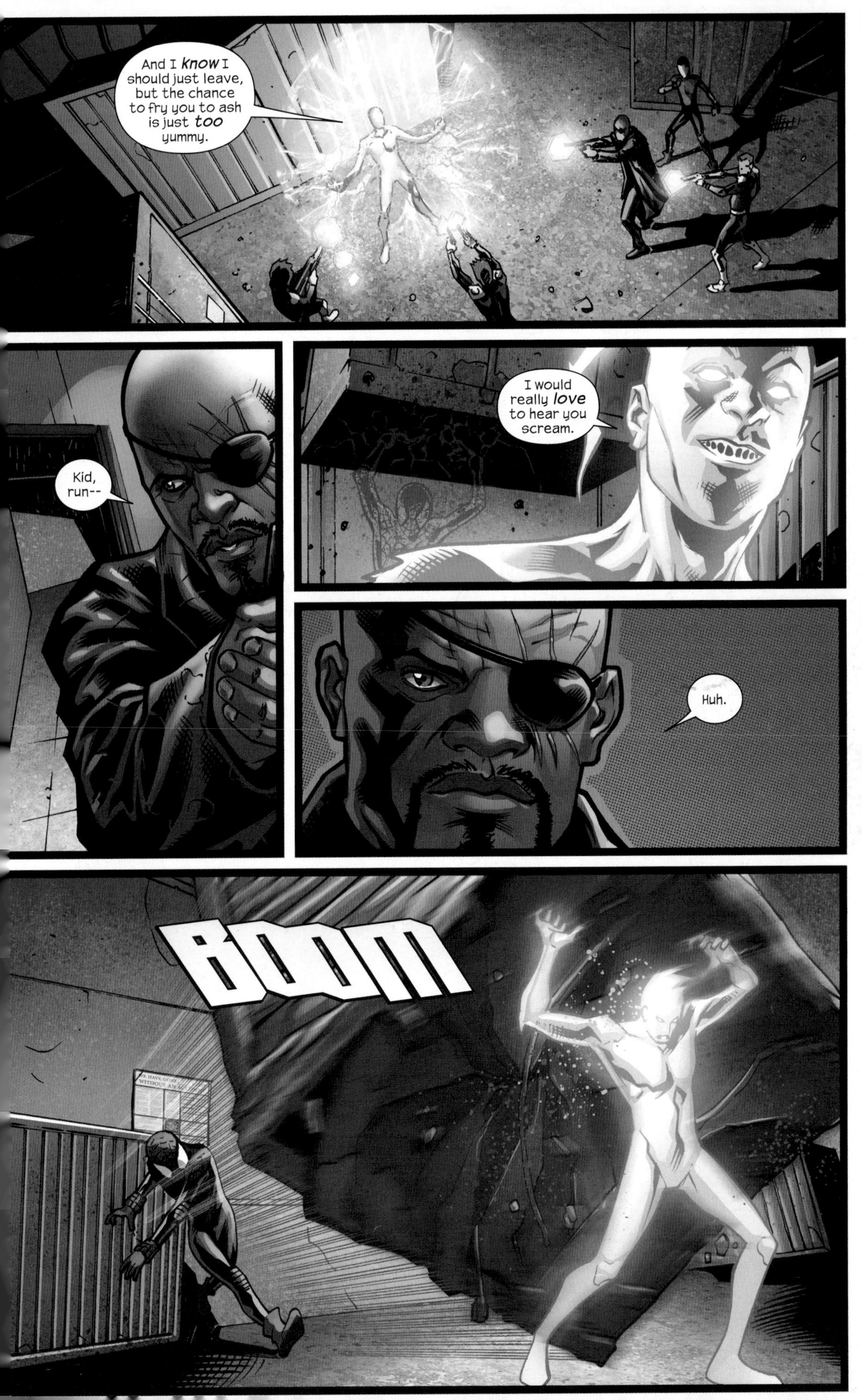
And I *know* I should just leave, but the chance to fry you to ash is just *too* yummy.
Kid, run--
I would really *love* to hear you scream.
Huh.
BOOM

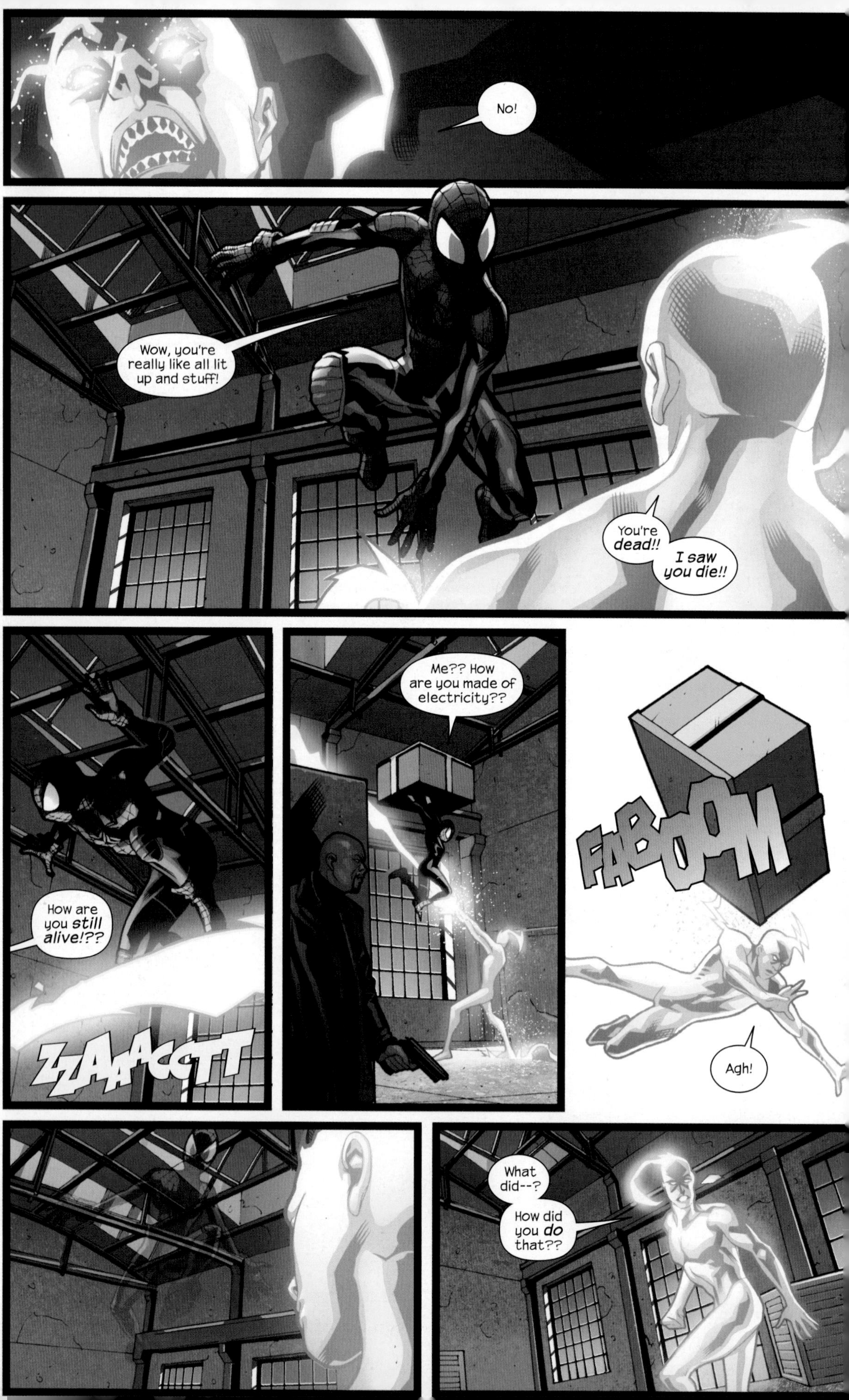
No!
Wow, you're really like all lit up and stuff!
You're dead!!
I saw you die!!
How are you still alive!??
ZZAAACCTT
Me?? How are you made of electricity??
FABOOM
Agh!
What did--?
How did you do that??

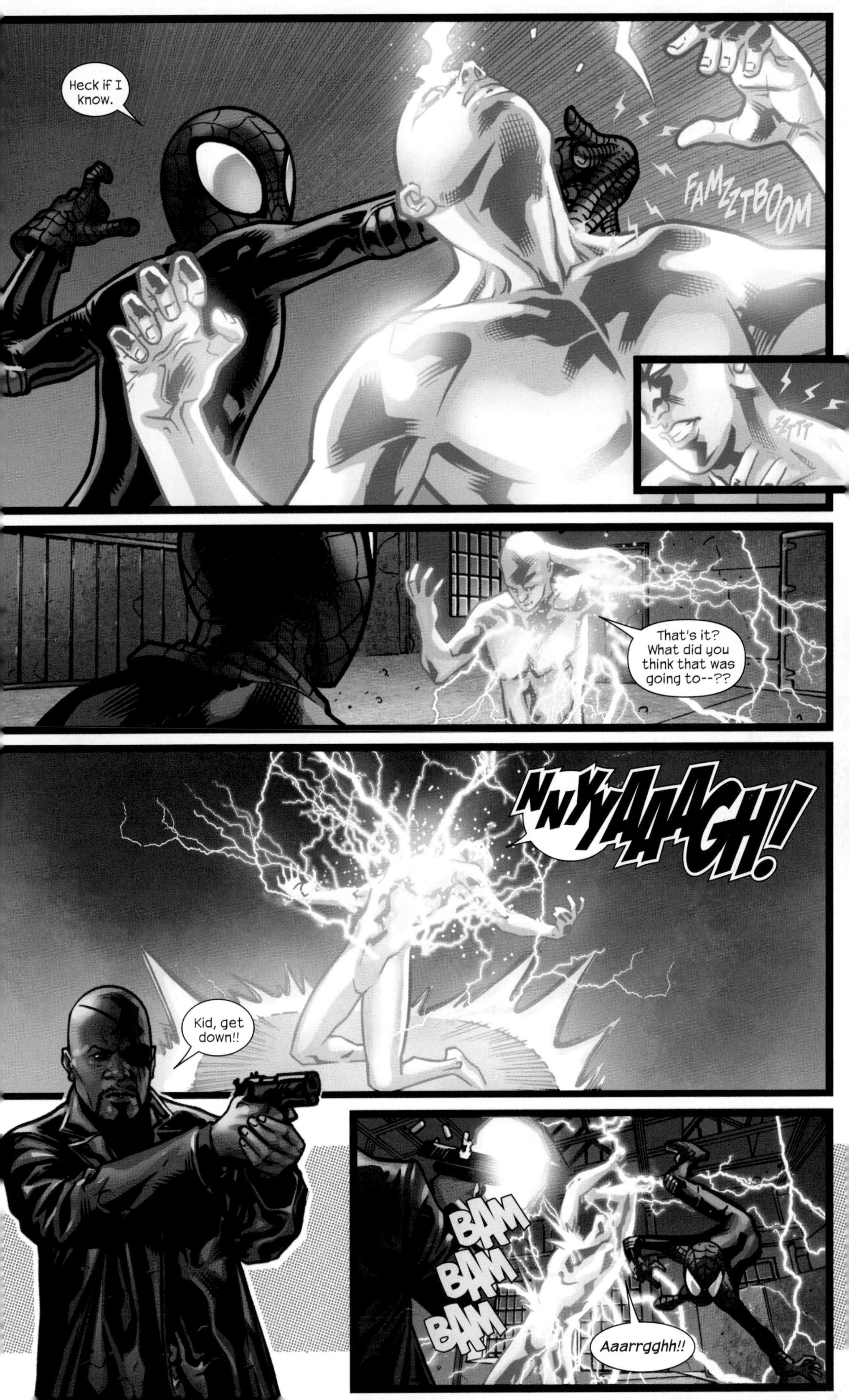
Heck if I know.
FAMZZTBOOM
ZZTTT
That's it? What did you think that was going to--??
NNYYAAAGH!
Kid, get down!!
BAM
BAM
BAM
Aaarrgghh!!

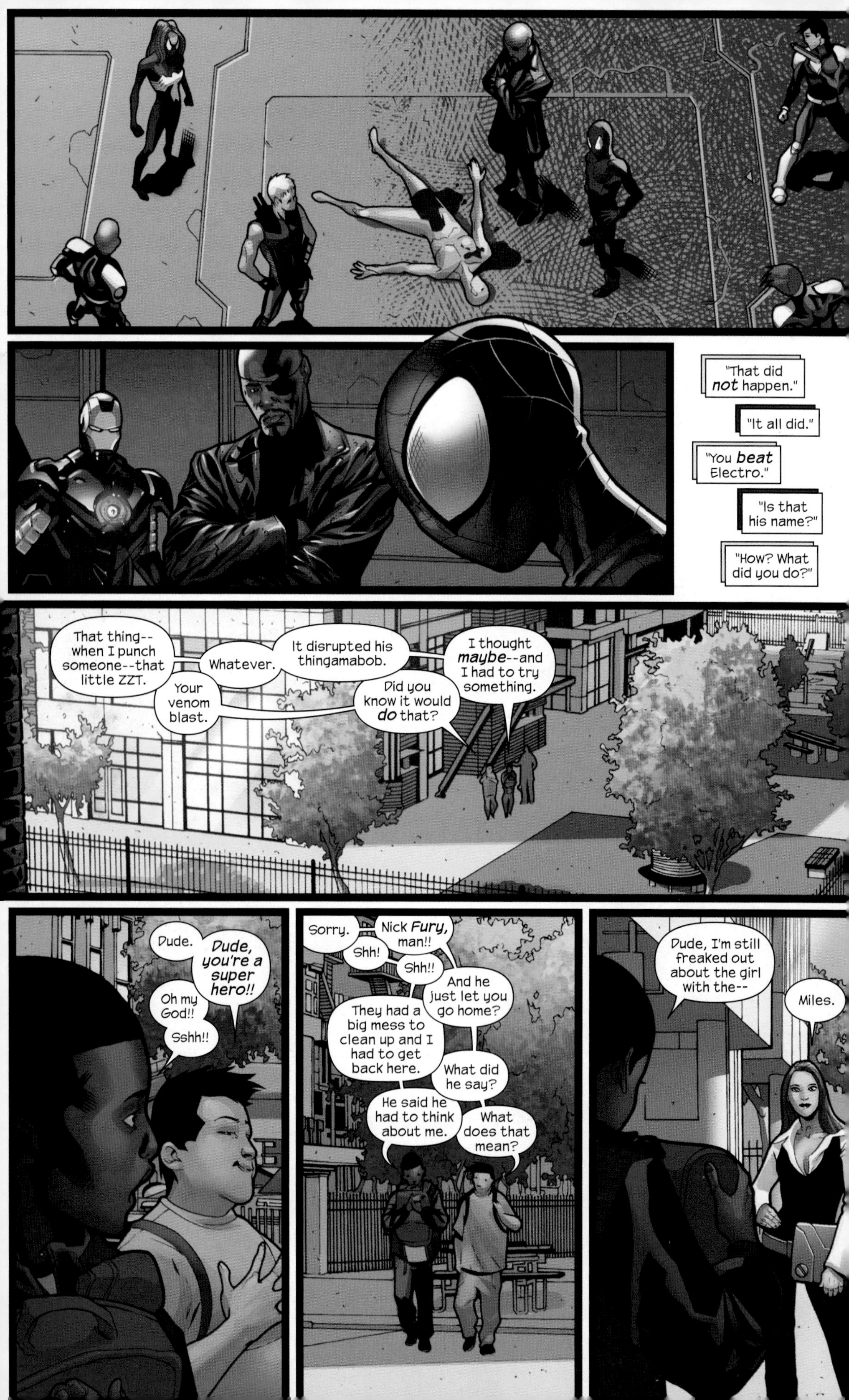
"That did not happen."
"It all did."
"You beat Electro."
"Is that his name?"
"How? What did you do?"
That thing--when I punch someone--that little ZZT.
Whatever.
Your venom blast.
It disrupted his thingamabob.
Did you know it would do that?
I thought maybe--and I had to try something.
Dude.
Dude, you're a super hero!!
Oh my God!!
Sshh!!
Sorry.
Nick Fury, man!!
Shh!
Shh!!
And he just let you go home?
They had a big mess to clean up and I had to get back here.
What did he say?
He said he had to think about me.
What does that mean?
Dude, I'm still freaked out about the girl with the--
Miles.

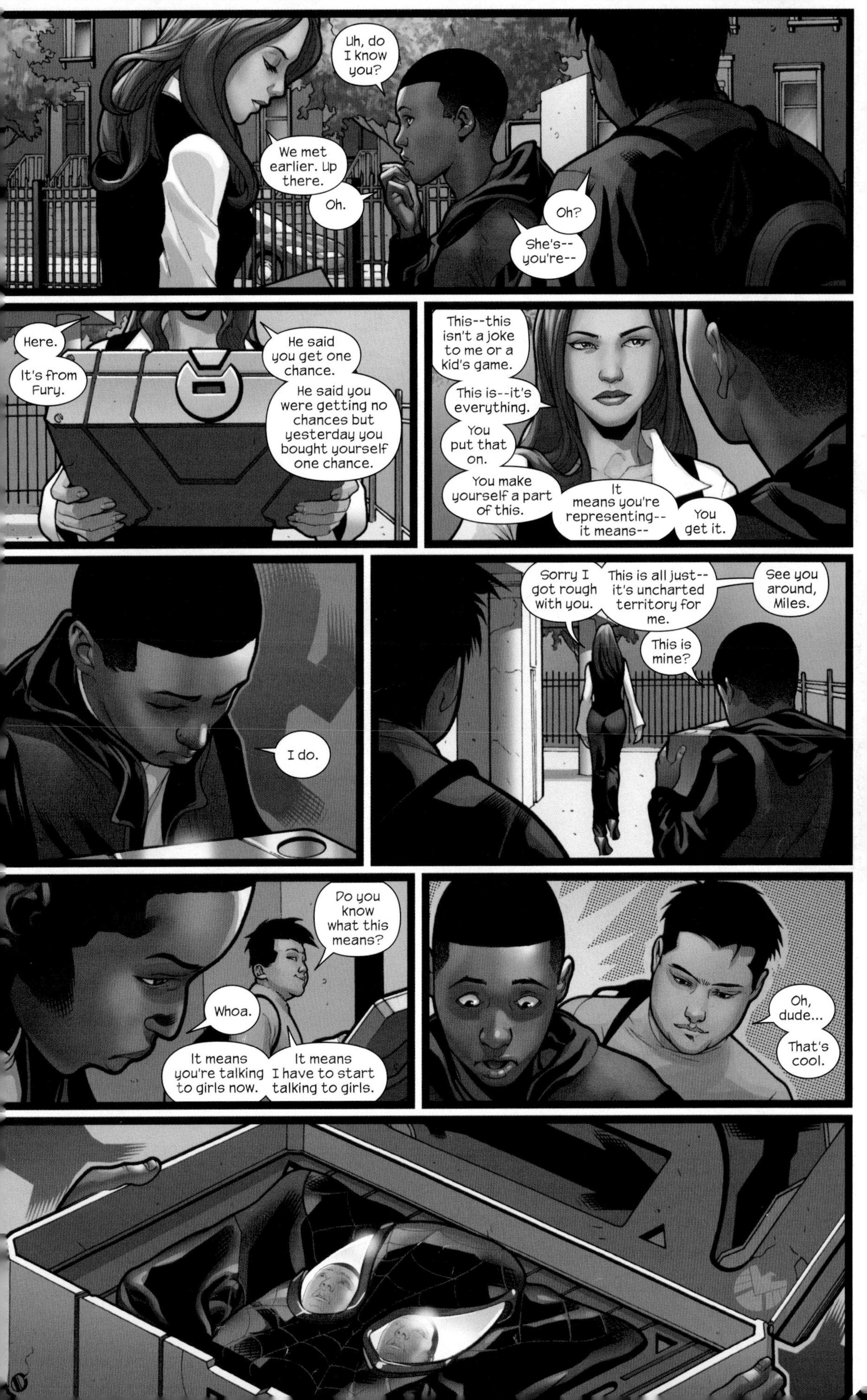
Uh, do I know you?
We met earlier. Up there.
Oh.
Oh?
She's-- you're--
Here.
It's from Fury.
He said you get one chance.
He said you were getting no chances but yesterday you bought yourself one chance.
This--this isn't a joke to me or a kid's game.
This is--it's everything.
You put that on.
You make yourself a part of this.
It means you're representing-- it means--
You get it.
I do.
Sorry I got rough with you.
This is all just-- it's uncharted territory for me.
See you around, Miles.
This is mine?
Do you know what this means?
Whoa.
It means you're talking to girls now.
It means I have to start talking to girls.
Oh, dude...
That's cool.

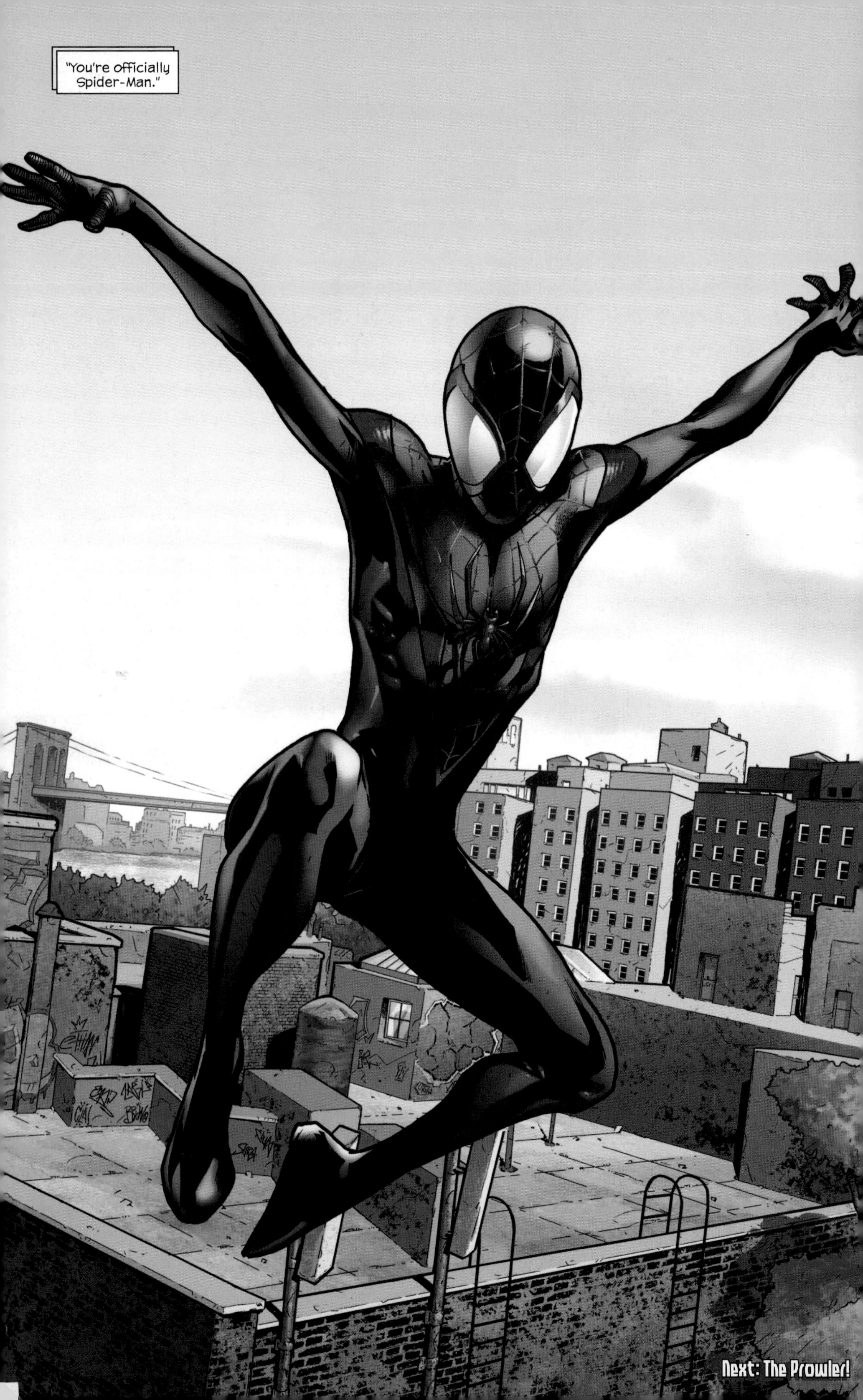
"You're officially Spider-Man."
Next: The Prowler!

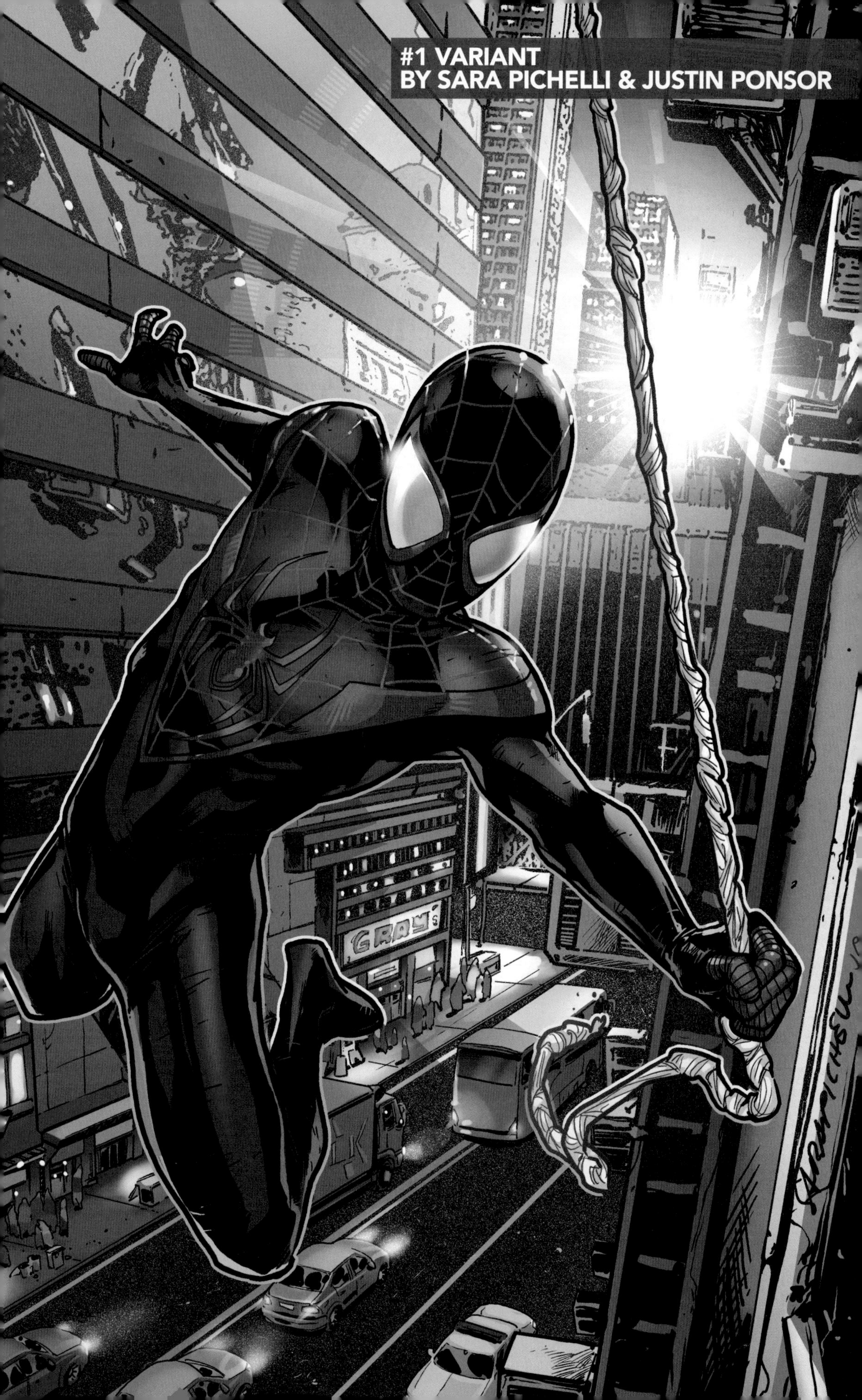
GRAY'S

#1 VARIANT
BY SARA PICHELLI & JUSTIN PONSOR

#1 SKETCH VARIANT
BY SARA PICHELLI

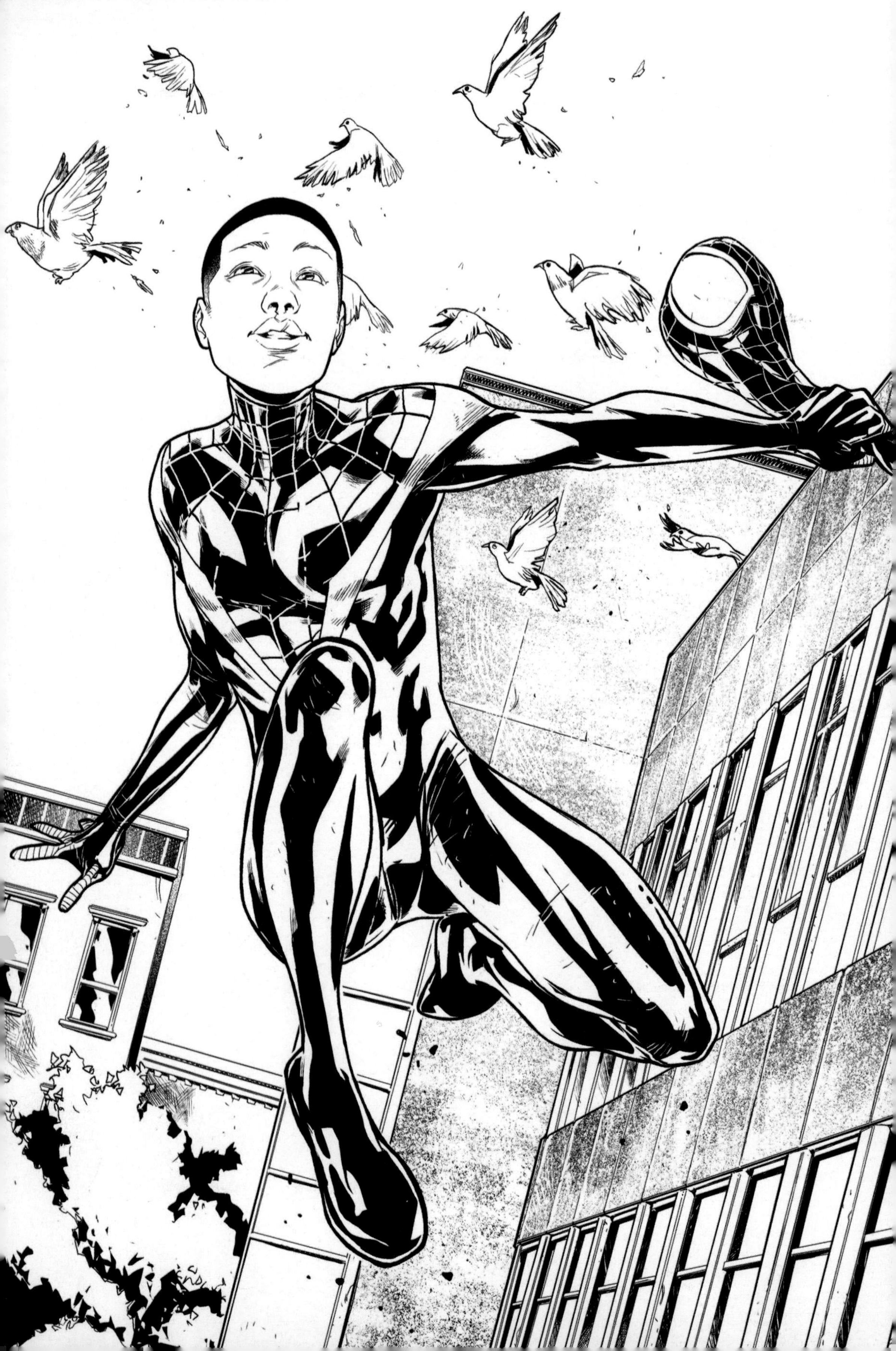

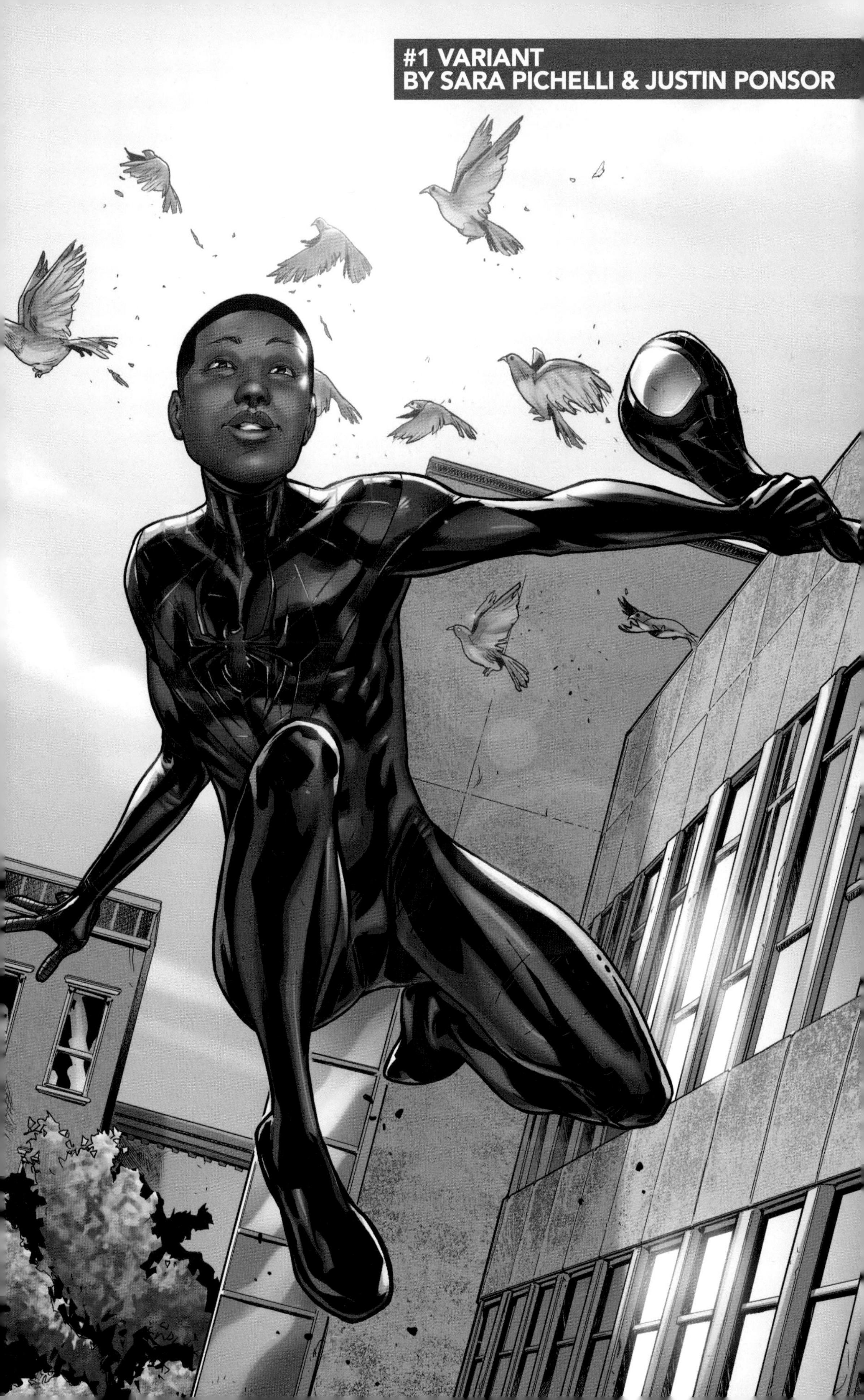
#1 VARIANT
BY SARA PICHELLI & JUSTIN PONSOR

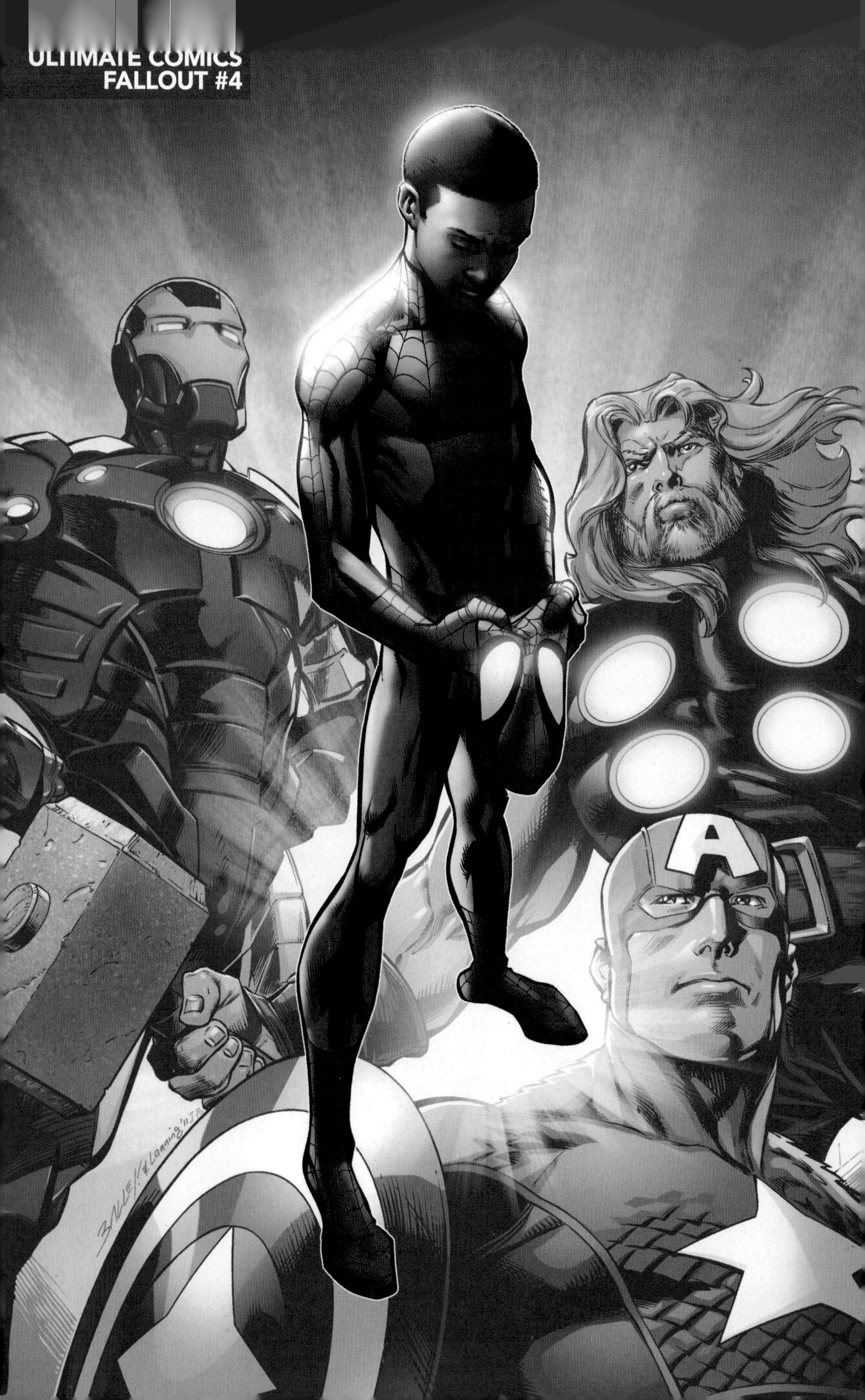
ULTIMATE COMICS
FALLOUT #4

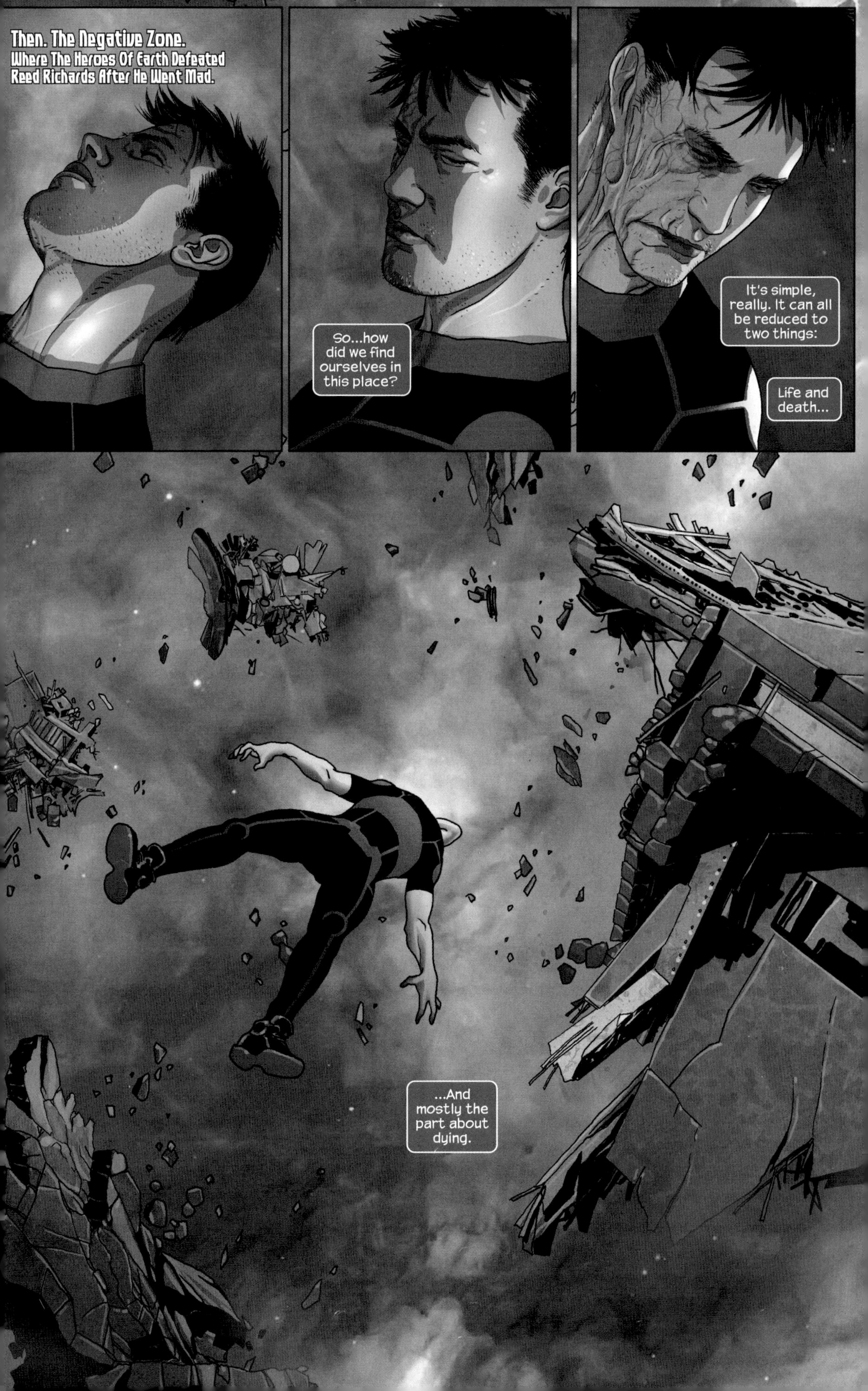
Then. The Negative Zone.
Where The Heroes Of Earth Defeated Reed Richards After He Went Mad.
So...how did we find ourselves in this place?
It's simple, really. It can all be reduced to two things:
Life and death...
...And mostly the part about dying.

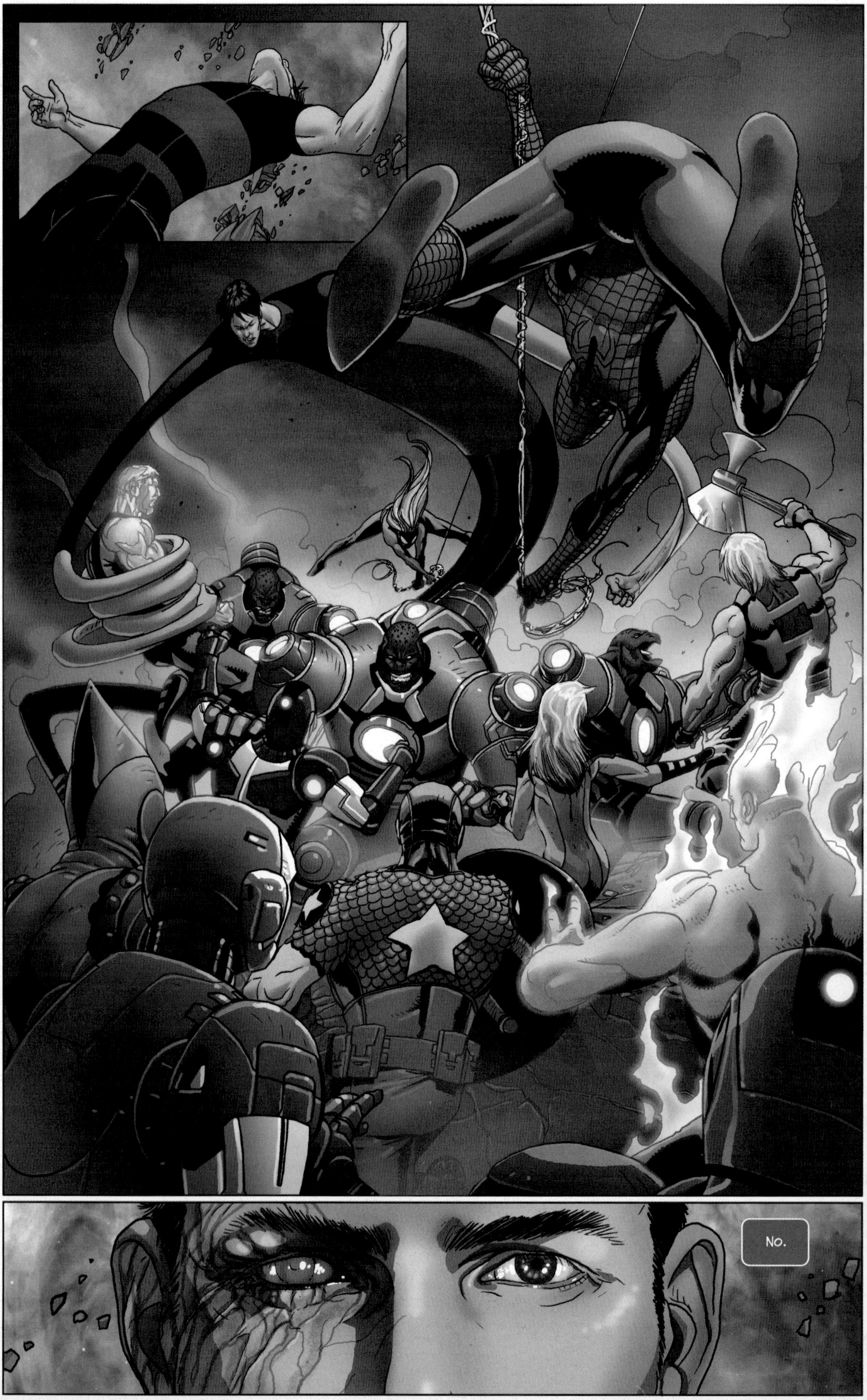
No.

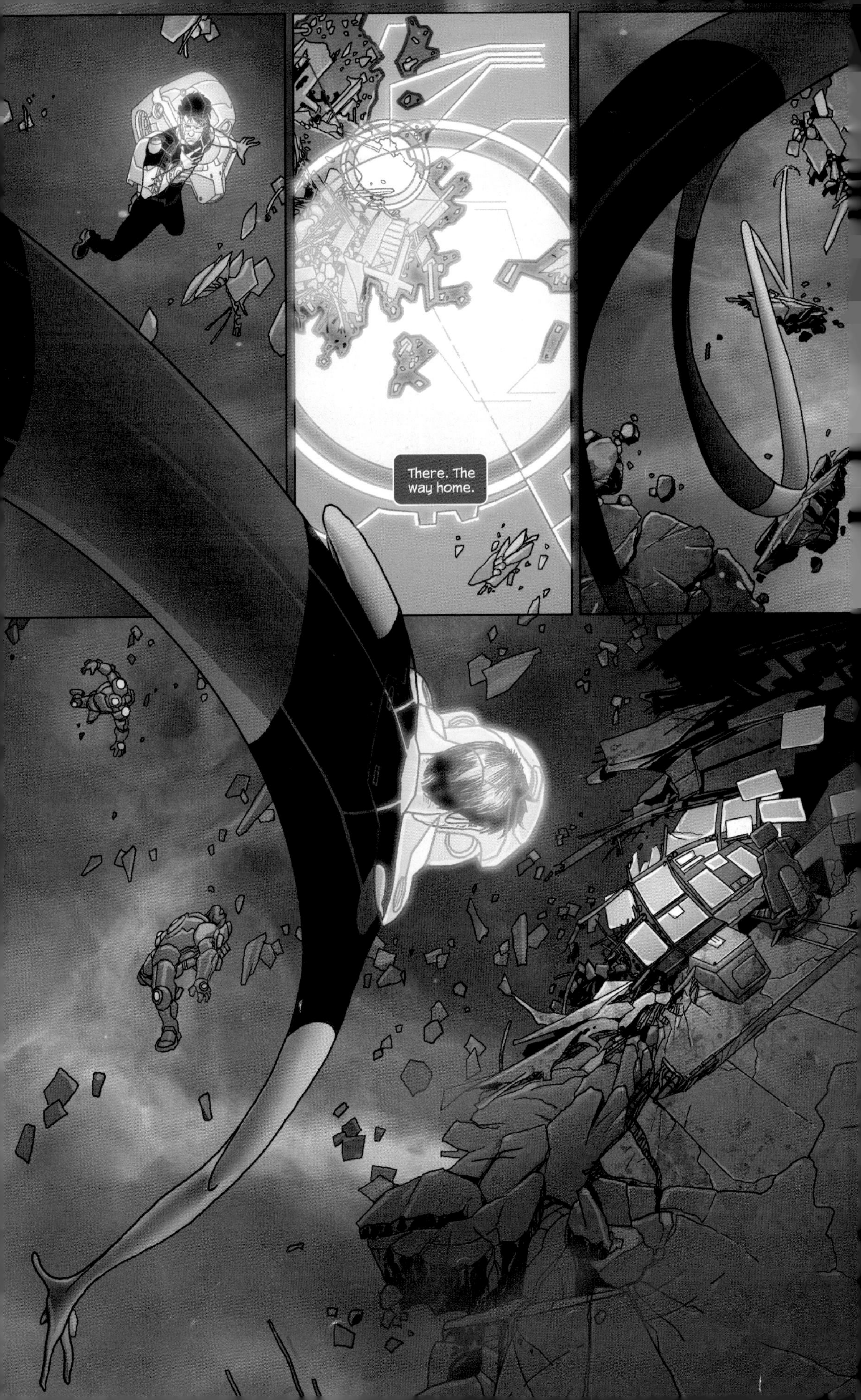
There. The way home.

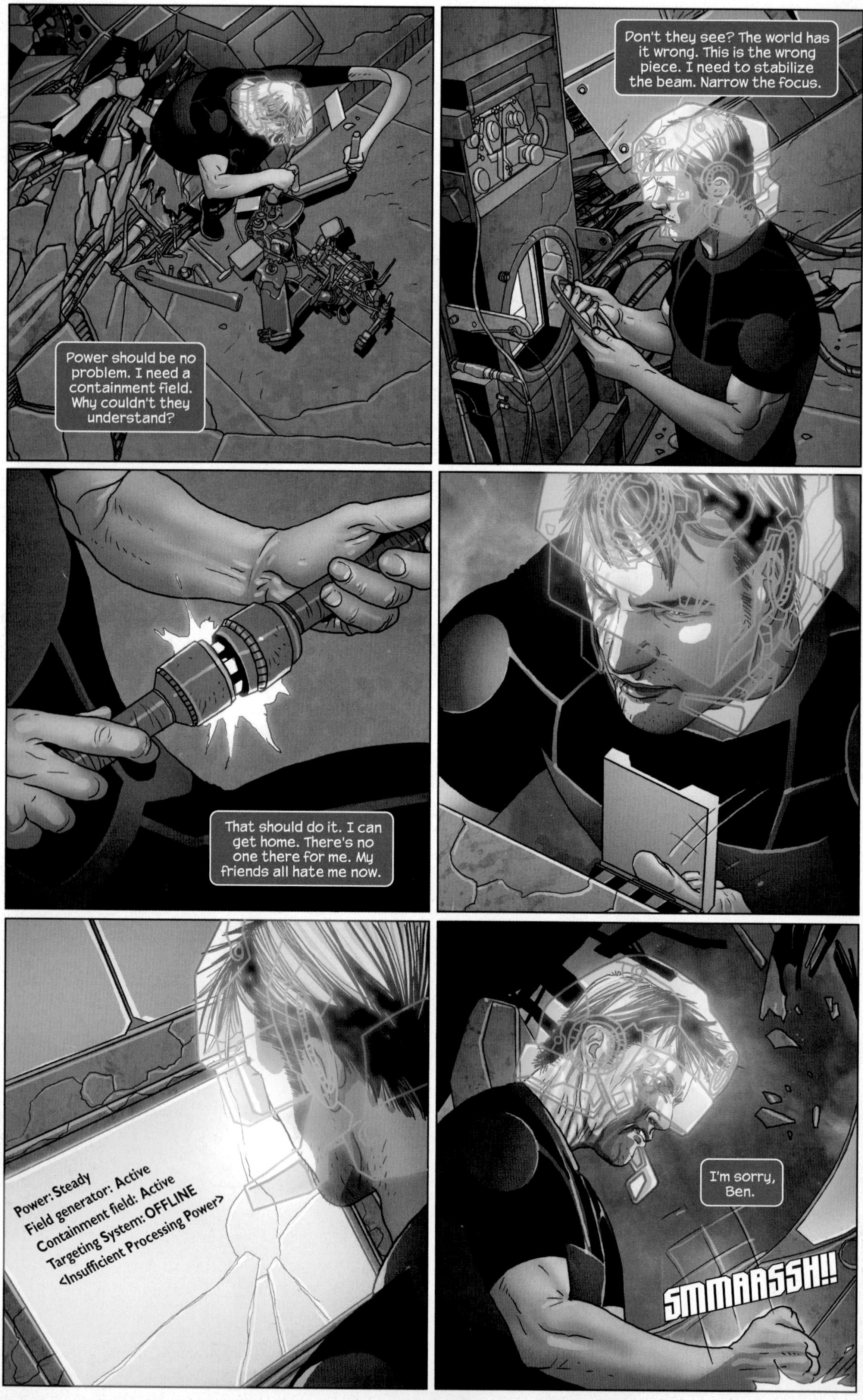
Power should be no problem. I need a containment field. Why couldn't they understand?
Don't they see? The world has it wrong. This is the wrong piece. I need to stabilize the beam. Narrow the focus.
That should do it. I can get home. There's no one there for me. My friends all hate me now.
Power: Steady
Field generator: Active
Containment field: Active
Targeting System: OFFLINE
<Insufficient Processing Power>
I'm sorry, Ben.
SMMAASSH!!

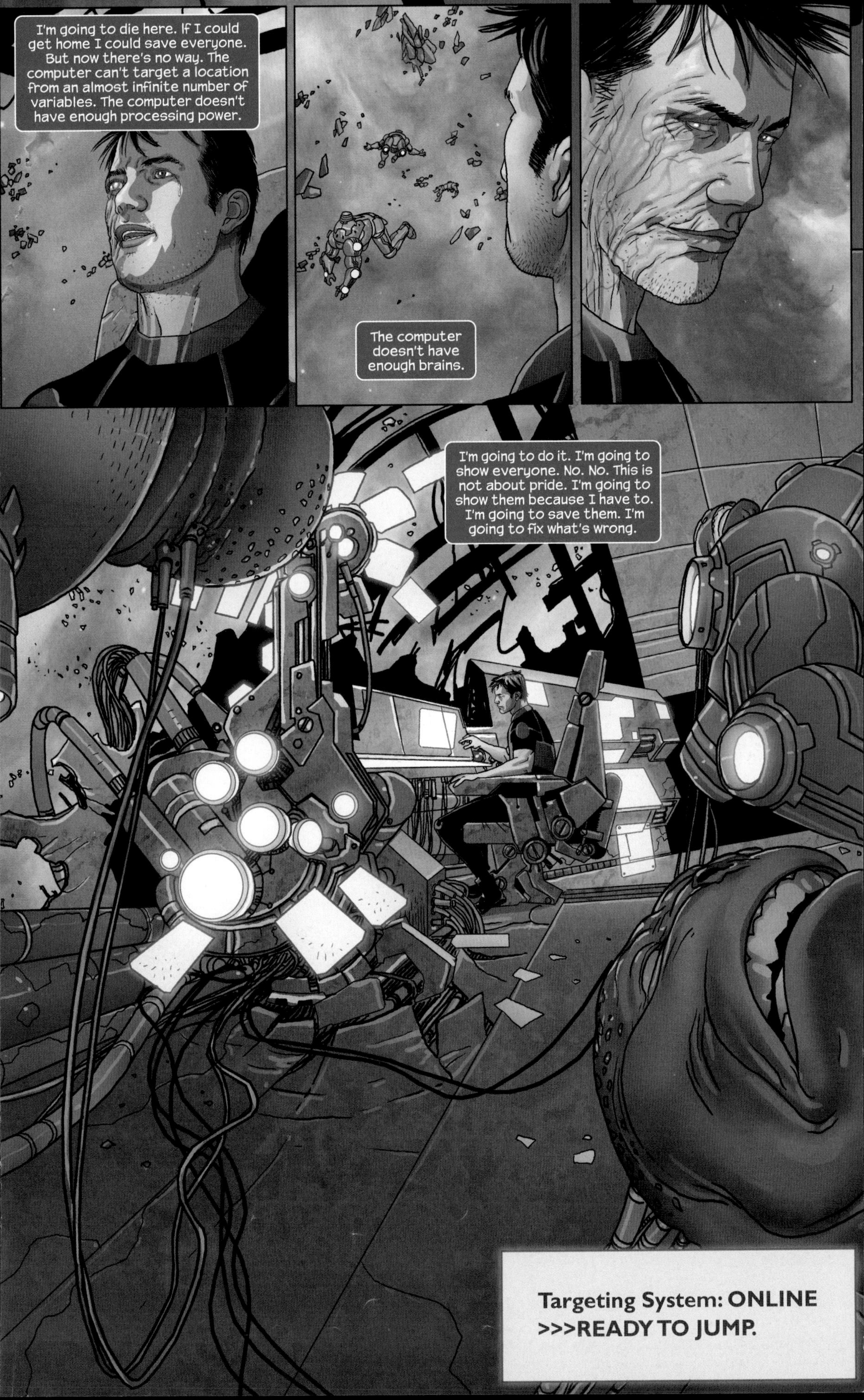
I'm going to die here. If I could get home I could save everyone. But now there's no way. The computer can't target a location from an almost infinite number of variables. The computer doesn't have enough processing power.
The computer doesn't have enough brains.
I'm going to do it. I'm going to show everyone. No. No. This is not about pride. I'm going to show them because I have to. I'm going to save them. I'm going to fix what's wrong.
Targeting System: ONLINE
>>>READY TO JUMP.

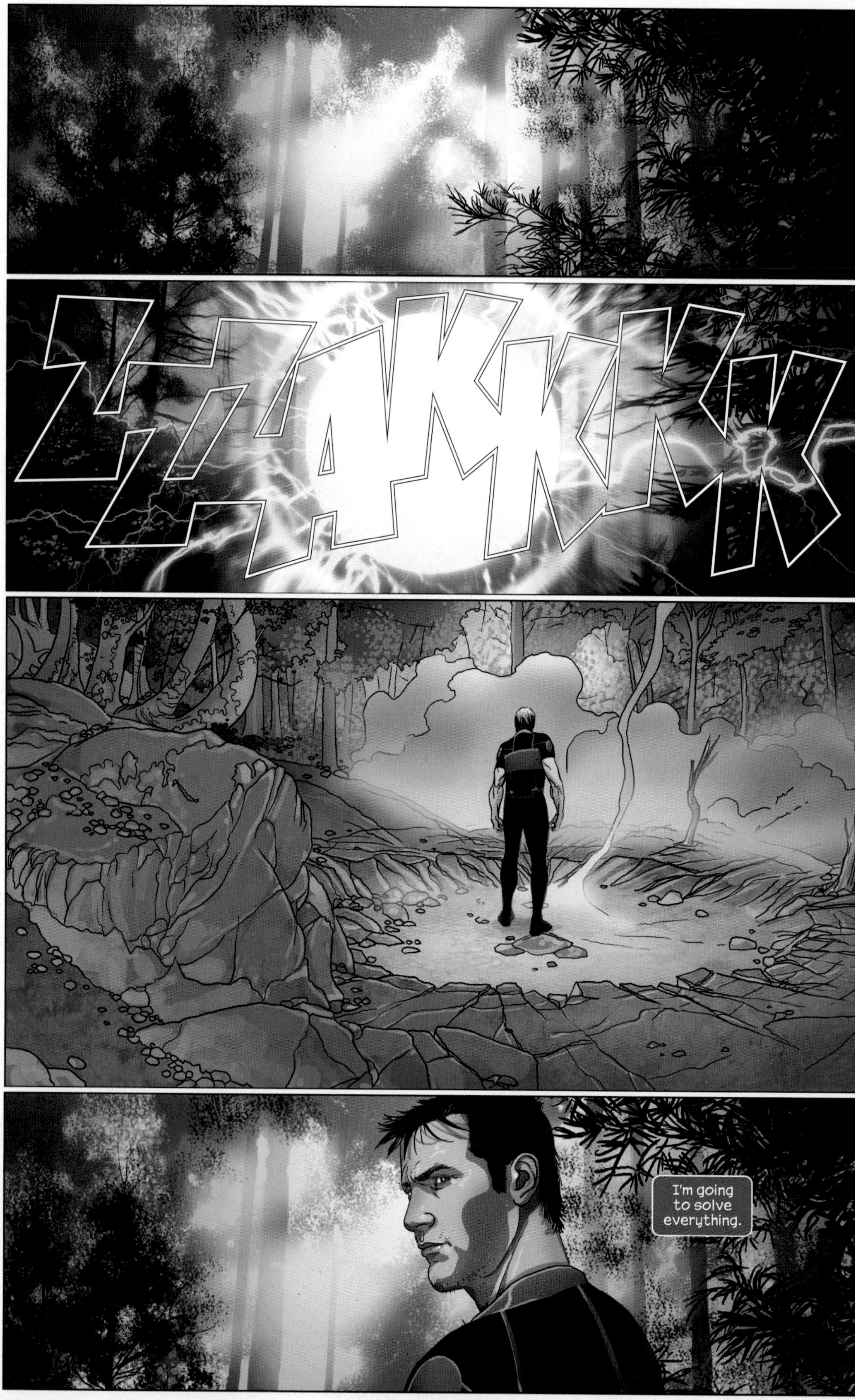
ZZAKKK
I'm going to solve everything.

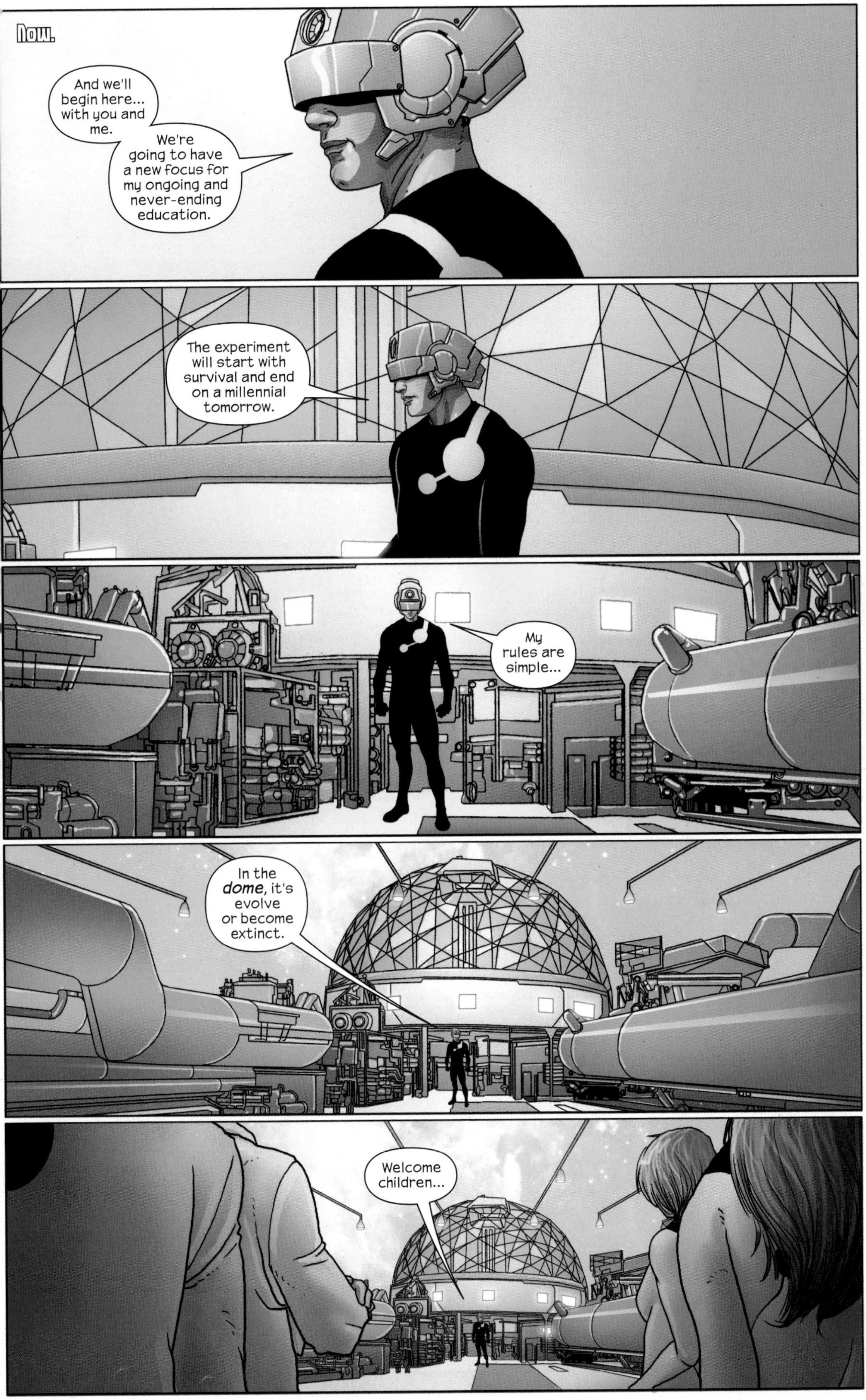
Now.
And we'll begin here... with you and me.
We're going to have a new focus for my ongoing and never-ending education.
The experiment will start with survival and end on a millennial tomorrow.
My rules are simple...
In the *dome*, it's evolve or become extinct.
Welcome children...

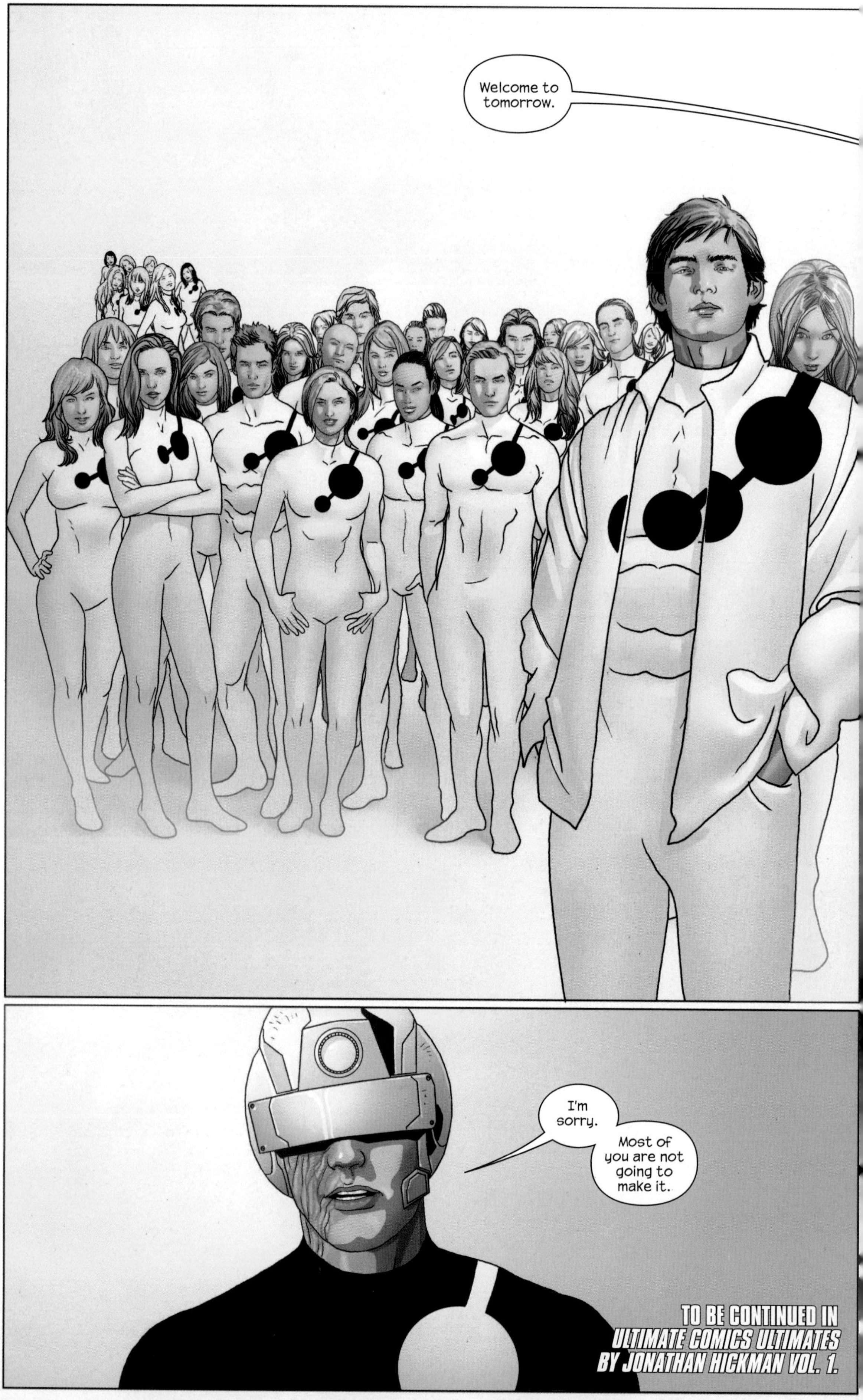
Welcome to tomorrow.
I'm sorry.
Most of you are not going to make it.
TO BE CONTINUED IN ULTIMATE COMICS ULTIMATES BY JONATHAN HICKMAN VOL. 1.

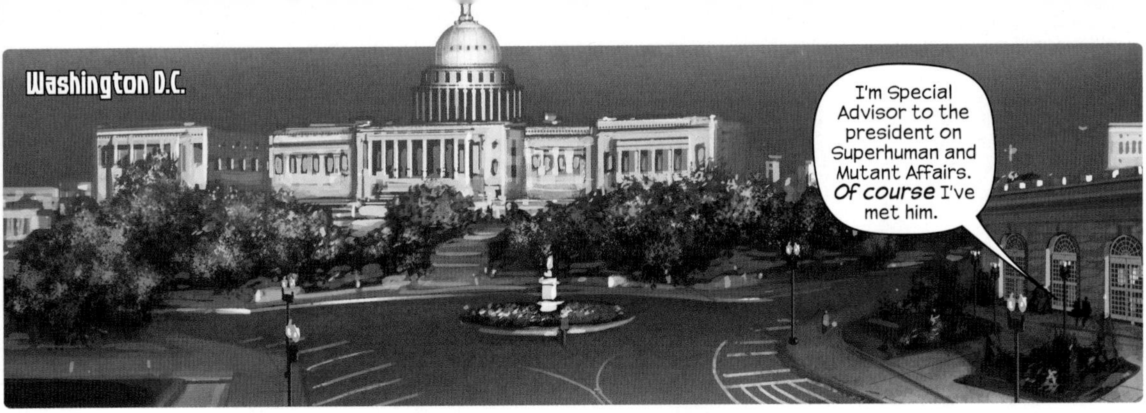
Washington D.C.
I'm Special Advisor to the president on Superhuman and Mutant Affairs. *Of course* I've met him.

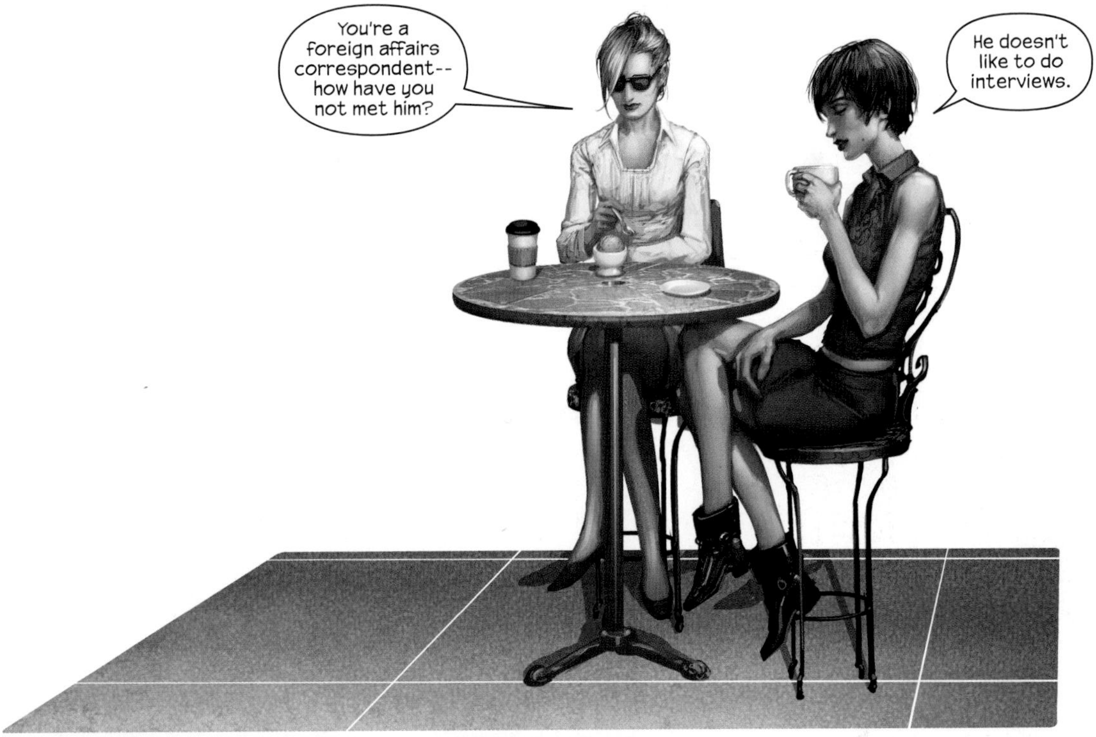
You're a foreign affairs correspondent--how have you not met him?
He doesn't like to do interviews.

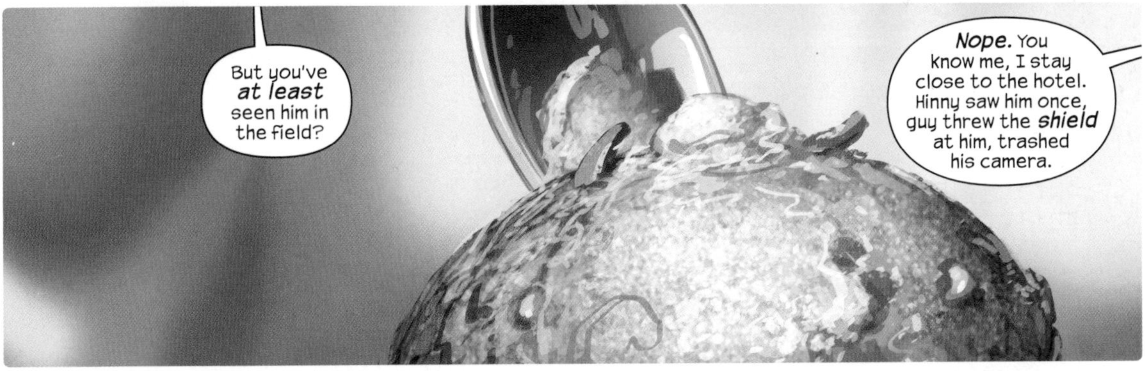
But you've *at least* seen him in the field?
Nope. You know me, I stay close to the hotel. Hinny saw him once, guy threw the *shield* at him, trashed his camera.

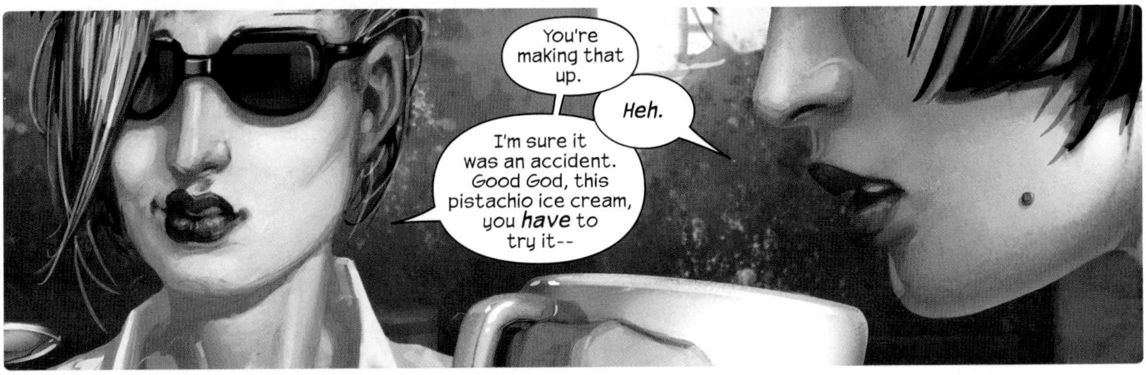
You're making that up.
Heh.
I'm sure it was an accident. Good God, this pistachio ice cream, you *have* to try it--

Maybe in a minute.

So is *this* why we're getting coffee? You want an interview with *Captain America*? He's not gonna want to talk about this Spider-kid thing.

I was in *Vancouver* over the weekend, Val.

Can you believe they film all those TV shows there? It doesn't look *anything* like New York.

Hm. No. There was an old man living up there, *burn victim.* Really ghastly. Just got diagnosed with terminal cancer, said he wanted to get his story out before he passed. Said he's tired of lying to the grandkids.

This some kind of human interest thing? I didn't know you had a soul. *Seriously,* you should try this--

He also happens to be a *mutant.* And he says he spent a bunch of years locked in a government research facility, getting experimented on.

Black Helicopters.

You know that saying comes from the fact that there were black helicopters, right?

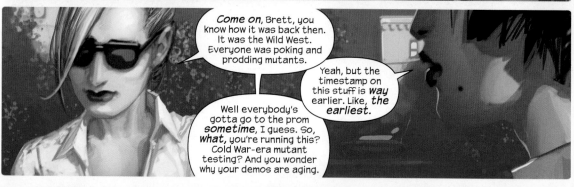

Come on, Brett, you know how it was back then. It was the Wild West. Everyone was poking and prodding mutants.

Yeah, but the timestamp on this stuff is *way* earlier. Like, *the earliest.*

Well everybody's gotta go to the prom *sometime,* I guess. So, *what,* you're running this? Cold War-era mutant testing? And you wonder why your demos are aging.

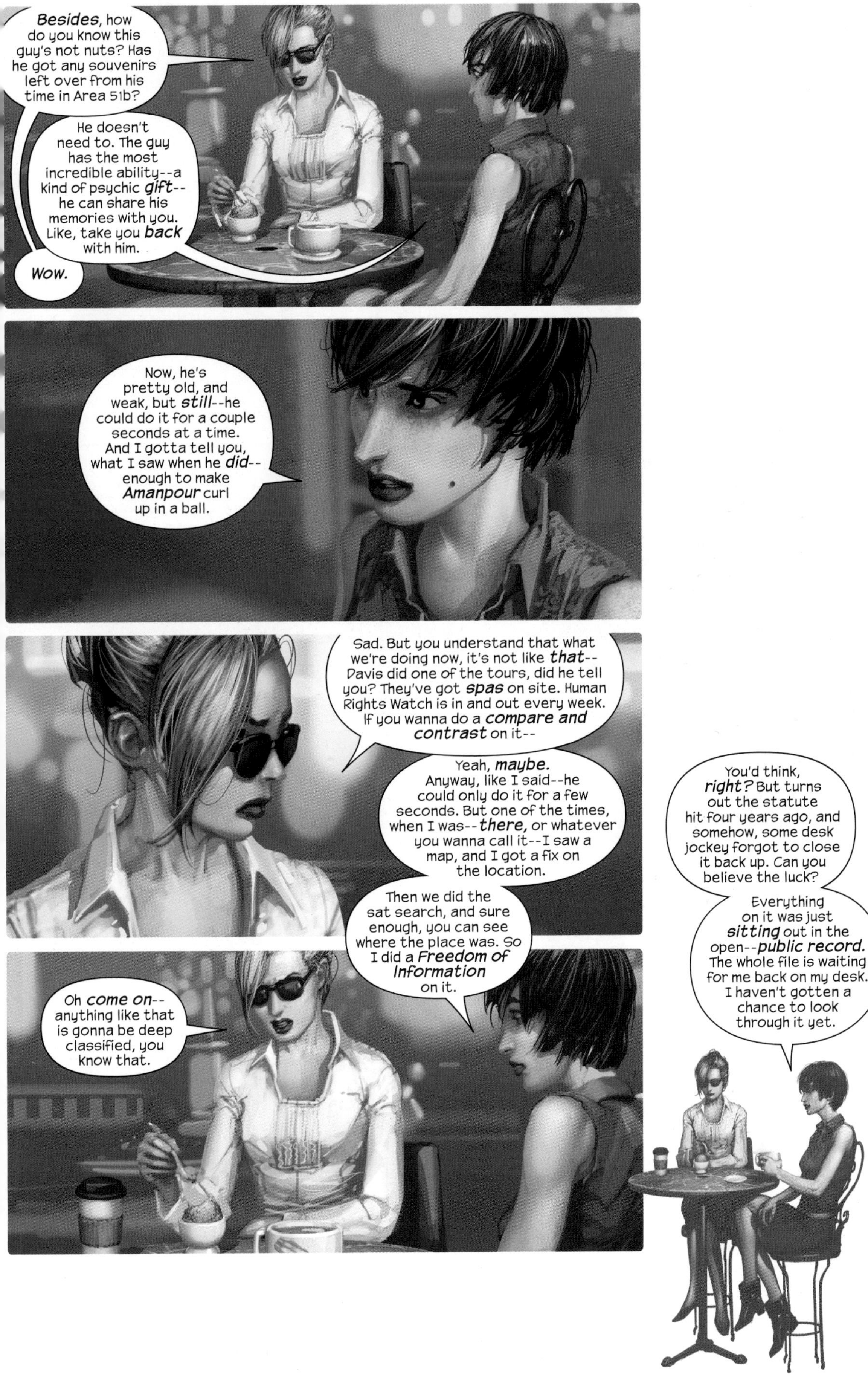
Besides, how do you know this guy's not nuts? Has he got any souvenirs left over from his time in Area 51b?
He doesn't need to. The guy has the most incredible ability--a kind of psychic gift--he can share his memories with you. Like, take you back with him.
Wow.
Now, he's pretty old, and weak, but still--he could do it for a couple seconds at a time. And I gotta tell you, what I saw when he did--enough to make Amanpour curl up in a ball.
Sad. But you understand that what we're doing now, it's not like that--Davis did one of the tours, did he tell you? They've got spas on site. Human Rights Watch is in and out every week. If you wanna do a compare and contrast on it--
Yeah, maybe. Anyway, like I said--he could only do it for a few seconds. But one of the times, when I was--there, or whatever you wanna call it--I saw a map, and I got a fix on the location.
Then we did the sat search, and sure enough, you can see where the place was. So I did a Freedom of Information on it.
Oh come on--anything like that is gonna be deep classified, you know that.
You'd think, right? But turns out the statute hit four years ago, and somehow, some desk jockey forgot to close it back up. Can you believe the luck?
Everything on it was just sitting out in the open--public record. The whole file is waiting for me back on my desk. I haven't gotten a chance to look through it yet.

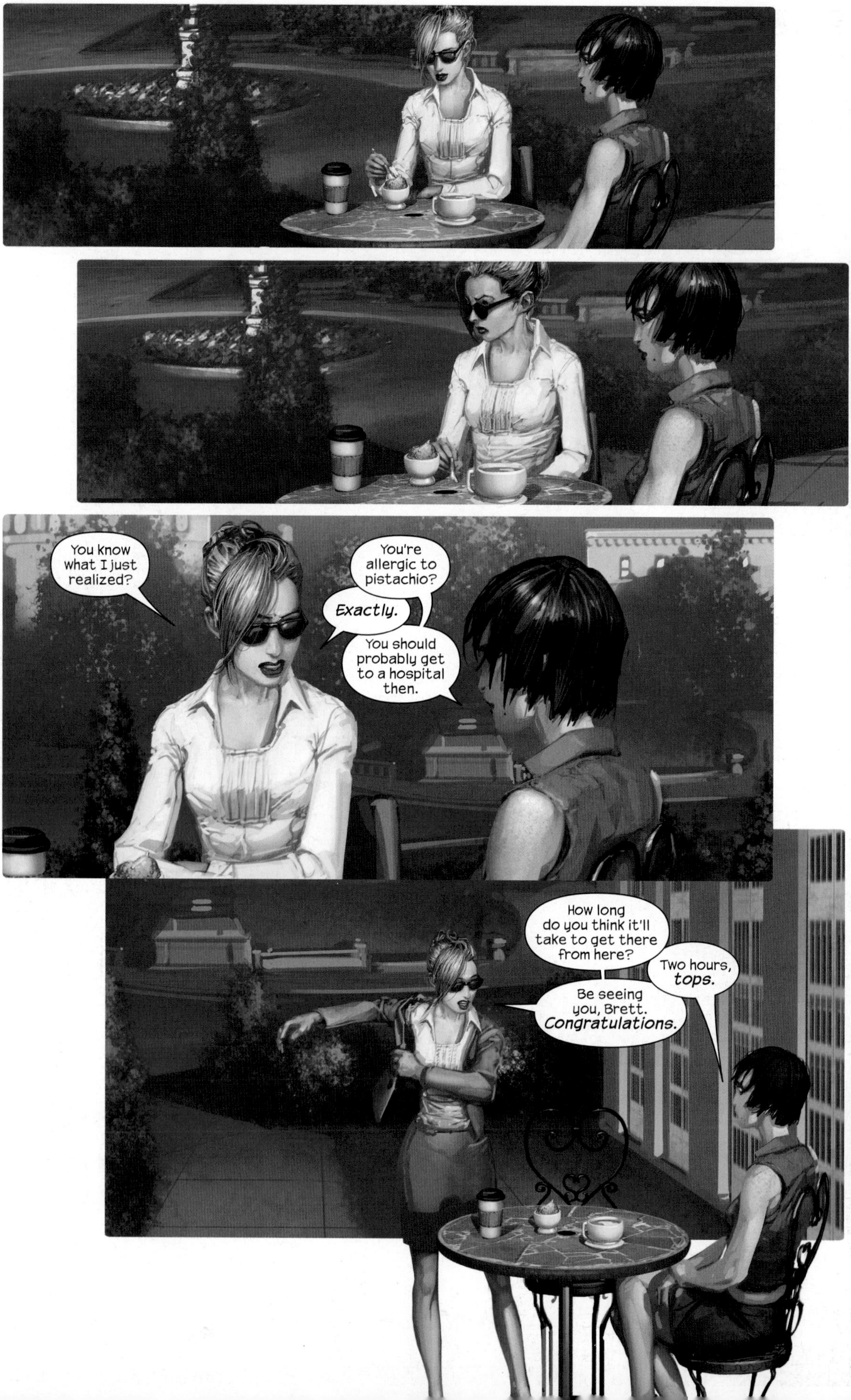
You know what I just realized?
You're allergic to pistachio?
Exactly.
You should probably get to a hospital then.
How long do you think it'll take to get there from here?
Two hours, tops.
Be seeing you, Brett. Congratulations.

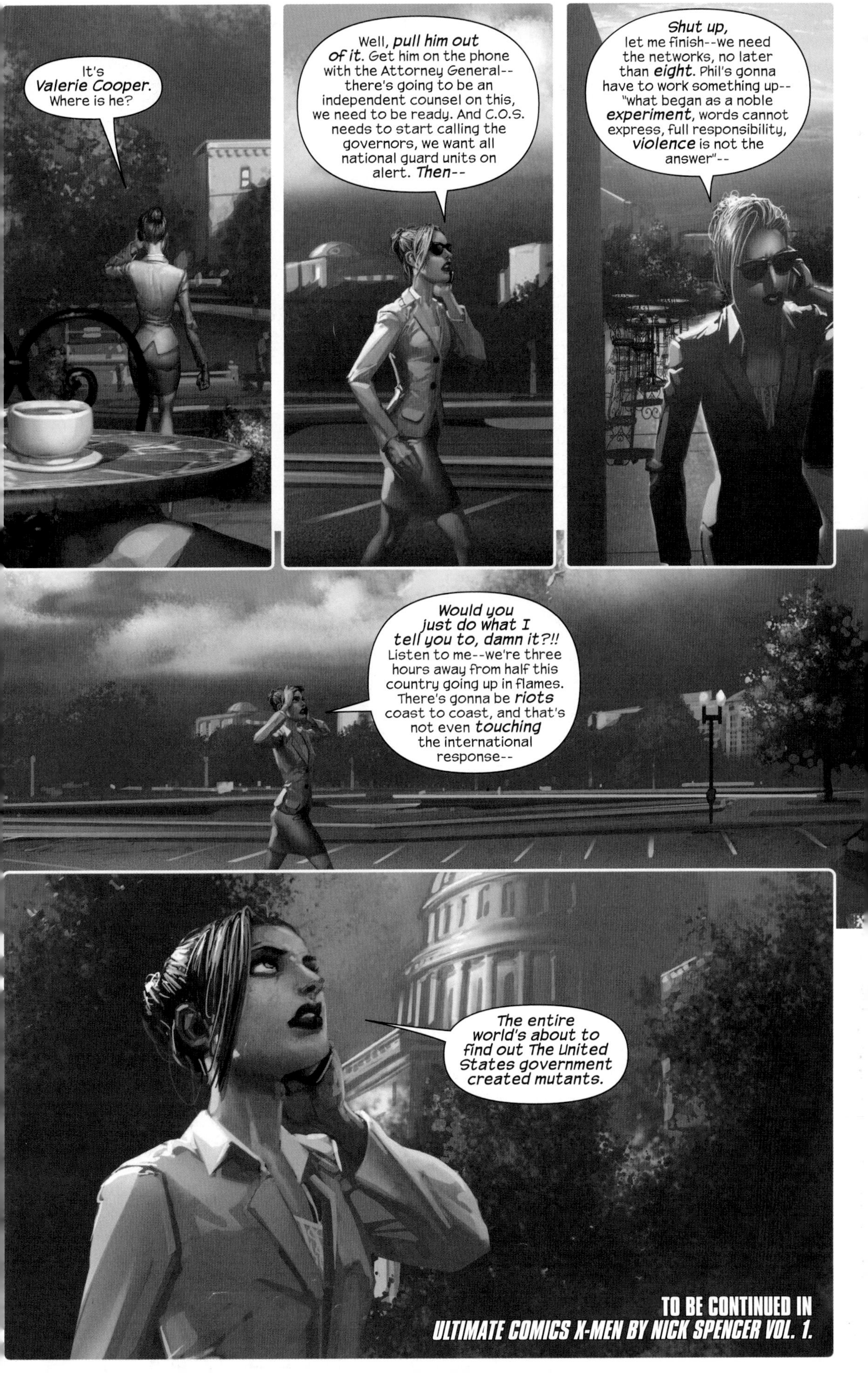
It's Valerie Cooper. Where is he?
Well, pull him out of it. Get him on the phone with the Attorney General--there's going to be an independent counsel on this, we need to be ready. And C.O.S. needs to start calling the governors, we want all national guard units on alert. Then--
Shut up, let me finish--we need the networks, no later than eight. Phil's gonna have to work something up--"what began as a noble experiment, words cannot express, full responsibility, violence is not the answer"--
Would you just do what I tell you to, damn it?!! Listen to me--we're three hours away from half this country going up in flames. There's gonna be riots coast to coast, and that's not even touching the international response--
The entire world's about to find out The United States government created mutants.
TO BE CONTINUED IN
ULTIMATE COMICS X-MEN BY NICK SPENCER VOL. 1.

ULTIMATE COMICS

In the wake of Ultimatum, the Ultimate Universe was overhauled with comics top writers and artists bringing a new energy to Ultimates characters!

➤ Ultimate Comics Iron Man: Armor Wars HC/TP

IRON MAN
ARMOR WARS

Collects *Ultimate Armor Wars* #1-4

By Warren Ellis and Steve Kurth

Tony's armor falls into the wrong hands in the wake of Ultimatum!

HC: JAN100637 • 978-0-7851-4250-8
TP: JUL100695 • 978-0-7851-4430-4

➤ Ultimate Comics Spider-Man Vol. 1: The World According to Peter Parker HC/TP

SPIDER-MAN

Collects *Ultimate Comics Spider-Man* #1-6

By Brian Michael Bendis and David Lafuente

Six months after Ultimatum, Spidey picks up the pieces on a new life!

HC: JAN100656 • 978-0-7851-4011-5
TP: APR100670 • 978-0-7851-4099-3

➤ Ultimate Comics Spider-Man Vol. 2: Chameleons HC/TP

SPIDER-MAN

Collects *Ultimate Comics Spider-Man* #7-14

By Brian Michael Bendis, Takeshi Miyazawa and David Lafuente

Rick Jones has some crazy new powers…and might just be crazy!

HC: SEP100695 • 978-0-7851-4012-2
TP: MAR110801 • 978-0-7851-4100-6

➤ Ultimate Comics Avengers: Next Generation HC/TP

AVENGERS

Collects *Ultimate Avengers* #1-6

By Mark Millar and Carlos Pacheco

Classified secrets threaten Captain America and only Nick Fury can help!

HC: APR100654 • 978-0-7851-4010-8
TP: AUG100701 • 978-0-7851-4097-9

➤ Ultimate Comics Avengers: Crime & Punishment HC/TP

AVENGERS

Collects *Ultimate Avengers 2* #1-6

By Mark Millar and Leinil Francis Yu

When the job is just too dirty, Nick Fury calls in the Avengers!

HC: AUG100688 • 978-0-7851-3670-5
TP: FEB110685 • 978-0-7851-3671-2

➤ Ultimate Comics Avengers: Blade vs. Avengers HC/TP

AVENGERS

Collects Ultimate Avengers 2 #1-6

By Mark Millar and Steve Dillon

Blade is back in a bad way, and that can only mean one thing: Vampires!

FEB110663 • 978-0-7851-4009-2

➤ Ultimate Comics X: Origins HC

ORIGINS

Collects *Ultimate Comics X* #1-5

By Jeph Loeb and Arthur Adams

Who is Ultimate X? The character who will change the Ultimate Universe forever!

978-0-7851-4014-6

➤ Ultimate Comics Thor HC

THOR

Collects *Ultimate Comics Thor* #1-4

By Jonathan Hickman and Carlos Pacheco

Origins revealed as Ultimates go back to the beginning of Thor, Loki and Asgard!

DEC100662 • 978-0-7851-5187-6

➤ Ultimate Comics New Ultimates: Thor Reborn HC/TP

THOR REBORN

Collects *New Ultimates* #1-5

By Jeph Loeb and Frank Cho

Thor returns from the underworld ready to destroy Loki for good!

JAN110838 • 978-0-7851-3994-2

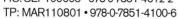